MARY

A CHAPEL HILL BOOK

MARY

AN AUTOBIOGRAPHY

Mary E. Mebane

The University of North Carolina Press
Chapel Hill & London

Library of Congress Cataloging-in-Publication Data
Mebane, Mary E., 1933–
Mary : an autobiography / by Mary E. Mebane.
p.   cm.
"Chapel Hill books."
Originally published: New York: Viking Press, c1981.
ISBN 0-8078-4821-2 (pbk.: alk. paper)
1. Mebane, Mary E., 1933–   .   2. Afro-American women—North Carolina—
Durham County—Biography.   3. Afro-Americans—North Carolina—Durham
County—Biography.   4. Durham County (N.C.)—Biography.   I. Title.
F262.D8M4   1998
975.6'56300496073'0092—dc21   98-49044
[b]   CIP

Grateful acknowledgment is made to Warner Bros. Music for permission to
reprint portions of lyrics to the song "I'll See You Then" by Jimmy Webb.
Copyright © 1969 by Canopy Music, Inc. All rights reserved.

03 02 01 00 99   5 4 3 2 1

To my aunt, Josephine Mebane,
who first believed in me,

and to C. Hugh Holman and Harrison E. Salisbury,
both of whom, at different stages of my life,
opened a lot of doors for me.

"And I believe I'm going to have to make a last try."
　　　　　　　　　—Sung by Roberta Flack

"The crooked straight and the rough places plain."
　　　　　　　　　—Handel's *Messiah*

Part
ONE

1

My name is Mary.

When I first opened my eyes to the world, on June 26, 1933, in the Wildwood community in Durham County, North Carolina, the world was a green Eden—and it was magic. My favorite place in the whole world was a big rock in the backyard that looked like the back of a buried elephant. I spent a lot of time squatting on that rock. I realize now that I probably selected it because it was in the *center* of our yard, and from it, by shifting ever so slightly, this way and that, I could see *everything.* I liked to look. Mama must have told me several thousand times that I was going to die with my eyes open, looking.

When I sat on the rock with my back to the house, the fields were in front of me. On the left was another lot that we called the Rock Pile, and to the right was an untended strip of land, strewn with rocks but cleared enough to be plowed sometimes. The Rock Pile, full of weeds and tall trees, was a place of mystery. It had so many rocks and some of them were so large that it was left uncleared with just a path through it. Behind me I could overhear voices coming from the back porch and kitchen. I could see who was chopping or picking something in the garden and I could see who was coming through the Rock Pile.

The road in front of our house was a dirty strip swirling with the thick red dust of state trucks going to and from the rock quarry. I saw the quarry once. To me it was one of the Seven Wonders of the World—a very wide hole, dug deep in the ground. The trucks around it looked like little toys. It was a mountain going in the wrong direction, with me standing at the top. Good-looking Edmund, the one with the limp from polio, died at the rock quarry. Explosives. They didn't want anyone to see his body. Someone said that they found only pieces. He was a grown man and I was a child at the time, but I remember him. He came down from Virginia to stay with his sister and find work. Like his sisters, he was very light-skinned and had thick, curly brown hair. I used to wonder about his hair. Did they find a lock of curly brown hair after the explosion?

Then there was the rich white contractor who lived on the highway. His oldest son had died as a young man, in another part of the state, backing a truck too near such an opening. The truck had started to slide and he couldn't stop it. I saw his picture once, when I went as a teenager to baby-sit at their house. His brother, then a grown man and my employer for the evening, told me about the accident. In the photograph the dead heir was still a child, about nine years old, sitting on a horse, smiling at the camera.

The world consisted of me at first; then, when Ruf Junior, the baby, was big enough to walk, he joined me on the rock. My older brother, Jesse, was a big boy who came dashing by to or from some adventure, and he might say something or he might not. My mother, Nonnie, and my father, Rufus, were the grown people who called me to dinner, to bed, or to do chores.

One day a car came up to the house and a lady got out, while a man put suitcases on the porch. The lady was Aunt Jo, and she stayed with us for several years. Sometimes other

4

people came, but they were visitors, and unless they had someone my age for me to play with, they didn't affect me one way or the other.

I would squat on that rock, my stick legs poking through the openings of my dirt-stained bloomers, my birdlike head turning from side to side, my gaze, unblinking, focusing up, down, in front of me, in back of me, now zooming in on the lower yard, then penetrating deeper into the garden, then rising up ever so slightly to where the corn was planted on the hill. I was in the center of life and I didn't miss a thing; nothing slipped by unobserved or unnoted. My problems started when I began to comment on what I saw. I insisted on being accurate. But the world I was born into didn't want that. Indeed, its very survival depended on not knowing, not seeing—and, certainly, not saying anything at all about what it was really like.

The whole backyard slanted down. It started at the well and sloped down to the lettuce patch. When it rained, water ran in gullies clear down to a ditch Daddy had dug parallel to the flow to make the water run off. Later he decided to stop the flow up higher, and Ruf Junior and Jesse and I toted rocks and formed a little dam between the big sloping rock and the two less-big rocks that lay on either side of it.

The rock on the left was big, but it looked like a rock, not like the back of a buried elephant. I could see all around it, but it was big. My brothers and I couldn't move it, not even when we all pushed together. The one on the right of the big sloping rock looked like its brother. You couldn't see where it started or stopped. Its back was like the back of a smaller gray buried elephant—the younger brother of the large gray sloping elephant that was buried in the middle.

The little dam, built up with sticks and rocks, held fast; later, when it rained, the running dirt stopped there and backed up and covered some of the hundreds of rocks that studded the backyard and on which we stubbed innumerable bare toes in the May-to-September, school-is-out summer.

5

The well was in the upper part of the backyard, before the slope started. The wooden box that was the superstructure of the well was partly rotted; there were wide spaces between the boards, and my brothers and I had been warned not to lean too hard on them when we pulled the bucket up or we would fall in. The bucket was beaten up from banging on the rocks that lined the narrow well, and when the bucket came out, water sloshed over the side and spurted out of the little holes in it. The rocks in the well had wet green moss on them as far down as the eye could see. The well was about the width of a giant inner tube, but rough where the rocks stuck out all the way down. When you looked over the boards, the water below looked like quicksilver in the sun. I would look into the well and think deep thoughts and smell the wet moss and rotting wood.

Hanging on a nail on the well was a gourd to drink out of. This was full and round at one end and tubular at the other, and had tiny ridges in its mud-brown interior. A drink of cool well water from a sweet-tasting gourd when you're thirsty is the best drink in the world.

Sometimes I liked to lean over the edge of the well and look past the box where the wood had rotted and splintered from the water, past the moss lining the bottom of the wood and the rocks paving the well. I thought that underneath the moving water was China. I read a story in the second grade that said that if you dug a deep, deep hole down from where you were and put your eye down, clear through the hole on the other side you would see China.

I believed stories like that. Just as once I read a story about Mexico and was struck by the bold designs on the pottery. That night I dreamed that I was in heaven and God looked like the father of a Mexican family, dark, with black hair and a long, colorful robe, with his wife and child by his side. They were standing in front of a clay house, and nearby were enormous pottery jars with bright designs on them.

Our well wasn't as deep as it should have been, and a couple of summers it went dry, so we would go to one of the springs. The nearest, at the bottom of a little slope, bubbled clear water up out of clean sand. The shallow encircling wall was about three hands high and a child could curl up and hold his feet with his hands around its circumference. The water there bubbled up endlessly, clear and sweet, shaded by tall North Carolina pines. The other spring was farther away. It was larger, more conventional, and not nearly so romantic.

In the morning the sun glistened on the long grass in the vacant lot that was never mowed. The cow ate the grass and kept it low, all except the spot where I emptied the peepots. She wouldn't eat there unless Mama sprinkled a lot of salt on it to fool her. Then sometimes she would eat it and sometimes she wouldn't. This grass was on the lot next to the main yard. Daddy sometimes plowed it all up and harrowed it and sowed it with grain and got mad when Mr. Jake's chickens came over from next door and ate it all up. But it was dry, hard, cracked land and never grew much of anything.

On the left side of the main yard was the Rock Pile, where I picked blackberries. Aunt Jo made purple dye from the poke-berries that also grew there, and sometimes she cooked poke salad, which I hated; it tasted like cooked leaves. But I liked the dye. When Aunt Jo dipped a white gunnysack in the dark water and it came up a beautiful purple, I was filled with wonder.

Sometimes my brothers and I played jumping from rock to rock. If you stepped off a rock you were "out." Sometimes snakes slid out of the Rock Pile. My brothers and I couldn't run through it; the briars tore too bad. But we had a path and as long as I stayed in the path I felt safe. One step either to the right or the left of the path and I felt scared. Not only of snakes and other natural dangers but of something else. I didn't know what.

At the bottom of the yard there was a vegetable garden with green growing things: lettuce and cabbage and cucumbers and squash. Little sticks held up the vines of tomatoes and string beans and butter beans. Beyond it, the field ran up a little hill from the garden a long way and then down

7

to some pines. After the rows of pines, the Bottom started. It was low there and wet most of the time, but I liked it; my father worked hard there with Suki, the mule, plowing. I followed him there all the time, but I liked mainly to play near the creek in the Bottom and on the pine-straw-covered mounds, where I slid down into the gullies.

I seldom went into the front yard. The front yard started in front of the well. It had level ground and tough grass and it ran to the dusty road. I played there on Sundays while my mother sat and talked with her friends. Three big trees in a row separated the front yard from the dusty, powdery road. Near the road was a bush that was yellow in the spring with tiny flowers on long stems. Closer to the house was a bush that had bell-shaped purple flowers that smelled sticky sweet, and a huge tree with a different kind of purple flower that ran all over the yard if you didn't cut it back, and it was always loaded with round, fat bumblebees.

2

Insects were our friends.

Lightning bugs hid from us in the deep grass around rocks. They tried to hide, but couldn't, for Ruf Junior and I found them. Jesse was good at knowing where things were, too. But he was a big boy and he didn't have time to play with us much. So we would seek out the lightning bugs around dusk, just as they began to light up. I thought that they had a lantern in their tail, for the light glowed like that in a lantern. Ruf Junior thought that someone had built a little fire in the tail of each lightning bug.

We would pick them up and cup our hands to create a little artificial darkness and the bug would light up! Like magic! Every time, he would light up! Then we would turn him loose and watch him fly away, lighting up all the time, while we searched out another. When dark came we didn't have to look anymore, for the whole yard was filled with the flickering fire.

Grasshoppers suffered a somewhat more difficult fate.

"Grasshopper, Grasshopper, give me some molasses."

We didn't doubt at all that they understood every word we were saying—those long, brittle creatures with bright, hard eyes.

"Grasshopper, Grasshopper, give me some molasses."

If he didn't come across right away, we would talk to him some more and have him to understand that we weren't going to let him go until he deposited some brown liquid in our hands, which he never failed to do.

"Doodlebug, Doodlebug, come out. Your house is on fire."

The best place to look for Doodlebug was in a sandy dry place. There was a good one under the shed where Daddy kept his car. You could tell where to look by the little mound of sand all around his hole. "Let's go and see if we can get Doodlebug to come out of his house," we would say.

It didn't seem incongruous to say "house," for I never doubted that he had a sofa and a chair and a bed and a table down in his hole—all small, of course—and I knew that if only I could see it, his bed would be made up and a bright quilt would be on it and Mrs. Doodlebug would probably have something on for supper.

"Doodlebug, Doodlebug, your house is on fire."

We would scare him enough and he would come up to see what was the matter. If he didn't come up, we would say that he was away for the day, that he and Mrs. Doodlebug had gone visiting and we would have to call on them again when they were home. But often Doodlebug heard us and rewarded us by coming up. You had to get down on the ground and put your eye real close to the hole, but he would come up, all covered with gray sand, if you called him enough and if he was not off visiting.

It took some expertise to converse with grasshoppers and doodlebugs, but anybody, including children from town, could get a fat white worm to come up. All you had to do was take a wild onion and bruise it until the smell got strong. Then you went to a large hole in the grass and put the green part of the onion down into the hole. You had to know exactly what type of hole to find, but usually that wasn't hard: a big round hole was the best. When you stuck the onion down, the worm would bite; then you could pull him up. After we got him out and examined him, all fat and curled up, we would put him back and then go find another one. Sometimes we would greet our friends the fat worms for a whole summer's evening, until my mother called and made us come up on the porch.

Town children could also play "June Bug, June Bug, fly away home." We would catch our fat blue friend with the green, shiny wings and make him sing for us. If you tied one of his legs to a string and attached him to the clothesline, he would fly in a great circle and sing for you. We didn't mean to be cruel, and after he sang for a while we would let him go. I once pulled a June bug's leg off to see what he would do. But he didn't fly away and I was so sorry for the June bug that I didn't do that anymore.

The snake doctor wasn't our friend. He had a long, keen nose, and when he flew overhead, we knew that he was in a hurry, going to see someone who was hurt. If we bothered him he would sting us, and the sting would kill, so grown people said. So when we saw a snake doctor we watched him quietly and were sure to keep out of his way.

Mama told us to stay away from toad frogs. If they peed on you, you would get a wart. But we played with them with sticks. We would never touch one of them. We took a stick and put it directly behind him. He would jump ahead and then jump again. Sometimes we would make him jump all over the whole yard until a grown person saw us and made us stop.

Chickens and pigs and Suki, the mule, weren't interesting, for they were part of the family. The chickens were nasty, dropping all over the yard and the porch steps; the pigs were far away in the field. The cow was a little bit interesting when she released enormous quantities of water, which we would stare at in amazement, wondering how she could hold so much. Suki was a friend. Sometimes, if we were good, Daddy would let us ride back from the field on her.

The world was nice and green. We ate the lettuce and tomatoes and squash that Daddy grew in the field—and green beans, corn, butter beans, cucumbers. The lettuce grew close to the ground, kind of flat. Its leaves were tough and had a sharp taste. The tomato bush had tomatoes of different colors; we picked those that were red and left the pink and green ones until tomorrow or the day after. The squash was greenish-white, and you tested it with your fingers to see if it was too hard. Green beans hung like long green plaits of hair all over the vine, so heavy that Mama put sticks underneath to prop them off the ground. Corn grew tall on hard stalks and had long, green, sharp leaves that cut you if you ran your hand over them. Cabbage was whitish-green in a hard round ball. You had to feel the butter beans to see if they were filled out enough; otherwise, when you shelled them, half the shell would be empty. You could tell if a cucumber was too hard by the color; if it was large and had started turning yellow, it was too hard and had best be left on the vine.

Daddy went to the Bottom every day. Tobacco and cotton grew there and were supposed to be money crops, but Daddy never made any money off them. As a matter of fact he never made much off anything.

In addition to the vegetables we planted, we made full use of things that grew wild. There were heartleaf tea (good for the heart) and other herbs that were believed good for various ailments. Jesse and the big boys pulled the gray rabbit tobacco and rolled it in brown paper and tried to smoke it. Sometimes Mama and Aunt Jo and Ruf Junior and I went over into "Sandy Land," beyond the Bottom, and picked gunnysacks full of cressy salad, stopping on the way back to pick wild grapes, with thick blue skins, and scuppernongs.

Some plants were medicine. Aunt Jo would go out in the woods and come back with her apron full of leaves and pieces of bark. She would boil them and swallow the mixture at night. When Mama wasn't looking she would give me some, too.

Then there was the dry, dark-green leaf called senna. It came in a yellow box, and we got a dose every Saturday night. It would cramp your stomach and send you flying down the yard to the smelly toilet early the next morning.

Life had a natural, inexorable rhythm. On weekdays, Mama went to work at a tobacco factory. On Saturdays, early in the morning, we washed clothes. We washed clothes outdoors. First Mama and Jesse drew buckets of water from the well and poured it into the washpot. It was a big iron pot that stood on three legs and was very black from soot. Mama put paper and twigs under it and poured kerosene on them. They blazed up and soon there was blue smoke curling all around the pot. She put all the "white" things in the pot—sheets and pillowcases and underwear—and put Oxydol in with the clothes. I was puzzled because most of the things she put in with the "white" clothes were colored. Our sheets were made from flour sacks and had red or green or blue patterns on them. Some of the underwear was colored, too.

My job was to stand over the pot and "chunk" the clothes down to keep the water from boiling over and putting out the fire. I loved my job. I had a big stick, and sometimes I stood there and "dobbed and dobbed" the clothes up and down all the morning.

Then Mama and Jesse drew water and filled up two large tin tubs. One was to wash clothes in; the other was the first rinse. Then there was a foot tub that was for the second rinse, the one with the bluing in it. Sometimes Mama let me melt the bluing, which came in a long, flat cake.

Then there was an even smaller pot, full of starch—cooked flour and water—with a heavy translucent skim on it. It was my job to skim it and throw the heavy part away. I loved that job, too.

After the clothes boiled and boiled, Mama would get a big stick and carry them a few at a time from the washpot to the washing and rinsing tubs. Then she would put more clothes in the washpot, add water and more Oxydol, and I would dob some more. Sometimes instead of dobbing I "jugged" the clothes—that is, dobbed from side to side.

While the second pot of clothes was boiling, I helped Mama with the wash. There was a big washboard in the first tub and a smaller one in the second tub (that was the first rinse). Mama washed with a big cake of lye soap that she had made, rubbing up and down on the washboard. The lye soap sometimes made tiny holes in her fingers. Then I rubbed the clothes up and down in the first rinse, which got the suds out; next I stirred them around and pulled them up and down in the bluing water. Then Mama wrung them out. Some things she starched. She hung them up high on the clothesline. By that time the second pot of boiling clothes was ready and we started all over again. Later in the morning she put in the "heavy things" to boil—overalls and her blue factory uniforms and the blankets. While they boiled, we ate dinner, the noon meal.

For dinner, Mama would send me to the field with a basket over my arm to get a dozen ears of corn, some cucumbers, and tomatoes. I would shuck the corn, pulling the long green hard leaves off, next the lighter-green inner leaves, then the silk in long yellow strands. Ruf Junior helped to silk it; then Mama would go over it again. She would let me slice the tomatoes and put mayonnaise on them, and slice the cucumbers and put vinegar, salt, and black pepper on them. But I didn't want to slice the onions because they made me cry, so Mama would slice them in with the cucumbers herself. She sliced the corn off the cob into a big frying pan, full of hot grease. Then we ate the fried corn with tomatoes and cucumber and onions, and a hunk of corn bread, and a big mayonnaise jar full of buttermilk, and a piece of pork.

Sometimes Mama put on a "pot." It cooked a long time on the back of the wood stove. Sometimes it cooked all day. It cooked all the while we were washing, and when we came in we had a steaming plate of turnip greens with tomatoes and cucumbers and onions. Sometimes it was cabbage, yellow from having cooked so long. (I didn't like the yellowish cabbage or the orangey rutabagas.) Sometimes it was string beans. If we didn't have a pot, we had something quick, like fried squash with onions. Mama put on a pot of meat to go with the pot of vegetables. Often it was neck bones or pig feet or pig ears. Sometimes we had pork slices, swimming in red gravy. She would put on a pie at dinner, blackberry or apple, so it would be ready at suppertime; we had lemon meringue pie only on Sunday. We sometimes had sweet-potato custard through the week, also.

After dinner we went back out in the yard. By then the heavy things had boiled and Mama took them on a large stick to the washtub. The water in the tub was gray now, with a high meringue of foam on it. But she rubbed and I rinsed, and she hung out the clothes high, but now she gave me the socks and sweaters to hang on the bushes. She sent me to see if any of the clothes were "hard," and I went to the line and lowered the stick that was holding it up. I took down the clothes that had been in the sun so long that they were dry and stiff. I took them in the house and put them on the bed. Then Mama went over to the field to look at her crop, leaving me to churn.

I put the gallon jars of sweet milk into the tall churn, using a stick shaped funny at the bottom. Then I jugged it up and down, up and down, looking every few minutes to see if the butter had come. If it hadn't, I jugged some more. Mama would be over in the field a long time and then she would come and say, "The butter come yet?" And I'd look up and say, "No, ma'am," and churn some more. When the butter came, she scooped it up and shaped it into a cake.

For supper we had what was left in the pot from dinner,

along with a pie Mama had put on then, and a glass of buttermilk, and corn bread.

Before supper, Mama would get out two heavy irons and put them on the hot part of the stove. Then she'd tell me to go sprinkle the clothes. I would take some water and wet the clothes down and then roll them into a ball. That would soften them up some and make the wrinkles come out easier. After supper, Mama would start to iron on a big ironing board that had burned places at the end where the iron stood. I couldn't lift the real heavy iron, but she would let me have the small iron and I would push it up and down a handkerchief or a pair of socks, glad to be a woman like Mama.

She would fold the clothes and put them in a drawer and put the sheets and pillowcases on the beds. By that time the flies and mosquitoes would be buzzing the lamp. When she finished she would go out on the porch and sit in the cool, with the basket of butter beans to be shelled for Sunday dinner. I would take a newspaper and shell right along with her, pausing occasionally to protest when Ruf Junior got a pod that I wanted.

After we finished shelling the beans, my eyes would have sand in them and Mama would tell me to go to bed. I would go into the house and fall asleep while I heard her still moving around.

I helped Mama pick the green tomatoes for chowchow. She cut up the green tomatoes, then a hill of onions while tears ran down her face. She put in green peppers and cup after cup of sugar and a bag of spice. Then she pushed the chowchow far back on the stove and let it cook. In a little while the kitchen and back porch smelled good. It was the chowchow cooking. Mama let it cook and cook until it "cooked down." By nightfall she was ready to put it in the jars that Ruf Junior and I had washed.

She canned vegetables after she came home from work. There were tomatoes, which she put in hot water and scalded, then peeled; peas and corn; corn and okra; and butter beans and string beans. She put down cucumbers in a large stone jar and filled it with brine for pickles. And after we finished eating watermelon, I peeled the rinds, front and back, and Mama cooked them with sugar and we had watermelon preserve.

I washed jars and Ruf Junior washed tops; and row after row of canned goods, looking just like pictures, formed on the shelves, around the sides of the back porch, and under the house.

When the truck came with the peaches, we stopped everything. If it was Saturday, we didn't wash anymore or gather vegetables; if it was during the week we worked until late at night. Everybody had to help because peaches spoiled so fast. Daddy and Jesse and even Aunt Jo helped. The grown folks and Jesse had big knives. Ruf Junior and I had small paring knives. Mama didn't like Ruf Junior and me to peel because she said we left more of the peach in the peel than we put in the pot. But she let us peel, too, because if she didn't we'd holler so loud and beg so hard that she wouldn't have any peace. She picked out the soft ones, near the bottom, that had bad places on them and let us peel those. We peeled and ate and peeled and ate and went to bed full of peaches, sometimes sick.

Slopping the hogs was Jesse's job when Daddy didn't do it. But sometimes if Jesse heard them squealing over in the pigpen before it was time, he'd let Ruf Junior and me take them something. We'd get water buckets; I'd take a full one and Ruf Junior would have half a one, and we'd carry slops— discarded vegetables cooked with "ship stuff," a coarse thickening substance about the consistency of sawdust. We'd pour it through the big spaces between the railings into the trough and watch them eat. There would always be four or five, and we'd beat the big ones away with sticks so the little ones could eat. We were careful not to make too much noise because Daddy would wonder what was happening to the hogs if he heard them squealing too much.

Sometimes Mama would get after Ruf Junior and me when

she'd hear a chicken squawking and would look out to see a hen flying across the yard with Ruf Junior and me running after it. We didn't want to hurt her; we wanted to play with her; but she didn't understand that and went running for her life.

Daddy and Jesse plowed in the Bottom in the tobacco and cotton. Mama and Aunt Jo hoed in the vegetables. I hoed until I started chopping up too many plants and Mama protested; then I joined Ruf Junior in running up and down the rows, feeling the hot sun on the dry dirt under my feet and the cool wet where the plow had just been. If Ruf Junior and I were good, we could go to the house and get cold water and bring it to the fields in half-gallon jars.

Daddy hauled away trash for people, to sell to the junkman. When he came back with the trash, he dumped it in a pile in the backyard. There were wonderful things—dresses, pocketbooks, shoes, and pink things that I held up to my chest, wondering what went into them. It didn't matter that the dresses had buttons off and torn places. I liked those with big flowers all over them. I liked stripes next; but I didn't like the solid-colored ones at all. I would put on a pair of high-heeled shoes and hold the pocketbooks with the broken handles under my arm and think that I was a fine lady.

Sometimes there would be magazines in the trash and I would save them to look at when I was by myself. I would sit quietly and look at the pictures. There were dresses and houses and mothers kissing children and men kissing women and beautiful things that I had never seen before. When I got to the end, I would start at the beginning again. Soon I learned not to turn the pages so fast; it would last longer if I looked at the same picture a long time.

Sometimes I would forget where I was and Mama would have to call me twice.

After Daddy sorted out what he could sell from the rest, he would say something about going to "Sid's"; I didn't know what that was. But he'd get up the iron pieces and clothes and magazines and go off, returning in a little while with his truck empty.

One day he took me and Ruf Junior with him. The sign said SID RANCER's and it was a fairyland. Everything was there: bedsprings and bottles and sinks like those in the magazines. And things I didn't know the names for, scattered high and low, all over the ground.

Daddy said he'd have to weigh the load and I started to get out, but the big man with the big cigar said, "Sit right there, young lady," and he smiled at me. I was pleased. It was the first time anyone had ever called me "young lady."

Soon the truck started up in the air. It was magic. I was scared, but very happy to be going up high like that. We sat there for a while and then came back down. He gave Daddy money and we left.

Sometimes grown people came on Sunday and brought children with them. They stayed until dark and then left. Mr. Edwards lived through the woods, and his two girls, one big like Jesse and one small, would come to ask my mother for some sugar or some flour.

3

It was Friday. Mama didn't have to work tomorrow, and it was berry-picking time. Berry-picking was a ritual, a part of the rhythm of summer life. I went to bed, excited.

Mama liked to leave early in the morning, before the sun got too hot. When I woke up, I reached under the bed and got my shoes. I hadn't worn them since school let out. They were my everyday high-tops. My black patent-leather shoes were reserved for Sunday.

Mama put out pots and pans to pick in. She herself used a water bucket, just like the one that hung in the well. Your status in the group was determined by the size of the container you had. Jesse went sometimes, and he got to carry a water bucket, too. He was a big boy. I got an aluminum pan. Ruf Junior got an even smaller one.

I had a glass of cold buttermilk for breakfast, wiped my mouth with the back of my hand, and ran, for I was afraid that they might leave without me. All of us went to the road and joined the other people who were coming down the road on their way to the berry patch, too. We were going Through-the-Woods; that's where the best berries were. I joined the other children in kicking up clouds of dust. Some of them were barefooted, and the wet dew and dust made interesting patterns on their brown feet and legs. But I felt safe because if I stepped on a snake he couldn't bite me through my high-tops.

Mama had on a great straw sundown, and she wore an old dress and her old shoes. She carried a hoe—for snakes. Berry-picking was serious business. She traded a few words with the other women who were going. They carried thick short branches to beat back the bushes and to hit snakes with.

I laughed and ran and kicked up dust with the other children until we got to the path that led through the woods. Then I went streaking ahead through the early-morning dew that glistened on my legs and soaked the tail of my dress. My legs already had two of the biggest dew sores in the crowd, and numerous smaller ones—and I was pleased. (Dew sores were tiny scratches or insect bites that were aggravated if early-morning dew got into them. The dew would keep any sore fresh and could make a new one out of the tiniest scratch.) I knew that when I went back to school I could sit on the rocks at recess and exhibit my sores along with the best of them. Some children had sores so large and so deep that they looked ulcerated. Other children would examine them with awe, and a favored few got to pull off the scabs while everybody crowded around, looking at the red edges and yellow pus inside. Mine never got that big, but I would make up for size with quantity.

It was dark among the trees, different from the road, where

19

the air seemed to shimmer with heat and the houses looked still. I liked to look straight up at the tall pines and wish that I could get up there, to the very top, and sit swaying as the wind blew. But then I tripped on a rock and went sprawling in the grass, got up with dew on my chest, and ran to the next stopping spot.

We didn't know whose berries they were; nobody had heard about the idea of private property. Besides, the berries grew wild—free for everybody. Berry bushes had dark-green vines with whitish flowers and sharp thorns all the way down. If you carefully started picking the ones nearest you, then mashed that plant down with your feet and stood on it so that it couldn't fly back up and scratch you, you could pick the blackberries on the plant a little deeper inside the patch. Soon you would have a little private space all your own. You had to be careful to push the bushes back on the sides, too, or they would fly up and scratch. The grown people picked up high and the children picked down low.

"There's a good patch here," someone shouted.

"Where?" those who didn't have such a promising patch said. Either the berries were still red, which meant that they weren't ripe, or someone had picked the bushes pretty clean the day before.

"Over here," the helpful one announced, and soon the crowd had shifted to another spot. The berries were long and cylindrical; and the blacker they were, the sweeter they were. Some that had started drying up were almost as sweet as candy. We children ate them on the spot, putting purple-stained fingers into our mouths, creating purple-stained tongues, while the grown people wiped sweat and dodged bumblebees.

Sometimes moments passed when there was no sound. That meant everybody had a "good" spot and was concentrating on filling a container. The grown people's containers didn't make a noise, for they quickly covered the bottom. The children plunked each individual berry into their pans, and each berry would go *plunk, plunk, plunk.* Sometimes the noise never stopped, for before the berries covered the bottom, they would have eaten the contents and would have to start over again, only to finish the day with the bottom of the container showing through the fruit.

"Yon he go!" someone yelled.

"Where? Where?" everybody shouted. They didn't need to ask what. It was a snake. The grown people reached for their sticks. Mama reached for the hoe. And the scared snake slithered away just as fast as he could. The excitement died down and berry-picking resumed.

I picked and ate and picked and ate, but I was a little unhappy; I wanted to fill my pot up to the top, yet I wanted to eat like the other children. But I wanted a full pot so that Mama would praise me. The other children didn't seem to care whether they filled their pots, and their mothers didn't care, either, except to say now and then, "Get out of my way, child, before I step on you."

When the sun got hot and all the grown people were wet with sweat, their dresses clinging to their arms and little rivers of sweat running down their necks, they murmured among themselves and we left the berry patch. Most of the children had pan showing through the berries; mine was three layers deep in berries, but my tongue was stained a deep purple.

"Get the jars," Mama said when we got home.

Ruf Junior and I went to the smokehouse to get last year's jars. They were sticky with the residue from the canning last year. Mama never washed them before putting them away. Other women did, but she didn't. I never have been able to figure out why; perhaps it never occurred to her.

We came out, carrying half-gallon Mason jars with heavy gray lids on them. The lids had glass inside. If the glass wasn't cracked, we would use the lid again. If it was cracked we would throw that top away, for it would cause the food to spoil.

Mama was already down in the yard, lighting a fire around the washpot. We drew buckets of water from the well and poured it into the washpot. Then we got the washtubs and filled them half full of water. When the water in the washpot boiled, Mama poured hot water into the half-filled tubs and put a hunk of lye soap in. I liked to stir it around and around until the water got cloudy and started to suds up.

I washed jar after jar, putting my hands down in the water to the elbow and scrubbing at the ridges on top where last year's berry stains remained. Ruf Junior washed the tops. Then we rinsed them in a smaller tub and set them up to dry. They were ready to be filled with the berries that we had picked.

In the kitchen Mama washed the berries through bucket after bucket of water and picked them. Then there was a small mountain of sugar that she poured in on top of them. I watched while the small mountain slowly dissolved and made the berries on top turn crusty white.

Before the berries cooked, I started to itch. "Chiggers," Mama said. I knew to get the kerosene. A chigger was hiding down under my skin, and he had raised bumps all over me. I tried to scratch him, but my skin got between me and him. But he didn't like kerosene and that would stop him.

It did for a while. But then he started itching again and I had to put more kerosene on him. He wasn't in my navel. If he got down in your navel he had won, for you couldn't reach him, and he stayed there and itched so bad that you couldn't sleep that night.

I rubbed all over in kerosene, and by the time Mama had started to pour the heavy blackberry liquid into the half-gallon jars, I had gone to bed.

Daddy was often sick, but when he felt all right he'd laugh and sometimes he'd play with us. One day he called me and Ruf Junior to the table. He had a piece of brown paper glued to a fingernail on each hand. I sat beside him on the bench. "Now watch," he said. Then he said, "Two little redbirds, sitting on a limb; one named Jack, the other named Jim. Fly away, Jack!" Then the brown paper disappeared. I asked him where it was. He said that the bird had flown away. I looked all around for the bird, but I didn't see him. Then he said,

"Fly away, Jim." And the brown paper on the other hand flew away. "Come back, Jack." And the brown-paper bird flew back and landed on the table. "Come back, Jim." And the other bird came back.

I wanted to know how he did it, but he said that it was magic. He did the trick all over again and the birds flew away. After he'd played it over and over with Ruf Junior and me, he showed us how he'd done it. He had changed fingers. I had been so intent on looking at the finger that was on the table and looking up in the air to see where the bird had flown that it had never occurred to me to look down and see the finger concealed beneath the table.

4

For a long time I had felt a chill wind blowing through this flower-bestrewn, green, vivid Eden. I would pause in my running and ponder on it a moment; then I would dismiss it from my mind and run on, hoping it would go away. The chill was my growing knowledge that my mother, Nonnie, had no warmth, no love, no human feeling for me. When her voice spoke, it was always a rebuke and there was the absolute refusal on her part to touch me—no hugs, no kisses, no pats, nothing. I had absorbed the knowledge that she didn't want me touching her or talking to her. If I did something, she scolded me; if she asked me a question, she wanted an answer. Nothing more. I hid this secret knowledge from myself and everybody else. For it meant that I had done something very bad, and that is why my mother didn't like me. But whatever it was I had done, I would be extra good to make up for it. And if that didn't seem to be enough, I would do more and then more.

Some people find themselves in the wrong grouping of human relationships. Often it's their own fault. They marry someone and think that they know what they are doing, that they know themselves and they know the other person. Only it doesn't work out that way. For often they find out things about themselves and sometimes they find out things about the other person that let them know that they are not a natural harmonious grouping at all, that they should never have tried to form so close a human relationship with each other. They deal with this situation in various ways, two of which are separation and divorce.

But sometimes the wrong grouping is not the result of a conscious choice—of marriage with a stranger. Sometimes one is a part of the wrong grouping because he or she was born into it and, far from being a stranger, is an intimate member of the grouping, with blood ties, family memories—an association from which there is no divorce, no separation. Then what do you do? You harbor the guilty knowledge that you do not belong. But even worse, you follow the group's belief that you do not belong because there is something intrinsically the matter with you; that all family groupings are just alike, and that if you can't function in this one, you can't function in any; that since other people seem to be living harmoniously in a grouping of some kind, while you are in misery all the time, something or someone has decreed that you must be an outsider, that something being God or Fate or whatever governs human affairs; that you must be an outsider for an unspecified length of time to atone for some secret sin that you somehow, somewhere in the past, committed; that you must submit to harsh accusations, cruel judgments, uncomplainingly. For only after this suffering can you find peace and reconcilement within the grouping, whether familial or ethnic.

What do you do in such a situation? Say: I divorce you, I divorce you, I divorce you. Strong ones do. I couldn't.

Violence and cruelty entered my world when I was quite small.

Something was attacking the chickens, sucking the blood

out of them. Daddy said it was a weasel and got down his double-barreled shotgun and put it on the unfinished sills of the back porch that he was working on. He set Ruf Junior and me to watch, but I never saw the weasel. We'd hear the chickens making noise; Daddy would grab the shotgun and run to the hen house, but by the time he got there a chicken would be dead and the weasel would be gone.

One day Ruf Junior and I were playing on the sills while Daddy was hammering nearby. Suddenly he stopped still and grabbed his gun. There was a loud noise. I was too scared to cry out. Then we saw him pick something up. In the sunlight the brown fur had sparkles on it, but it was torn and covered with thick blood. The weasel had gotten bold and ventured too far.

On Saturdays Mama would throw a handful of chicken feed and call, "Here, chickee, chickee. Here, chickee-chick. Come on." When they came, she would quickly stoop and select one, carry it, squawking, to the chopping block, and chop its head off with the ax. The chicken would run all over the yard with no head on, splattering blood everywhere, while my mother threw its head in the bushes. Then, exhausted, it would fall. Sometimes I couldn't eat the chicken I had seen killed.

On Friday afternoons about dusk I would go to my rock and sit; I was waiting for the hollering to start in the little house over on the hill. I couldn't see the house; a stand of trees prevented that. But even though we were separated by at least three acres of land, I could always hear the screams clearly—mainly, I suppose, because the house was on a hill and the sounds carried clearly through the woods.

Every Friday after Ol' Dan'ul got home, the screaming started; first the wife, then the children. I could sometimes make out words she was saying, mainly calling for him to stop. But I never heard him say anything. The children didn't say anything, either; just cried. I never knew when it ended, for my mother would call me when it got dark, and make me go to bed.

At dusk one day the sky toward town turned red. At first it looked like a very bright sunset, but after the sun went down, the sky was still red. The color didn't come from the sky; it reached up from the ground. We wondered why the sky was red. Folks walked up the road, talked to each other about it, but no one knew the reason. I stood and watched the sky long after it got dark. Then the news began to come from town. I heard the words "soldier," "bus driver," "shot." I figured out that a bus driver had shot a soldier and somehow something was burning down in Durham. The next day, people talked. A white bus driver had ordered a black soldier to the back of the bus. The soldier wouldn't move. They argued and the driver shot and killed him. There was talk of the black soldiers coming from Camp Butner with machine guns. Later that night, a warehouse near the heart of downtown Durham burned to the ground. Nobody said that the blacks had burned the building, but somehow I understood what had happened.

One Sunday afternoon I was sitting on the porch. A man and a woman, both solid, round figures, she dressed in her Sunday blue-crepe dress and he in his Sunday gray suit, white shirt, dark tie, both disheveled, slowly walked up the red-brown dirt road in front of our house. They were methodically beating on each other. His tie was twisted and his hat was on backwards and nearly off his head. Her face was swollen and sweaty, but she clung to her black patent-leather pocketbook.

He punched her in the head. She staggered to the edge of the road, but didn't fall down. He lurched over after her and she swung out with her left hand holding the pocketbook and hit him so hard that he lost his balance. Both of them stood weaving in the road for a minute, trying to get their balance; then he hauled off and hit her again. This time she

26

lurched forward, almost tipping over into the dirt. He followed up with a punch in her back, but somehow she managed to lurch farther to the side rather than continue to fall over. The punch was so hard that it unbalanced him for a while and they both just stood there. Finally he got his breath and started to hit her on the head, but just at that moment she swung the pocketbook, hitting him and knocking him off balance. They stood weaving for a while and lurched a little farther up the road. They fought in silence, as if they had said all the words before the fight started and now they just fought.

I wanted to cry. They were grown, and grown people weren't supposed to do things like that. When you got grown you did the right things just like you had been taught in Sunday school.

Traney was coming through the Rock Pile. I looked out the window and saw her. "Traney's coming," I said. I was glad, for though she was bigger than I was, she played with me sometimes. I ran to the door to let her in. "Come in, Traney," I said, just like I heard Mama say to her friends. She had a cup in her hands.

"Miss Nonnie?" she said. "Mama said, 'Do you have a cup of sugar?' "

"Naw, honey," Mama said, "tell your mama I ain't got no sugar."

Traney had turned to go when I said, "Mama, we've got sugar."

"Naw, we ain't," Mama said.

"No, we don't have any," Aunt Jo said.

"Yes," I said. "I know where it is."

Aunt Jo and Mama looked at each other. There was Traney standing there.

Then Mama said, "Where is it?"

I pointed to the top of the shelves, where just over behind the little curving part there was a bag of sugar.

Mama got it down and gave Traney a cup. Traney left.

Then Mama reached in the corner and got her switch and said, "Come here."

"What for, Mama?" I started to cry. "I didn't do nothing."

She started to switch me. "What for?" I said.

"For [dis]puting my word," she said.

I knew I was being whipped because I had told we had sugar when she said we didn't have any. But Mama had always told me never to tell a story, and in Sunday school they said never to tell a story. But I was being whipped for *not* telling a story.

Nothing was ever enough; Mama's coldness never ceased and I never ceased trying to prove to be good. That is, I didn't until the third decade of my life, when I was so tired and worn out that I just didn't care one way or the other anymore.

This nightmarish relationship created a giant raw scar across my life.

But first I had to learn for certain that what I sometimes felt and paused briefly to wonder about before I skipped away and tried to dismiss it was real. And I did the summer we built another house, in 1938.

I don't remember our old house at all, except the front porch. It was wooden and brown and low to the ground. That was where I went into a screaming rage once when Miss Zula, the midwife who came to stay when Ruf Junior was born, locked me out of the house so she and the baby could sleep. I hollered and carried on so on the front porch that Daddy had to come to the house from the fields.

That summer, however, this house was torn down so another one could be put there. We all moved down into the backyard. Mama, Aunt Jo, Ruf Junior (who was just a baby), and I slept under the shed. It was open on three sides and usually held Daddy's car and the washtubs. Daddy and Jesse and some men slept in the barn. I don't know who all the men were, but they were helping Daddy, and I remember that one was a cousin who was feebleminded.

I have no recollection of hardship about sleeping under the

shed. To me it was a magical adventure. To lie there in the dark and see fireflies flickering just outside the reach of your arm was really wonderful, as it was to see the insects that came to buzz the yellow flame of the lamp, which burned all night.

The stove was on the little hill just above the rock that looked like a buried elephant, and food was cooked there, with red sparks licking out of the jagged pipe that had no chimney. The men came and stood around the stove, laughing and eating and talking.

It rained that summer. Every day. In the morning the ground was dark brown, soft like chocolate pudding. I liked the rain. The leaves of the trees and the poke salad and the bushes were a bright, shiny dark-green when it rained. Every day there was a thunderstorm. The mornings I can't remember, but in the evening the sky would fill up with clouds that would slowly turn gray and a deeper gray and then get lower and lower, so that if I stood on tiptoe I could almost touch them. They looked like a cow's udder.

Then the noise would start and something bright would hurry through the low, soft, dark-gray clouds. We all rushed with what we were doing. Aunt Jo would give orders. I ran around, as happy as I could be, in a short dress, dirty bloomers, bare feet, hair uncombed—it was plaited once a week, on Saturday night—over the wet rocks, the rain falling on my head, the mud, very cool, coming between my toes. The world was bright and laughing and I was always running, dancing, wanting to see everything. To me it was truly wonderful. The nicest thing that had ever happened.

One night it poured down rain. There was thunder and lightning everywhere.

Perhaps it was a loud clap of thunder that woke me up. I was a little wet, for I slept on the outside, near the open side, but I didn't really care; that made the adventure even nicer. But I was worried, for I had to "go." And *it* was out there in the dark, and I was afraid to go alone.

So I called my mother to go with me.

"Mama."

But she didn't say anything.

I half rose up in bed and looked around in the yellow lamp-light. The tail of my nightgown was wet from the rain that had run off the tin roof of the shed. Every now and then the world outside the shed was illuminated for a second, and then it was dark again, sometimes accompanied by a loud crash of thunder. When the world lit up, I could see *it*, where I had to go, through the sheets of rain. But when it was dark again, I couldn't see anything. It looked like a velvet cloak that I would have to push my way through.

"Mama," I called, almost crying.

"What is the matter with you, girl?" She was sleepy and mad.

"I've got to go."

"Well, go on, then."

I didn't say anything, but lay back in despair, hoping that maybe I could wait until morning, when it wouldn't be dark and thundering and lightning anymore. I was quiet for a while, and it must have occurred to my mother that I would mess up the bed, for she rose up.

"Go on, girl."

"But Mama, I'm scared."

"You had better go on," Mama said, really mad now.

I was scared of the thunder and lightning, but I was even more scared of my mother now that she was mad; so I went running out into the rain in my nightgown. While I was out there—I don't remember whether I was coming back or still going—something happened. Something scared me to death. I still can't say what it was. I fell down in the wet, or something or someone came up behind me and pushed me down. I jumped up fast, running to get away from it. I had been hurt. I found myself running all over the yard in a world that was now dark, now light, and full of rain. And somehow I couldn't find my way back to the shed. I went flying across the yard to the barn where my father slept, and called, "Daddy! Daddy!"

He rose up sleepily and said, "Go back to your mother."

He didn't know that there was something after me. He only knew that I was in the wrong place at the wrong time. I went running across the yard in the rain again, and this time I made it. I was safe in the glow of the yellow lamplight.

I tried to recall what had happened, but I could not. But I knew that it was bad and that the one person whom I had called on to help me hadn't, but had sent me out in the dark alone and in the pouring rain.

I was five years old. Eden had ended for me.

5

Aunt Jo was a tall, slim lady. She held herself very straight. She had long black hair that hung to her waist when she let it down, but she wore it parted in the middle, with a little bun in the back. She was ivory-colored and had a sharp nose. She also had a sharp temper and would cuss if you made her mad.

Aunt Jo came to live with us when she got tired of the North. She had left Durham when she was a young girl because she was disappointed in love. In her teens she had married a man, only to find out shortly afterwards that he had a wife from whom he had never been divorced. She soured on men and swore that she would never marry, and she didn't.

She adored me.

Though we couldn't have looked more unlike each other, she insisted that I was just like her. One day she called me to her.

"Let me see your hands," she said.

She took them and examined the fingers one by one.

"See, you have long, slender fingers. You are going to be a pianist."

Until then I had never thought of playing the piano. Marguerita had a piano, but then her father was a building contractor and they had a whole lot. After that I started worrying Mama for a piano so that I could take piano lessons. Marguerita had a piano and I wanted one. I pleaded and begged. I asked Daddy, although even then I knew that he didn't have the money and that Mama would have to pay for it. Mama never quite forgave Aunt Jo for that. But she bought the piano. It was a short upright, secondhand. It was not tall, like the player piano that one of the families in Wildwood had, nor was it low and sleek, like Marguerita's. Still, it was mine and I loved it, polishing it often with clear red furniture polish and admiring the figured maroon scarf with the heavy gray crocheted border that Aunt Jo made for it.

A piano was a fixture in many black homes in Wildwood; it was even a sign of refinement. A guitar was not. A song played on a piano was all right with the good Baptists who dominated the community; the same song played on a guitar was Satan's message, luring people to their damnation and death. Banjos were not mentioned at all. I suspect that in some way they were reminders of the slavery past and thus were regarded as signs of an outcast's status.

Aunt Jo was also determined that I was going to college someday. Nobody on either side of the family had ever gone to college, but she knew that I would. She was going to send me herself. I didn't know what she wanted me to be. I doubt if even she knew.

Mama would get after her about it: "Jo, you're always putting ideas into that girl's head. Nothing but foolishness."

Aunt Jo wouldn't say anything. She and Daddy didn't get along very well, but she wanted to stay with us because he was her brother and her closest relative. So she tried to keep on the good side of Mama. She used to say that she didn't want to stay with her nieces and nephews because they wanted to get what money she had and she wasn't going to give it to them because they wouldn't do anything with it but waste it up. So she put all her hopes on me. Daddy's mother had married twice, having children by her second husband quite late in life, so that he and his nephews and nieces were nearly the same age, while I was closer in age to my second cousins. My first cousins resented Aunt Jo's interest in me.

Sometimes Aunt Jo liked to do a little something special in the kitchen. We often had chicken feet. Mama knew a shop in Durham that sold poultry and let the workers at the tobacco factory and other blacks—and, I suppose, anybody else who wanted them—have bags and bags of chicken feet for very little or nothing. Mama brought some home and Aunt Jo cooked them. But she put all kinds of things in with them and made dumplings also, thus turning it into an exotic dish. This didn't sit too well with Mama. Then there were Aunt Jo's exercises with poke salad—which no one would eat. It wasn't long before Mama said, "Jo, don't bother about cooking supper. I'll fix it when I get home."

Aunt Jo had brought a lot of great big trunks when she came to live with us. One day she let me see one of her dresses. It was black, but around the neck and each sleeve there was a heavy collar of silver. It formed a crust and hung down in raindrops all around. The dress looked like the ones worn by the queens in one of my schoolbooks. She had other fine things that she never took out, except for one special occasion—a family reunion.

Aunt Jo wanted to invite all her and Daddy's kin to our house for Sunday dinner. Mama didn't want her to. She said that Aunt Camellia had consumption and she might give it to everybody. The talk went on nightly: Dinner. Consumption. I didn't know what consumption was, but I knew it was bad and that people died from it. Still Aunt Jo persisted. She would see to it that Camellia ate out of special plates; she'd put paper down outside so that if Camellia had to spit she wouldn't contaminate anything; and she'd wash Camellia's plates, fork, and spoon in a special pot separate from the others and sterilize them afterwards. Finally Aunt Jo prevailed.

I was excited. We had never had a dinner party and never had company for a meal, except about once a year when Aunt

Donna came down from Philadelphia or Uncle Josh and Aunt Eula came over from Virginia.

Aunt Jo reached into her trunk and came out with strange-looking utensils that I had never seen before. There was a fork that she said was a pickle fork. And she had a bowl-shaped deep spoon for gravy. And there were long forks and shorter forks, and ordinary knives and broad knives that were cake servers. She called them silver, not knives and forks. She let me help her polish them. When we rubbed them hard with a soft gray paste, they started gleaming, not bright, but soft; and the longer we rubbed, the more they gleamed. Magic. I wondered what they were going to be used for, for I had never seen anything like it. Then she got out big plates with soft colors and silver around the edges. She called them china. There was a bowl shaped like Aladdin's lamp that she said was for gravy. And a cut-glass dish for pickles, and a dish with many hollows for eggs. She wouldn't let me help wash the dishes; she was afraid I might break them.

On Sunday, two carloads of people came from town. The children ate at a separate table, but I ate with the grown people. Most of them had never been to our house before, though I had visited them with Daddy; he went to town nearly every week to see one or the other.

Aunt Jo had been cooking for two days. We had strange dishes like lamb, along with fried chicken and ham. In addition to ordinary pickles, she put on the table green things with red coming out, called olives. She had celery stalks with soft orangy cheese in the large end. The whole table looked like a picture in a magazine. The silver gleamed, the dishes sparkled, and the food looked like a picture. My aunt had done that, and I wanted to be just like her.

Parties among the black folk were the main source of entertainment. I say "were" because with the coming of integration many more blacks started going out to movies, to restaurants, to other events. But prior to the civil rights movement of the early 1960s in the United States, and even up to the end of the 1960s, most blacks found their amusement exclusively within the black community, and the party was one of its major forms. It was communal; it was considered "clean," as opposed to the evil of going to "joints." A joint is a place, usually a dark hole of a building, often out in the woods, where beer, and often illegal liquor, can be obtained. There is usually a jukebox present; thus the name "juke joint." Sometimes older people call such places "roadhouses." "Roadhouse" was also a term of opprobrium, carrying with it a strong sense that the house was out in the woods and was used for immoral, and frequently illegal, purposes. So, nice people didn't go to juke joints. But if they sat around and drank "a little something" at a party, it was all right.

A party was an event for which one carefully prepared. Everybody took a fresh bath. There is something beautifying about a bath—the whole personality seems to glow. For rural people with no running water, a bath was an undertaking of considerable proportions.

We would go to the well and get water, bring it in and put it in a big tub on the wood stove and heat it and take a bath, washing one section of the body at a time with a rag torn from a sheet and some of Mama's lye soap. We finished clean and sweet-smelling. Taking a bath was a ritual every Saturday night. One stopped to ponder one's body, what one walked around in and exhibited to the world. With the introduction of running water, much of the drama surrounding the ritual has been lost.

If you were going to a party, or going riding in a car, that meant that you would dress extra-special nice.

Black girls all over the South would sit while a mother or sister patiently pulled a hot metal comb with a wooden handle through small bunches of hair, each segment of which had been carefully lubricated with some type of heavy oil, sometimes green, most often pale yellow and sweet-smelling. If the metal teeth were too hot, a cloud of smoke would rise from the hair and the black ends would singe brown. If the wielder of the comb was unskilled, the owner of the hair would wince and jump when the hot comb touched her scalp or ear. Sometimes burns on the top of the ear were so severe that they blistered and peeled. A skillful straightener was much in demand because she saved the price of a hairdresser. No one foresaw that the time was near when the natural texture of black hair would be thought beautiful and it would be worn and even flaunted everywhere.

Next, hot curlers were introduced and the hair ends were curled; if the procedure was successful, a curl could last for a month. If a girl's hair would not hold a curl, she soon became short-haired, for the incessant straightening and curling took its toll.

Fashions changed. At one time, glossy uncombed curls were considered high style. Then they started combing them together. Next they started combing them all the way out and by a series of pushing motions reintroduced a calmer version. New pomades were introduced that produced a dull finish, rather than the high gloss that was characteristic of straightened hair.

Bathed, hair straightened, a girl put on a bright-colored dress to finish the dressing. If her mother was worldly she let her wear Cutex fingernail polish, and lipstick, and nut-brown powder. Sometimes the mother didn't approve of makeup and the unlucky girl was left with an unpowdered face glowing in the heat.

Boys got themselves together in sports jackets and dark pants and shined shoes. They brushed and brushed their hair and smiled in the mirror to make sure that their teeth gleamed.

Then they were ready for the party.

"Aunt" Laura was my mother's best friend. I wouldn't have known that she drank except that I once heard my mother telling someone about it in a soft voice, the same voice that she used when she talked about "it" that Laura was dying of. "It" was cancer. The world became sunless when "it" was talked about. "It" was a very, very bad thing to happen to anyone.

I somehow figured out that when Mama said things like "messing with that stuff" or "likes a little taste" it meant that Aunt Laura liked whiskey. I couldn't understand it. Whiskey—and all alcohol was called whiskey—meant loud voices, men standing up in the house with their hats on and in their Sunday clothes, as Daddy and Uncle Josh did when Uncle Josh and Aunt Eula came down from the woods in Virginia several times a year to visit. Uncle Josh would bring a bottle of red-eye with him and Daddy would laugh and they would joke about how strong it was. It was a dark, clear red, like red Kool-Aid, only the liquid looked heavier than Kool-Aid and Uncle Josh would bring it in a half-gallon jar. Sometimes Aunt Eula would take a taste, but I never saw my mother take any. Sometimes when Uncle Josh didn't have any red-eye, he'd bring white lightning, but red-eye was the most highly prized.

When Uncle Josh and Daddy drank and talked, it was happy; they both had very long legs and I would look straight up until I saw their mouths laughing and talking.

One Christmas it was happy, too; this time it was beer. My father took us all to visit Aunt Camellia, who had consumption, and he and the men sat around a table and I sat with him. Someone went out to get something called "beer," and when it was poured into clear glasses I thought that it was the most beautiful drink I had ever seen. It was clear and sparkling in some places and cloudy in others, and it smelled good.

I wanted some and was mad at being left out, so Daddy poured me a full, sparkling glass with crystal bubbles in it and foam at the top. I knew sheer bliss. That wonderful drink was going to be mine.

One huge sip and I was to be forever cured of the taste of beer. It wasted like a mouthful of alum.

Alcohol to me, however, usually meant trouble.

"He drinks." I would see in my mind shouting, cussing men. They beat women, broke the furniture, and sent the children hollering to the neighbor's.

6

I started school.

The night before I was to go to school, Mama called me to her. "When you want to go, raise your hand and say, 'May I be excused?' " she said.

"Excused?" I said. "What is excused?"

"When you want to go," Mama said.

I couldn't figure out this "excused." It was the first time that I had heard the word and I wondered what it meant. I didn't know the meaning of a word I couldn't see, touch, feel, or taste. What was it? "Excused." "Excused." I said it over and over because I didn't want to forget. When I wanted to go I had to raise my hand and say, "May I be excused? May I be excused?" I was so scared that I was going to forget that word. It meant that I could go when I had to, so I mustn't forget, but I didn't know what it looked like.

It was magic. "Excused," and I could go when I had to.

There were a lot of children, and I was scared. The big lady was called the "teacher," and I was scared of her, too.

Each of us had to go up to her desk and tell her when we were born. I was panicked. I didn't know when I was born. I listened closely to what the others were saying. I would be born when they were born. But each one said something different. "February," I heard one say. February, I thought to myself. What is February? Then they said things like "nineteenth" and "sixth" and "twenty-third." What was it they were saying? Those were magic words, like "excused." You said them and they meant something. But I didn't know any of those magic words. When was I born? What did that mean?

The teacher called my name and I went up to the desk. I was scared to death.

"When were you born?" she said.

"I don't know," I said. I couldn't get my breath. Some of the children laughed; others didn't because they didn't know when they were born, either.

"What did your mother tell you?"

"Nothing."

"Can you point to the calendar?"

"Yes, ma'am," I said, glad to get away from her desk. I went to the calendar and pointed to a date.

"What month?" she asked.

"Month" was another one of the magic words. I didn't know what "month" meant. The game was up. I didn't know.

"Ask your mother tonight when you were born and tell her to write it on a piece of paper," she said.

"All right'm," I said and went back to my seat, not looking at anybody.

I sat there in a fog. "Excused." "Month." "Date." "Born." All these magic words, and I didn't know what they meant. I was glad when it was time to go.

Soon everybody said "ABCDEFGHIJKLMNOPQRSTUV-WXYZ," and I said it, too. It was a game called "alphabet." We said it together every morning after something called "devotion," which was like Sunday school. We copied the big letters off the board and then we copied the small letters. The big letters were easy; they were lines with a few curves. The little letters were harder; they had a lot of curves. Mrs. Johnson gave us paper with lines, and I patiently drew the curving letters. If it looked like the letter on the board, she said, "Good." If it went too far above the line or below the line, she told me to do it again. It was called "writing."

Then we said, "One times one is one, two times one is two," until we got to ten; then we started over on "Two times one is two, two times two is four, two times three is six, two times four is eight," until we got to ten. I didn't know what I was saying, but I said it right along with the others. This was school and this was what you were supposed to do. I used to wonder, though, how some of the other children knew things and I didn't know them. Where had they learned them?

"Did Dick Tracy get out yet?" Mama said to Jesse.

"No'm," Jesse said. "They've still got him in there."

"How long's he been in there?"

"He's been in there two weeks. I sure hope he gets out all right."

"You don't have to worry about old Dick. He gets out every time," Mama said.

Mama had just got in from work at the tobacco factory, and still in her blue uniform, she was talking with Jesse about the "funnies." They were something in the paper that came in the evening. Mama and Jesse liked the funnies. I didn't know what the "funnies" were, for Mama and Jesse talked about people, and when I got the paper and turned the pages, no real people fell out of the paper. Where was Dick Tracy? Where did he hide when I turned the pages trying to find him?

"Jesse, show me the funnies," I would beg. He would keep on reading and laughing. "Hear, Jesse. Hear. Show me the funnies."

Finally one day he showed me a page covered with a lot of drawings. These were the funnies that he and Mama talked about. But they didn't make sense to me.

"Where is Dick Tracy?" I asked. I expected to see a man emerge from his hiding place in the paper. Jesse showed me a drawing that was like a squiggly line. These were the funnies. I was disappointed. All the drawings looked alike to me. I started pointing to the pictures.

"This is Dick Tracy," I said. And I went from frame to frame, on down the page. "Dick Tracy." I was a big girl now and I should know what Jesse and Mama were talking about.

"No, girl," Jesse said. "This is Dick Tracy." And he pointed to just one part of the page.

"How do you know?" I said.

"See the hat? And he's got a square jaw," Jesse said.

I looked closely at the page. He did have a hat and his jaw was big. But I couldn't find what Mama and Jesse talked about every evening when she came home from work.

In school, Mrs. Johnson turned the pages of a big book and we all said, "Run, Spot, run," and "This is Dick," "This is Jane," "Run, Spot, run," "See Spot run."

One day I looked over the squiggly lines called "Dick Tracy" and something stopped my finger. It was "see." I looked at it for a long time. That was the word in the big book that Mrs. Johnson turned the pages in every day. It was "see." Magic. From then on, I could read.

The teacher would call me to her desk and I would take my book and stand beside her. I would read until she told me to stop and go back to my seat; then she would call somebody else. The book was smaller than the big one that stood on a stand in front of the class, and I never knew what it was about because I read where she pointed and stopped when she said stop; then the next student took up from there. It was something you did, like brushing your teeth.

One day a big, broad-chested woman came to our room. She was very black and clean. She was the cleanest woman I had ever seen. Her dress was clean, her shoes were clean, and she herself was clean. We stared at her and she looked back at us, stern, unsmiling, through very clean square glasses. I was scared of her. Mrs. Johnson said that she was the "nurse." Nurse, I thought. What is a nurse? Why were they always saying these magic words that I didn't know? The whole class lined up and followed her up the hall to the auditorium. There were glass bottles, and cotton and clear fluids in jars. Each child went to her and she took his or her head in her hands and looked and did something that I couldn't see. They turned around with a piece of cotton on their arm. Sometimes she took something from around somebody's neck, and it made a sound as she threw it in the wastebasket. "Asfesda," I thought she said. Some of the children wore small bags around their necks. I had never thought about it. I thought that they were born that way. But the nurse was throwing the bags in the wastebasket. I breathed a sigh. I didn't have one. I was all right.

When I got to the head of the line, she turned my face this way and that, looked at my chest, and then got mad. "What's this?" she asked. She was looking at a square piece of cloth, plastered to my chest, that was brown with salve and constant wearing.

"It's my flannel cloth," I said.

"Flannel cloth?" she said. "What are you doing wearing a flannel cloth?"

"Mama says so's I won't catch a cold." My chest felt tight. I could barely speak.

"Such ignorance!" she said and grabbed the cloth, balled it up, and threw it in the wastebasket. I was heartbroken and terrified. I always wore a flannel cloth. Mama put it on us when the first chilly morning came. She greased it on the side next to the chest with a brown salve and we wore it all the time, day and night, until it got warm again, never removing it at all except for the Saturday-night bath. It was never washed, so by the time the weather got warm again, the flannel, which had originally been soft pink and blue and gray, was very brown.

While I was wondering what to tell Mama, I looked to see what was the cold that was going on my arm. It was alcohol. Then the nurse reached for some sharp, shiny needles and I knew that this was the "shot" that some of the older children had talked about. What was I going to do? Daddy had told Mama that he didn't want any of his children taking shots.

"Don't let 'em give you no shots," he'd said to me.

"No sir," I'd said.

What was a shot? I had never seen a shot. I tried to open

my mouth to tell the nurse what Daddy had said, but I couldn't get my breath. I felt a sharp tingle in my arm and she gave me the cotton to hold over the spot. My words, down in my chest, had not come up.

The world was bewildering. I thought that all grown people were the same, but the nurse had thrown away my flannel cloth that Mama told me to wear and don't lose. Then she had given me a shot when Daddy had told me not to take any. What was I going to do? The nurse was grown like Mama and Daddy, but she did things different from them. Something was wrong.

Mama told me not to tell Daddy about the shot, and Aunt Jo made me another flannel cloth.

"Who'd like to sweep the hall?" Mrs. Johnson said. A daily ritual. A dozen hands shot up instantly, mine among them. I wanted to sweep the hall today. The hall was a mysterious place that led between two rooms to the entrance of the auditorium. It was a little dark because no windows opened on it. To us it represented freedom, and it was a great honor to be chosen. So far I hadn't got a chance to sweep the hall, though I had swept around in the room. Sweeping the room, cleaning out paper from under the seats, and straightening up the chairs were mundane activities. What everybody really prized was going outside to clean the erasers by hitting them on a rock, and sweeping the hall.

Mrs. Johnson pointed to me, and I ran to the cloakroom to get the broom.

I would make the hall twice as clean as anybody else ever had, and then I would get to sweep it again. I wielded the broom that was twice as tall as I was, and swept and swept. One or two people passed at the end of the hall, going into the auditorium/classroom, but I was alone.

Then I looked up and saw him.

Calvin was a big boy. He must have been eight years old. He was brown and smooth, like creamy chocolate, and he had black curls all over his head. I liked him. They said that he hugged and kissed the girls, but he had never hugged me.

I wondered what it must be like to be hugged. Or kissed. No one ever hugged me. Sometimes in church I saw mothers hug their children to them when they wanted them to be quiet during the sermon. Or children would crawl up on their mothers' laps and kiss them and the mothers would kiss back. But Mama never kissed me and she drew back if I wanted to touch her. I was not huggable. That was the way things were. I didn't like it. I wished that things were different.

Calvin looked at me and I stopped sweeping. Then I saw him look back to see if anyone was coming. There wasn't; and he ran down the hall, while I ran up to meet him. I was careful to pick up the broom because I didn't want to cause any noise and have Mrs. Johnson send someone into the hall after me.

We met halfway and he started hugging me and the broom. I held it close because I didn't want to drop it. It was warm and I felt happy, the way babies in church jump in their mother's lap and lean backwards way over, knowing that she will hold them and not let them fall. I wanted him to hug me forever, but I was scared. I had been out sweeping the hall a long time and Mrs. Johnson might send someone after me. Or someone could pass at the end of the hall. He was scared, too, for we parted real fast and ran in opposite directions.

I ran into the room, out of breath and scared. I must have looked funny, for Mrs. Johnson asked me what was the matter. "Nothing," I managed. I put the broom away and sat down, and didn't hear anything else that was said the rest of the day. I didn't tell anybody.

I saw Calvin after that, but I didn't talk to him when he came around me. I had heard that some girls went under the house with Calvin, and I knew I couldn't go. Then I saw him talking with Rebecca. She was a big girl and she went under the house with boys. So I backed off, but I always wished that Calvin would hug me again.

I drew a big circle with a smaller one on top, put on a tail, and called it a cat, then patiently filled it in with yellow, purple, green. Mrs. Johnson called it beautiful and I was satisfied. Then I drew a big circle and put a smaller one on top, drew some ears, and called it a rabbit. Then I filled it in with red, brown, black, trying not to color it over the edge, and showed it to Mrs. Johnson. She said it was just like Mr. Bunny, and I went back to my seat quite pleased with myself.

Recess came often. We played games. Sometimes the teachers would play dodge ball with us. They would take a big rubber ball that bounced, and stand far apart. All of us would get in the middle and they would throw it at us while we dodged. If the ball hit you, you were out. Soon there would be just two or three left and it would be hard to get them out, for they were the fastest and it was hard to hit them.

I liked hopscotch. With a stick we drew on the ground three boxes on top of each other and put 1, 2, 3 on them. Then we drew two boxes on their sides over them, so that it looked like a _T;_ they were 4 and 5. Then we drew another box like the first three and called it 6. Then we drew two more boxes like 4 and 5 and called them 7 and 8. You took a piece of glass or a rock or a bottle cap and threw it in 1, then hopped over that box on one leg. You could put both feet down in 4 and 5 and in 7 and 8. The object was to hop over the whole design on one foot without stepping in the box into which you'd tossed the glass or rock or bottle cap. If you wavered and put a foot down, you were out. It was easy for 1, 2, and 3. But when the glass was in 4 or 5, you couldn't put both feet down to rest and you had to hop on to 7 and 8 and back again. The one who could do the whole design was the winner.

I liked a game called last-one-squats-shall-tell-his-name. We formed a circle, held hands, and sang, "Last one squats shall tell his name, tell his name, tell his name. Last one squats shall tell his name, so early in the morning." At the last word, you sat down fast. The last one down was "it" and had to tell the name of the one he loved. Everybody had a love. Often the recipient of this affection was totally unaware of the giver's existence.

I learned another ritual:

"What's your name?" "Puddin' Taine. Ask me again and I'll tell you the same."

Most of all, we liked to run. At recess we ran everywhere—around the schoolhouse; up in the woods, where we jumped from rock to rock and swung around the trees; then deep down in the yard, where the big boys played baseball. Running, dodging the big children, some of whom were standing talking like grown people. Hitting those we thought we could outrun—otherwise the victim would catch up with you and knock you down. Boys, girls, running, running, far, far away from Mrs. Johnson.

One hot day we ran and played, then ran sweating back to the room and continued in the cloakroom. Mrs. Johnson came in, slapping us right and left. She hit me.

That evening Mama said, "What's that on your face?"

"I don't know," I said.

"It looks like fingerprints."

I was surprised and a little shy. This was the first time Mama had ever talked to me with something like sympathy.

"Mrs. Johnson slapped me," I said. I had forgotten all about it.

"Why?"

"We were playing in the cloakroom."

"Well, don't let your daddy see it." Daddy had a quick temper where his children were concerned and he would have gone to school to see about it.

I had been hurt, but I must not show it.

7

It turned colder and we put on sweaters and ran, then coats. Then it was Christmas.

We were going up to my Aunt Claudia's. I liked Aunt Claudia. She lived in a big dark house on the hill. The windows had long filmy curtains and there was a big hall that ran right through the house. When you sat on the porch, you could see the cars far down the hill. Aunt Claudia always took me up on her lap and asked me if I had been a good girl. I nodded yes, and she said, "Let's see what we can find for the good girl." She gave me milk and cake. Her cake was pretty. It had pink layers and green frosting. The chocolate cake had pink-and-white patterns on top of the brown chocolate.

Mama got out a shopping bag. She was going to take Aunt Claudia the walnut cake that she had made for her. I was very proud of that cake. Ruf Junior and I had picked up the walnuts under the tree over to Mr. Harvey's. It was a big tall tree. You couldn't see to the sky when you stood under the branches, close to the trunk. The limbs came down real low to the ground. A grown person could touch them if he jumped up.

Nuts were all over the ground. They had black hair all over. We picked them up and went home bent over on the side, carrying a big bucketful. Then we took a hammer and a shoe last and cracked them. They were very hard. Sometimes they would fly out from under our hands and we would hit our fingers instead; then we would holler and shake our fingers, ashamed to cry because others would laugh. Under the hairy coat was a smooth brown nut. Then we would crack it and take a safety pin and pull out the meat, which was dark brown on the outside and light brown inside.

Mama took the small bowl of nuts that we had picked out

and put it in the frosting, which looked yellowish-brown. This was the walnut cake, and every year she made one for Aunt Claudia.

I wanted to give Aunt Claudia a present. I wanted to hear how she would talk to me when I gave her a present. So I ran around the house looking for something to take to her. I thought about the doll that I had just got for Christmas, but Aunt Claudia was grown; she wouldn't know how to play with a doll. And she had dishes bigger than my tea set. We had nuts and apples and oranges. But Aunt Claudia had more. Her children were big and when they came from town they brought her a whole lot of things. What to get her? I went from room to room. I had to hurry because I was afraid Mama would leave without me.

Then I found something. It was a statue of Christ. He had on a robe and he looked like the picture on the Sunday school card. The statue had been around the house for a long time, but it wasn't any good because it had fallen and broken, and a fine white powder fell off the place where one arm had been.

"Can I have it, Mama? Can I have it?" I begged.

"What are you going to do with it?" she said.

"I want to give it to Aunt Claudia for Christmas," I said.

"Claudia doesn't want that old thing. It's broken."

"Yes, she will, Mama. Please let me have it."

She nodded her head and I went running to find something to wrap it in. I found some white tissue paper under the tree and carefully wrapped the statue in it. I walked up the hill with the statue cradled in my arms. I had a present for Aunt Claudia, too.

"I've brought you a present, Claudia," Mama said. "A walnut cake."

"Well, Nonnie," Aunt Claudia said, "you never forget me. I sure do appreciate it."

We were in the kitchen, and Aunt Claudia put the walnut cake on the table with all kinds of cakes; some were chocolate, some were green, some were pink, coconut, pineapple—all kinds of cake. I was jumping up and down with excitement, but I was waiting until the grown people stopped talking.

"What did old Santa bring you?" Aunt Claudia said.

"I brought you a present," I said, shifting from one foot to the other as I handed it to her.

"A present. For me?" She seemed to be astonished. Her mouth flew open and she said, "Oooooooohhhhhhh! It is so pretty! A present for me! A statue of Christ. Wait until I tell the others about this. It's the nicest present I've got this Christmas."

Aunt Claudia kept talking about my present while I stood there looking up at her, listening, so happy. Aunt Claudia liked my present.

"We've had that old thing around the house so long," Mama said. "It's broken. She wanted to bring something, so I told her to bring that. It ain't no good."

I hurt so bad in my chest. I wanted to cry but couldn't. Aunt Claudia hugged me to her side.

After Christmas we clustered at recess. "What you get?" "What you get?" Doll. Electric train. Tea set. Some clothes.

I asked one girl, "What did you get?"

"I didn't get anything," she said. "I'll get mine 'Old Christmas.'"

"Old Christmas?" I asked. "What is 'Old Christmas'?"

"It's after Christmas and I'm going to get something then," she answered. (Old Christmas, I have since learned, is Epiphany, January 6.)

I stopped for a moment, listening. It was my first realization that everybody didn't do everything the same way.

"No school today! No school today!" The road was full of black and brown children slopping through the mud on the road that led to the rock quarry, where trucks went to get rocks. When a truck almost ran over them, the children jumped the ditch and scattered on the soft mudbanks on the other side.

"I'm glad we got out early," one said.

"Thank God for the snow," one bold boy said.

"You're taking the Lord's name in vain," a youngster told him.

Boys and girls were on their way home from school. They were laughing and talking, glad that they didn't have to stay at school, for if the roads were so bad that the buses couldn't get through, those children who had walked to school—and had pulled on their galoshes and rubbers and gone splashing through the mud puddles or the snow and ice—could come home very early in the morning, and there would be no school until the roads got better.

I watched the boys and girls in the road. Even though Jesse and Ruf Junior had gone to school, I hadn't. Daddy figured that since it was bad weather, the children would probably come home early, anyway, and I had just gotten well from a cold; so he thought that it was better that I not go. But I loved school and had waited anxiously near the road, so that if the children hadn't appeared over the little hump soon, I would have begged him and he would have let me go. Though I was standing on the side of the road, I was actually among the laughing boys and girls. I laughed along with them.

Everything was in fun until Rat, the boldest of the boys, sang out, "Marguerita wears homemade drawers." Everybody stopped laughing and backed up, for they knew that a fight was about to start.

"What did you say about my sister?" T. J. said.

Rat was scared but wouldn't back off. "I said Marguerita wears homemade drawers, and what's more, your mama does, too." He was triumphant.

The other boys and girls went "Ohhhhhhh" and "Ahhhhhhh."

"They gonna fight. It means a fight," a girl said.

"It sure do. If you talk about somebody's sister, he'll sure fight you," said a boy with a bibbed cap.

"You right. When Leo talked about my sister, I went to

the playground and beat him up," Lee said. Lee was so tough that the grown folks said he was made of pig iron.

"What did he say about your sister?" another girl asked Lee.

"He said she smelled bad. Talking about my sister. I beat him up."

Roy backed Lee up. "You're supposed to do that if somebody talks about your sister."

At that moment Rat and T. J., who had been circling each other, lunged. The children formed a ring around them, boys on the inside and girls on the outside.

I stood frozen and cold, watching. I couldn't see anything but the circle moving until I saw two forms in the mud of the road. T. J. was on top.

"Look out, a truck's coming," they all yelled, and T. J. let Rat go and they all scattered to the side.

T. J. pointed a finger at Rat. "That'll teach you to talk about my sister." Rat, shamed, ran off.

Jesse, my big brother, peeled off from the group and came running to where I was standing and watching the boys and girls go down the road.

"The children were talking about you." He was laughing. I hung back and looked fearfully at him. Jesse said, laughing and pointing, "Marguerita said that you looked like a frozen turkey standing out here." He doubled over with laughter.

"And you didn't take up for me! You didn't take up for me!" I ran into the house, crying.

One day when I got home from school, there was a beautiful fresh pile of trash that my father had collected. I was happy. There would be dresses and shoes and pocketbooks for me to play with, but best of all, new magazines to look at. Ruf Junior was playing with a beautiful cup. It was the most beautiful cup I had ever seen.

"Let me see it," I said.

"Naw," he said, holding it behind his back.

"Please let me see it," I said.

"Naw," he said, laughing, and held it so I could almost touch it, but jerked it back when I reached for it.

"Let me see it." This time I grabbed him and started to take it away from him.

"Mama! Mama!" he hollered, and started crying.

"Leave him alone," she said.

"I just want to see the cup," I said.

It was a beautiful cup. Prettier than the mayonnaise and peanut-butter jars that we drank out of. It was deep green on the outside and white inside, and it had a handle.

Ruf Junior ran off, laughing, his prize still his.

When Daddy came in from the field, Mama said, "Where'd Ruf Junior get the cup?"

"The lady gave it to him," Daddy said. But he didn't sound happy.

"Why?"

"He wanted some water and she gave him some. Then she told him he could have the cup."

"She didn't want the cup back?"

"Not after he drunk out of it."

They both stood there for a while and didn't say anything.

I knew that it was something wrong. But I didn't know what. It was a beautiful cup, and the white lady had given it to Ruf Junior; but there was something wrong.

Daddy cleaned out something called septic tanks. He often went to Mr. McDougald's. He lived on the highway in the not-large house next to the big house where the Ransoms lived. Daddy said Mr. Ransom had made a million dollars and could buy and sell Mr. McDougald.

One night Mr. McDougald came to our house when Daddy wasn't there. Mama was sitting at the kitchen table and had Ruf Junior on her lap. I was sitting at the table, too.

"Where's Ruf?" he said. In the lamplight he looked tall and real big. He had on a brown overcoat and a brown hat.

I opened my mouth to speak. "You're—" I had started to

say, "You're not supposed to have your hat on in the house." Mama had gotten after Jesse about wearing his cap in the house. But here was this big tall white man standing up in our kitchen with his hat on and Mama didn't say anything. I tried to attract her attention to tell her so she could get after him. But she didn't seem to see it. Mama didn't say anything.

Daddy and Aunt Jo didn't like white people. Daddy couldn't work in the tobacco factory because of them, and Mama had to bring in the money by working there. One time, when Daddy and Aunt Jo were on friendly terms, Aunt Jo came in from town very mad. Though she had had to walk nearly two miles from the bus line, she was still very angry-looking when she got home. "I started walking to the back of the bus and that cracker stuck his foot out," Aunt Jo said.

Daddy looked at her, but he didn't say anything.

"I told him that if he didn't take his foot out of my way, I'd take my knife and cut his head off." She spat the words out.

I was surprised. It was the first time that I knew that Aunt Jo carried a knife when she went to town.

I knew who she meant by "crackers." They were all white people.

The photographer came to school to take our pictures. When they came back, mine had a streak like lightning on it. It was wide just over the part in my hair and it stopped short at my eyebrow. Mrs. Johnson didn't know what had caused it and she didn't know if my mother wanted the picture or not. But Mama sent the money to school.

It was a mark. A sign. The camera had recorded it. All my life it would make me a target.

We got our report cards and I was promoted to the second grade.

8

I was scared all the time in second grade.

On the first day of school Mrs. Ross let three of us girls take the books out of the boxes. We were laughing as we traded secrets of the summer. The boys took the books from us to distribute to the class. I bent over the box to get a book, and grasped it the wrong way; it fell open to a page that had yellow tape on it. I was about to close the book when I saw the words PROPERTY OF BRAGGTOWN SCHOOL. Stunned, I sat down, while the others continued to talk and laugh. I looked in the front of the book, and there were two names and the same words: PROPERTY OF BRAGGTOWN SCHOOL. We were paying book rent for books that the white children at the brick school had used last year. I looked at the books as the others picked them up. *All of them were secondhand.* They felt dirty to me. I wondered about the girl who had had my book last year. She was smug and laughing at me. I had to use her old book. It wasn't right. I was very quiet for a long time.

Mrs. Ross scrambled words on the board for spelling. "Dacny"—I fixed the letters and it was "candy." "Uynfn" became "funny." It was a magic game and I loved it.

Mrs. Ross started reading us a story called "The Ugly Duckling." I was not paying much attention at first. I was scared of her, so I seldom said anything, hoping she wouldn't see me. But today she started to read, and somehow something she read caught my attention and I started to listen. I was enthralled. She read and read, and I didn't see the other children anymore. I didn't see Mrs. Ross. I saw the Ugly Duckling and I wanted to know what was going to happen to him. I went somewhere far out of the classroom. Just then Mrs. Ross said, "It's time for recess. I'll finish the story when we come back." I hurt from wanting to know what would happen to the Ugly Duckling. I hung back, wanting to go up to her to ask what happened, but I was afraid of her.

At recess I didn't play with the other children. I sat down and thought about the Ugly Duckling and became the Ugly Duckling. I couldn't wait for the bell to ring. This was one day that I didn't join the others in begging the big girl who rang the bell not to ring it for a little while. I wanted recess to be over so I could find out what happened to the Ugly Duckling.

Quiet period was torture for me. I put my head down on the desk like the other children, but I didn't close my eyes until I looked and saw Mrs. Ross looking right at me. After a long time she told us to put our heads up. She started to read again, and in a few moments the classroom disappeared and I was again the Ugly Duckling, following his adventures. When he became a swan, I felt that it was fitting, somehow. I would become a beautiful swan, too.

From that day on I loved stories, and a story was good or bad depending on whether it would draw me over into it. If it couldn't, it wasn't so good. But if I got over into the book and moved around with the characters—seeing what they saw, hearing what they heard—it was a good story. I saw the key that had the blood that wouldn't wash off but slid around from side to side, and when Bluebeard came home I trembled. He'd know I had looked in the forbidden place and seen all his dead wives.

Then Mrs. Ross read to us about "Tobe," who was a black boy. That book was different. It had photographs instead of drawings like the books in the first grade. Tobe lived on a farm. His family worked in tobacco, and there was a picture of Tobe in the fields. Mrs. Ross showed us the picture, but she wouldn't let us touch the book.

Hazel liked stories, too. She lived at the Richardses', who owned a big farm on the highway. Her parents worked for them. Their daughters listened to *Let's Pretend,* a radio program on Saturday morning that featured fairy tales. Hazel told me about it and I started listening, too. I heard all the fairy tales, some of which I enjoyed but most of which I didn't believe. The only fairy tale I ever got absorbed in was "Bluebeard"— a precursor, perhaps, of my lifelong interest in detective stories. But on Mondays at recess, Hazel and I would talk about the stories on *Let's Pretend*.

Mrs. Ross liked to whip you.

If you missed a word in spelling, you got a lick in the hand with a paddle; if you didn't have a ribbon in your hair, you got a lick with the paddle. Mrs. Ross assigned one of the boys to give the licks. One day I was standing at the board when she sent John to hit me because I hadn't finished my problem. It didn't seem right that John should be hitting me. He couldn't do a problem any better than I could. I think she sent him because he was husky and could hit hard. For the first time, I protested. I screamed as loud as I could.

"What's the matter with you, girl?" she said. "That lick didn't hurt you."

She was right; it hadn't hurt much. She was upset because, as loud as I was screaming, some of the other teachers might hear and wonder what was going on.

I learned a valuable lesson but one that, unfortunately, I had to keep learning over and over. Protest is the most effective way of stopping unfair treatment. People who treat you unfairly don't want others to know. I never got another lick from her.

Our interest in "love" fed on the teachers, all of whom were said to be going with each other. I didn't know what "going with" meant, but it was something you weren't supposed to do. They said Mrs. Ross went with Mr. Jackson. One day during recess I went back to the room and walked in quietly, hoping she wouldn't see me. Mrs. Ross was sitting on her desk, while Mr. Jackson was in a child's seat directly in front of her. She had her legs open. She had big legs, like two pillars, and the big boys made sly jokes about them. I was scared to death when I saw her and Mr. Jackson. But they didn't notice me and I ran out.

The locust fell in the fall—dark-purple, crescent-shaped fruit full of seeds on the lower half, brownish pulp on top. It turned sweet when the grass in the morning wore a coating of whitish ice. The frost made the orange persimmon turn a dark, crusty brown. It fell from the trees by the handfuls—sweet as sugar.

When it got to be winter the night was cold. If you sat on the floor near the window with your feet stretched out toward the fireplace, you could lean back and hear the wind blow and feel little circles blow across your neck. At the same time your feet, encased in high-top shoes and long cotton socks, would burn at the bottom—they were so hot from the fire.

Aunt Jo would stand with her back to the fireplace and pull up her long dark dress behind her, while the front stayed down, and warm her "hind parts," as she called them.

The whole house would be dark and mysterious when the wind cried outside and everybody sat around the fire. There were lamps burning in each room—yellow at the bottom where the globe was full and fat, and dark at the top where the chimney narrowed and smoked. Often half the room was in darkness, when a big hole in the globe was plastered over with a chunk of brown paper put on with water-and-flour glue.

We children sat around the fire while the grown people murmured and the room was reddish warm. Occasionally Mama or Aunt Jo would spit in the fire and a spear of flame would shoot up; then a black spot would appear in the ashes where the spit landed.

And I would look in the fire and see strange things, and then I would lean back and listen to the wind blow.

In the fall, too, we played baseball. The pitcher stood in the middle of the driveway facing the hitter, and the shortstop stood behind the hitter. First base was a rock or tree on the right of the driveway facing the hitter. Second base was on the left. Often there was no third base like the one at school—the yard was too small.

Everyone got a chance to hit—down to the littlest ones who couldn't hold up the bat but were allowed to swing with a plank. Sometimes the pitcher let them get on first just to let them have the pleasure of doing so. The pitcher knew very well he was going to get them out before they got to second. The game lasted hours and hours, until it got too dark to see. No one cared who won.

When May Day drew near, there was talk of the Queen and her Court, but I didn't pay much attention. I had learned who was pretty and who was not. I was one of the bluebells, a sort of backup chorus of the girls who had to be fitted into the dances somewhere. My costume was a blue dress with blue socks and a blue ribbon in my hair.

I was eight years old.

Mrs. Richardson, the third-grade teacher, was a pretty lady. She had a gold chip between her teeth and she smiled a lot. She had light-brown skin and wore her hair pulled back in a bun. She liked to say, "Now, boys and girls . . ." She liked me.

This time we got a geography book and an arithmetic book along with our reader and speller.

I hardly ever missed a word in spelling, so Mrs. Richardson often let me call out the words. Then the class exchanged papers and corrected them, and sometimes she corrected them herself.

We did arithmetic problems at the board.

Dorothy was very light-skinned and had long red hair with gold sparkles in it. Her eyes were green. I liked to look at her hair and wonder where it came from. She looked like a white girl. She had a lot of freckles on her face. They puzzled me. But she was Dorothy and she was friendly. She came to our room after school had started. She had been going to another school.

"What grade were you in?" I asked.

"The fourth," she said.

"This is the third."

"I know." Dorothy sighed like a grown woman. "They put me back."

It took Dorothy longer than the others to do arithmetic problems. She was always at the board when the others went back to their seats.

One day Dorothy and I were standing side by side, working arithmetic problems. Mrs. Richardson called out four sets of numbers. We had to add numbers, then subtract some, then multiply, then divide. If we did them all right, we could take our seat. I had four problems on the board and had done mine when Dorothy said, "I work so hard, but I just can't do these problems." She sighed. I looked to see if Mrs. Richardson was watching because she would get you if you helped somebody or if somebody helped you. She wasn't looking, so I quickly worked all of Dorothy's problems, too.

Then Mrs. Richardson went around the board checking problems. When she got to Dorothy's she looked at them and said, "Well, Dorothy, did you do these?"

"Yes'm," Dorothy said.

Mrs. Richardson looked at me, but she didn't say anything. When everybody had finished, she called me to her desk and gave me another book, different from the one we were using. Some days I worked problems out of that book.

Then one day she showed me a book called a "dictionary" and said, "I'm going to show you how to look up a word." She wrote one down for me to look up, and when I did, she smiled, showing the pretty teeth with a gold chip between them, and gave me a note to take to Mr. Harrison's room. He was the eighth-grade teacher.

I took the note, and after he'd read it, he said, "You're a smart girl. You can use the dictionary."

Mrs. Richardson brought me a story that she liked very much. That night I read it, entranced with the magic carpet that could fly high over cities, wishing that somehow, somewhere there were a real magic carpet and that I could get on it.

We took turns being in charge of the class on Friday afternoons, which was free time. Mrs. Richardson went out of the room. Mostly we told riddles. One day I was in charge when Dorothy raised her hand and asked to tell a riddle:

"When a boy's on top and the girl's on the bottom, what are they doing?"

Nobody said anything.

Then Dorothy said, "Something nasty," and laughed.

Henry said out loud, "Dorothy is a fast old girl."

I couldn't for the life of me figure out what Dorothy was talking about. In my mind's eye, I saw a tall boy standing upright on a girl's shoulders, so that he was as high as a tree. I thought that he would be too heavy and hurt the girl. But I didn't see anything nasty about it. Then I imagined the girl lying flat, with the boy standing upright on her stomach. I thought that that would hurt her stomach, but I didn't see anything nasty about that. Yet Henry knew, and the way some of the others looked, they knew. I wanted to ask Dorothy, but I didn't want her and the others to know that I didn't know, so I didn't say anything.

There was more that I had to find out about than what was in the stories I read.

Another May Day was coming and the whole school started practicing for it. Everybody was in May Day. The girls were buttercups, bluebirds, Hawaiian maidens, and assorted pretty things—birds, flowers, nationalities. The boys were Indian chiefs and did a rain dance, or they practiced playing ball in the afternoon, for May Day was an all-day celebration. A group of boys and girls, carefully trained, wrapped the Maypole in many-colored ribbons. Every girl wore a dress of crepe paper or organdy with matching socks and black patent-leather or white shoes. They wore matching ribbons and crepe-paper flowers in their hair. The whole class dressed alike, so if the class was buttercups, there was a field of yellow flowers bobbing and dancing.

This year I wasn't in the dance. My music teacher asked me to play for one of the dances. Each girl had to hop up to the Queen's Court and bow and hop back again, still facing the Queen, to the tune of Schumann's "The Happy Farmer." We rehearsed for days outside in the rocky yard at school. Our whole school went to Little River School to have one big May Day with both schools. May Day was on Friday.

The Sunday after May Day, Mama sat on the lawn and talked with her friends in the evening after church. When they left, she called me to her. "You played for May Day," she said. Her voice sounded funny and she looked different. I felt like I felt when she asked me about the marks from the slap Mrs. Johnson had given me.

"Yes'm," I said. I swallowed but I couldn't think of anything else to say.

"You didn't tell me," she said. I looked at her face, but I didn't know what to say. I knew her friends had told her and she felt bad that she hadn't known I was going to play. It had never crossed my mind to tell her.

"No'm," I said, and backed off.

That year on awards night they called my name and I went up to the stage. I got a medal for being the best scholar in the primary grades.

The next day Daddy called me to him. "I heard you got a medal last night," he said.

I paused, wondering how I should answer. I listened to his voice to hear whether he was happy about it or mad, before

I answered. There was a whole lot about the school that Daddy didn't like. I couldn't figure it out, so I didn't say anything.

"That's mighty nice," he said. "I want you to win one every year."

"Yes sir," I said. I stopped holding my breath. I was overjoyed and ran up the road to catch the other boys and girls on their way to school.

Daddy hadn't been there; he hardly ever went anywhere because he was sick all the time. He had a bad ulcer. Mama had gone to the ceremony, but she didn't say anything to me about the medal. In looking back, I realize she must have been the one who told him what went on at the program.

I was in the fifth grade, and our class was to arrange a program for assembly. We decided to have a raffle. Mrs. Harper chose three of us to be in charge: Dionne, Hazel, and me. We were considered to be the most reliable. We filled a jar with dry black-eyed peas and then sold chances; the person who bought a chance put his name and the number of peas he guessed to be in the jar on a ticket in another jar. On Friday during our assembly the winner would be announced and the prize was going to be a coconut cake. Only we three knew the number of peas in the jar, for we had laboriously counted every one.

At recess every day for a week, we went all over the school grounds, one girl with the jar of peas, another with the jar of chances, and one soliciting buyers. We also visited classrooms. The chances were a nickel and we were going to put the money in our class treasury for an end-of-school party. Not too many students had nickels to spend on chances for a coconut cake, but our sales moved right along.

Flossie was not a member of our group, but I played with her sometimes. She used to tease me about my dimple. "Ah, you've got a pretty dimple," she used to say, and I would smile, a bit puzzled. At first I didn't know what she was talking about, for no one had ever told me about dimples. Finally

I learned that a dimple was the little place on my cheek that went in when I laughed.

Flossie referred to it again and again. I wondered why until one day I looked at her and noticed that she had three or four. Then I knew why she always pointed mine out to me. She wanted me to say something about hers. Some grown people must have told her that they were beautiful, and she wanted them established as grounds of beauty at school, too, but no one had noticed. Flossie was a very black girl with black hair that shone when it was pressed. Her eyebrows were dark and shiny, and she had long, heavy lashes and smooth chocolate skin.

Flossie had another group that she went around with sometimes. The King girls.

"How many peas are in the jar?" Flossie said, running up to me on Monday.

"I can't tell you, Flossie," I said. "It's a secret."

"You can tell me. We're friends."

"No, I can't."

At every recess period every day that week, Flossie would try to catch me by myself, and she would plead and beg until she saw Dionne or Hazel coming: "How many peas in the jar?"

"I can't tell you. It's a secret."

"You can tell me. I won't tell anybody. I just want to know. Hear. How many peas in the jar?"

"I can't tell you."

And she would run off, for she had seen Dionne and Hazel looking.

By noon Friday we had sold four dollars' worth of chances. The jar with the names was almost full. And best of all, Lisa had brought the cake that Miss Sarah had made to be the prize. Miss Sarah knew how to make beautiful fancy cakes like the ones in magazines. We sold a lot of chances, once everybody saw the cake they were going to get.

Near the end of recess, when I was by myself for a moment,

Flossie came up to me. "How many peas are in the jar?" she said. "Come on. You can tell me. We're having assembly right after recess. I haven't bought a chance and I'm not going to buy one. I just want to know. Please tell me. You're my friend."

I thought about what Flossie said and thought it was all right. Dionne, Hazel, and I already knew the one who had guessed closest, and so far that day no one had come as close, so we knew who the winner was. I told Flossie how many peas were in the jar. She smiled a big smile, showing all of her dimples, and ran off to get some water before the bell rang.

In a few minutes Hazel and Dionne came, and they looked worried. "Did you tell anybody how many peas were in the jar?"

I felt bad. "Flossie was just here and she asked. She said that she wasn't going to try, so I told her."

"You know that little King girl that she runs around with sometimes?" Dionne said.

"Yes." I already knew what was coming.

"Well, she came and guessed two peas from the exact number."

I was heartbroken. Flossie and her friends had plotted together to get the cake. I was so hurt and so ashamed.

We had to do something. We decided to change the count of the peas so that the girl who had already guessed closest would still be the winner.

We did.

Flossie avoided me on the playground after that.

When Mama came home from work in the evening and Daddy came in from the fields, she'd read the paper to him. He could read, but he had to get his round glasses with the yellow rims, the ones he used when he was working mathematics problems. Mama wore her glasses all the time, so when she was reading, she'd read aloud to him. They both talked about the part that said: "Roosevelt said." And when

President Roosevelt was going to be on the radio, Daddy pulled up close; he liked to sit right by the radio with his head bent down to the long slots where the sound came out.

Mama and Daddy sometimes said something about a wheelchair. So when the president came on with the music like lightning, I could see him rolling up to our radio in his wheelchair to speak through the slots. I looked in sometimes, trying to see him sitting there, but all I saw was a bright red glow. I never doubted, however, that he had been there and now was gone.

He was going to get rid of hard times. "Yes, he is," Daddy would say and slap his long, bony leg. He always said that Roosevelt was going to make himself a king, that that was his aim, and Mama would say, "Oh, Ruf," and Daddy would defend his position. "Oh, yes, he is," he would say.

Daddy would talk for a long time when Ol' Joe was going to fight. To me Joe Louis was someone far away who fought a lot. When people came to visit, sometimes in the evening, sometimes on Sunday, they'd talk about Joe Louis. "Ol' Joe can beat him," they'd say. "Oh, yes," someone else would agree, "no one can stop him." I wondered how Joe Louis could be such a good fighter if he was old and who it was he was going to beat. We got whipped for fighting. But he was a fighter and it was a good thing and he was going to beat. He always beat. Gradually I came to realize that it was a good thing because he was "colored" and the other man wasn't, and Joe Louis *had* to beat.

On the night of a fight, Mama and Daddy would let us stay up late. They'd finish everything early, and a little while before the fight Daddy would turn the dial to get the right station. Then he'd sit down.

"All right, ya'll," Mama would say. "If I hear airy word out of you, you're going to bed." Even Aunt Jo would come in from her room to listen, standing tall in the light in her dark dress.

I liked to hear the noise in the auditorium, which sounded like the noise at baseball games. I thought that the bell that rang was a cowbell, like the one around Suki's neck. Then there was the announcer saying, "A right and a left and an uppercut." I had no idea of what any of it meant, but I would look at Daddy's face. When the announcer said it was Joe Louis, he'd smile a big smile. When the announcer mentioned the other man's name, the look on Daddy's face would be painful to see. When the announcer said, "A right and a left and— Ladies and gentlemen, he's on the ropes!" Daddy would look so worried I was scared for him that Joe Louis was going to lose. I didn't know what would happen to Daddy if Joe Louis lost, but it would be very bad, I was sure.

The room would get very quiet between rounds; Daddy would be so quiet that no one else would say anything. Then the bell would ring and Joe Louis would come out again and the announcer would start talking faster and faster and Daddy would whoop, "Joe Louis got him this time!" And sure enough, the announcer would soon say, "Still champeen!" Daddy would stand up, jubilant; Mama and Aunt Jo would smile; Jesse would look smug, as if he'd known all along.

During recess the next day, the big children would talk about the fight and the teachers standing in the playground would talk about it, too. I was glad that Joe Louis had won because it meant so much to Daddy.

If Joe Louis, a black man, won, Daddy had won. He could hold his head up, looking the look that said, "Joe Louis won. He is black like me; therefore, that means that I won, too. I am not nothing. I am something."

Admirable as his accomplishment was, it is a sad commentary on American life at that time that the only positive self-image that millions of black Americans had was wrapped up in the image projected by one black athlete.

Mrs. Graham, my sixth-grade teacher, brought loads of newspapers and magazines to school. There were the Norfolk *Journal and Guide*, the Baltimore *Afro-American*, the Pittsburgh *Courier*, the Chicago *Defender*, and others. Every week there would be pictures of outstanding black people, and I had the job of reading the newspapers and cutting out the pictures and articles and fixing the bulletin board. I loved the job and spent part of every day reading the news, for Mrs. Graham believed that each of us should know what was going on in the world. We had a current-events quiz every Friday, and I liked that. Every student had to tell something of importance that had happened in the world that week—no murders, car wrecks, no crimes of any kind, but instead news about the president or Congress or important blacks. Without knowing it, I had tuned in on the twentieth century. It didn't sit so well with everybody, though.

One Friday the tenth grade, Jesse's class, was in charge of assembly. Every week there was an activity in the assembly, which was really two classrooms with a divider that had been pushed back. Sometimes there would be a talent show; other times a class play; sometimes a visitor would come. The tenth grade had a special treat that day—a quiz show with pennies for prizes. The whole school was there, since there were less than two hundred in all twelve grades. When the committee from the tenth grade came in, I was so proud; my brother was with them. After the singing and announcements, the program started. Questions were taken from the news. Three students took turns reading the questions, while it was Jesse's duty to point out the one to answer.

The questions were all from the current news. Speaker of the House? I raised my hand. *Life* magazine had done a cover story on Sam Rayburn. Jesse reluctantly called on me when no one else raised a hand. Senators? Generals? Important people in national life? I knew them all, but Jesse wouldn't call on me until everybody who had raised a hand had tried. Then he'd call on me, looking meaner every time. I collected my pennies happily, wondering what was the matter. Others collected some pennies, but at the end of the hour I was the winner. I had more pennies than anybody. I must have had twenty cents. I was elated.

When Jesse got home after school, I turned to him eagerly, knowing that now my big brother would like me and pay some attention to me.

"What did you answer all those questions for?" he said, real hard. "The others thought I had given you the answers."

I was too hurt and stunned to say anything. That was the tenor of our relationship from then on—he, harsh and attacking me for something I had done that I thought would gain approval. There was a divide between me and the world—what I thought was valuable they hated. What was wrong? How could I fit in?

One day I had a number of clippings on the desk by the bulletin board and was taking down last week's clippings and putting up this week's when Jennie came over.

"Who's that?" she said.

"Marian Anderson," I said.

"What does she do?"

"She's a singer."

Jennie looked puzzled. "Blues?"

"No, she's a concert singer. She started singing in Europe because they wouldn't let her sing over here." Mrs. Graham had told us about the Daughters of the American Revolution refusing to permit Marian Anderson to sing in their auditorium because she was black. Mrs. Graham had been indignant.

Jennie looked the strangest sort of look at me. I felt as if a chasm had opened up between us. I knew the blues singers—Ruth Brown, Ella Johnson, and LaVerne Baker. But I had also heard of Marian Anderson, and that made a difference between Jennie and me. I didn't know it then, but that look was the first of many I was to get over the years.

Jennie was a "bad" girl. So were Rebecca and Grace. Vicki was terrible—that was extra bad. Being bad always had something to do with boys.

By the time she was in the sixth grade Jennie had become so experienced on the little boys that she was now ready for older ones. Mr. James, a high-school teacher, knew it. He had a brother still in high school in town who wanted to meet a girl who was willing and undemanding. Some of the town girls expected something more in return from him than a ride in his brother's newest car. So sometimes he would ride with his brother out to Wildwood, pick up Jennie at the school grounds, take her off for several hours, and then bring her back. Sometimes they would stay even longer, returning only in the afternoon when school let out.

This went on and nobody said anything about it. Jennie would come in, her hair piled high in a pompadour, feeling quite important in her United Department Store shoes and dress. I wanted to tell her that Mr. James's brother considered himself above her, that neither one of them considered her their "equal," that he would never take her to a dance or to the movies or invite her to his home for dinner to meet his parents. But she seemed so content and acted so superior that I was afraid to say anything. Years later when I read of the sons of the manor house and the peasant girls and their attitudes toward them, I remembered Jennie and Mr. James's brother. I've known for a long time that blacks are just as capable of exploiting blacks as whites are.

Rebecca had a number of boyfriends, often changing weekly, all of whom she had "something to do with." What that "something" was I could never quite figure out. I could imagine and wonder, but I was never certain. It had something to do with "down there," and I knew you had better not let a boy have something to do with you down there or you would get a baby. Just how this took place, I couldn't tell, and all of my reading didn't help because it never told me exactly what was done.

Vicki would let the boys have something to do with her for a cold drink, which they'd slip off through the woods and across the highway to get. Sometimes the big boys and some girls would form a circle around Vicki and a boy right on the school grounds and she would do "it" during recess. I would listen to these tales in wonder and look very knowledgeable, but I really didn't know what was taking place.

Sometimes those girls were called "fast-ass girls" and sometimes they were called "hot tails." But I noticed that even when a grown person was saying one of these phrases, there was an undercurrent of affection there. They were "bad" girls, but not really; the grown people were approving and disapproving at the same time. Something was wrong here. Why did the grown people mean two things at once?

Just before my eleventh birthday I felt warm blood inside my thighs and looked down and knew that I was a woman.

I used to stand and look at myself in the mirror. What I saw looked all right to me, but at school it was not beautiful. My hair wasn't long. Girls who had thick long hair were considered pretty. "Long" hair was shoulder-length hair. If the hair "took" straightening well, so that it had a sheen on it, it was okay. Girls with naturally "straight" hair (which could be combed easily without being straightened) were considered the most attractive of all. My hair, as was the case with most girls in the school, was not shoulder-length and was not naturally straight.

Facial features that were not typically black were felt to be beautiful: lips that were not full and a nose that was not broad. My mouth and nose were full and I had "healthy" feet.

But canceling out all "defects" for a girl was "light skin." Light skin was really banana-colored, though often a girl with caramel-colored skin could make it over into the beautiful category if she had long or straight hair. I varied in color from a fade-out black in winter to a reddish-chocolate after a summer in the sun.

Complicating my problems was the fact that Aunt Jo, worried about my thinness and my long winter colds, and mindful of the fact that TB was in the family, persuaded my mother to take me to old Dr. Boone to get a tonic to build me up. It did. In one summer I turned from a frail child into a chunky girl.

One day I was reading in my mother's home-remedy book and in the section devoted to flat chests I read that massaging one's breasts with cocoa butter was good for remedying that condition. I looked on top of the cabinet where my mother had some cocoa butter, and every day would secretly massage my breasts with it. My mother was as flat as a pancake in front, as was Aunt Jo. I wanted to be different. The treatment was effective; while other girls my age were flat all around, I developed full breasts, so much so that they were the cause of much comment and caused me deep embarrassment.

10

Religion went on and on. It provided the main sense of community in Wildwood.

Every Sunday morning the road was full of children going to Sunday school. The girls had on pink, yellow, blue, or white dresses when it was warm. The dresses were starched so stiffly that they stood out all around, revealing knees often covered with fresh or healing dew sores and an expanse of polished bone that extended from the knees to the top of their turned-down socks. They wore black patent-leather slippers with a little strap across the instep. If it was a little chilly, they wore light-colored sweaters, sometimes in a contrasting color. Their hair was often plaited in three braids: a big one on top that leaned toward the right or left side, and two behind. They always wore a bow on the top plait. Sometimes it was a soft ribbon, sometimes a hard, store-bought plastic bow. It always matched the socks. (It was thought to be very "country" not to have a matching bow.) In their hands they carried a little pocketbook, often of artificial leather. If a girl didn't have one, she tied her collection money up in a handkerchief and twirled it casually around as she walked and skipped.

The boys had on coats and pants, sometimes matching, but always a shirt with a starched collar and tie. Sunday meant a tie.

So the road would be full of many-colored legs, socks, and hairbows, faces freshly washed, teeth clean and visible. The older girls walked together. They had secrets to discuss and they would run off any little girl who was not yet one of the group. Sometimes the boys would have a walk race. They would walk stiff-legged as fast as they could without running. They looked like lunging robots.

Though an older boy was supposed to protect his sister, he would let her know that he didn't appreciate her calling on him unless she couldn't possibly defend herself. He would be disgraced if his little sister or brother came crying to him, though he might have washed their faces and dressed them both an hour earlier.

If it had rained, some brave boys would carefully splash the rainbows left by oil slicks in mud puddles on their way back from church. But everyone tried to get to church spick-and-span. Tragedy sometimes occurred if a car went speeding along and splattered somebody with mud. Little children would cry and big boys and girls would stop and try to get the stain off.

When it was dry weather, it was nice to walk crunchingly over rocks that had fallen from trucks going to and from the quarry. If a car passed and dust swirled everywhere, we could always dust it off when we got to church.

The superintendent would toll the bell, and everybody would assemble for a song, Scripture, and a prayer. Then we would go to classes according to our grades.

Classes were held in various parts of the auditorium; there were no Sunday-school rooms. Little children who couldn't read were taught by a big girl, someone in the eighth or ninth grade or in high school. She would decide when someone was ready for the next class and recommend the child to the superintendent. It was always a big day when a child was promoted from one class to another. Other classes had books called "quarterlies," and the teacher was grown and had read over the lesson before coming to class.

The lessons for all age groups went on simultaneously and

no one seemed disturbed: young adults sat in the missionary sisters' amen corner; grown people conducted their class in the deacon's corner; another group sat in the middle of the center aisle; and the little children with their picture cards of Jesus and a Bible verse sat at the back under the clock.

After the lesson was over, the whole school came together for a song, painfully picked out by some piano hopeful, the reading of the minutes by whoever was a good reader and writer, and Bible verses and the collection. Everyone had to say a verse. It was considered an honor to know a long passage and be able to quote book, chapter, and verse. Small children who forgot their longer verses fell back on the standard one: "Jesus wept." The class that raised the most money got the banner, a pennant that hung over their section until the next Sunday. Then there was a final song. After benediction, during the walk home, secrets were shared and comments made about the day's events.

It was in Sunday school that I played my first hymn for others to sing by. It was "Steal away, steal away, steal away to Jesus. Steal away, steal away, steal away home, I ain't got long to stay here." (One church lady was reported to have said that I looked so thin and sickly sitting on the bench that she thought I was going to steal away for real.)

It was also in Sunday school that I did my first writing— I was the secretary. And I liked the Bible stories—the people and what they did. The pictures that the preacher drew were so vivid that they made an indelible impression on my mind; they were, in fact, verbal film. And, as in a favorite film, you enjoyed what was coming next, although you might have heard it twenty times. And the sermons were all in color on a big wide screen, full of drama and action.

Once a month everyone stayed for "service." The pastor was a farmer from a neighboring county and he had two or three churches. But our community was fortunate. He was with us on the first Sunday of the month. So Sunday school got out on time the first Sunday, and when the Sunday-school "scholars" got out, there were already dark-suited men on the grounds waiting for the morning service to start. Their clothes were always dark, winter and summer; only the hats changed. In the summer they were straw; sometimes they were hard and glazed, and sometimes they looked as if they were woven. No one had heard the term "boater" and few had heard the term "Panama," but that's what they were. The hats were always yellowish-looking, as if they had been worn for many years—like maybe half a century.

The men's shoes were shined and their white shirts were starched stiffly, with dark ties neatly tucked inside their jackets. They always wore vests, and often a gold chain snaked across their chests and they pulled on it to extricate a round gold watch whose cover they lifted seriously to study the time. Time didn't seem to matter much, though. They shook hands and stood in clusters and murmured to each other. What they talked about would be heard later in church during announcements. If somebody's tobacco barn had burned down and he had lost some of his crop, or if his smokehouse had burned and he had lost his meat, a special collection would be raised. Special collections were also raised for the sick, and deaths were faithfully recorded.

The women wore enormous flowered hats. Flowers sprouted all around the wide brims and high crowns: red flowers, yellow flowers, orange flowers, blue flowers. On Easter the flowers were fresh and gay, but as the summer grew older, they got tired and listless. The dresses were summery in warm weather and darkish in winter. The women had matching handbags and shoes, and some of the more fashionable ladies carried gloves.

With the tolling of the bells, service began. First there was a song, then the testimony meeting, which was conducted by the missionary sisters. Several ladies gave testimonies about God's goodness to them. These were interspersed with thin, dry songs. "Shall we gather at the river, the beautiful, the beautiful river /Gather with the saints at the river /That flows by the throne of God." The sisters' voices were high-pitched and cracked, and they held each vowel as long as they could.

They also liked "In the Sweet By and By." Not a one of them could sing. Occasionally a visitor would come who was used to a more evangelical approach and would launch a spirited song in a big, melodious voice. She wouldn't get much support, though, and after five minutes of unrewarding labor she would cease.

After the preliminaries, which included a prayer in which the speaker invariably thanked God that when he woke up that morning his bed was not his cooling board (dead people, at one time, were placed on boards to "cool"), the pastor would launch into his sermon. Reverend Waters, a short, dark, chunky man, was a farmer during the week, but he picked up his Bible on Sunday. He retained some of his earthy humor, though, and always started off with a joke. Some of the members thought this unbecoming. They were the same ones who resisted so long the introduction of a piano into the church. To them it was the devil's handiwork. Dance halls had pianos, therefore pianos couldn't be used for God's service. They finally gave in, but they wouldn't budge an inch on the guitar issue. (Someone had brought it to the attention of the congregation that on one occasion, when a male quartet was invited to sing, one of the members had accompanied the group on a guitar. The "old heads" were scandalized, and that was the end of the quartet and its guitar.)

The old heads liked plain, unaccompanied singing, especially "old hundreds," songs torturously spelled out, line by line. "That Awful Day Will Surely Come" was "lined" and sung so slowly that you felt sure that by the time it was over, Judgment Day, that awful day, would surely be here.

Deacon Woods, a tall, dark, skinny man who was the leading "liner," used to punish his enemies with old hundreds. If something went not according to his liking, he would pull out his thick old-hundreds book and line out a song that must have had a thousand verses. Being pious people, the congregation could not object. Deacon Woods didn't like Reverend Waters's jokes. But the pastor was undeterred. He liked the one about the baby boy who never crawled—he developed whooping cough and he coughed so hard that he gave one powerful whoop and jumped right out of the bed and started walking. Reverend Waters always laughed appreciatively at his own jokes. Kindly members chuckled a bit, and others just endured.

(His jokes were mild in comparison to those of his friend and fellow farmer Reverend Benjamin, whom he let preach occasionally. The congregation had the misfortune once of unexpectedly having Reverend Benjamin as the main speaker on a Sunday when the school principal and his wife were making their yearly visit. Everybody was honored and wanted everything to go just right. The two visitors represented the epitome of learning and culture in Wildwood, and it was necessary that they be impressed. So Reverend Benjamin, who looked ten feet tall, got up and read about the Prodigal Son and took his text from that story. Everybody got still. What was he going to say? He said, "Come out of the hog pen. You've got all that hog mud on you." Those who weren't speechless laughed in embarrassment.)

Reverend Waters, after his usual joke, would be silent for a moment, take off his gold-rimmed glasses and wipe them, and search for his text. Sometimes it was Daniel in the Lions' Den and didn't my Lord deliver him, and the congregation could see Daniel down in there making friends with the lions and the surprise of the king's men when they saw old Daniel at peace with the lions. And Shadrach, Meshach, and Abednego and how they would *not* bow down at the sounding of the trumpet and how they were put into the fiery furnace and when the king looked there was a fourth man in the furnace. Here some sister would shriek and another would moan. And, of course, there was Ezekiel and the Dry Bones and can these bones live. Often it was a "the-Lord-will-provide" sermon with Abraham and Isaac, and he was about to sacrifice his son when God sent a ram. Then there was the test of which God to serve and the decision was to serve the God that answered by fire. Then fire came down and licked up the water and slew the unbelievers.

The Seven Plagues of Egypt; the Whited Sepulcher; the Prodigal Son; the Parable of the Talents; the Five Wise and Five Foolish Virgins; and John on the Island of Patmos and the Number That No Man Could Number (a big shouting sermon—some people who never said a word would get up on that one)—all were favorites, and were preached over and over, as were the Separation of the Wheat from the Chaff and the Seeds Falling on Stony Ground. The congregation always murmured their approval of the Handwriting on the Wall and the Downfall of a Wicked Race (we all knew who *they* were). The Cloud on the Horizon That Was No Bigger Than a Man's Hand was a shouting sermon.

Every preacher's style was different. Each had his own rhetorical devices and physical mannerisms. For instance, Reverend Waters, in the heat of his sermon, would cup his ear with one hand and go into a part-spoken, part-sung delivery, punctuated by intermittent glottal "hahs." Sometimes he would lose his breath altogether and the congregation would hum and tap their feet until he got it back. He also liked to preach two—often unrelated—sermons. He would bring one of them to a climax, slow down and talk in a conversational voice for a while, and then start another. His congregation had grown to expect this. Often the sermons lasted more than an hour.

Since distinctive mannerisms and rhetorical devices marked each preacher, good church people would go miles to hear an unusual preacher. It was these devices, more than the subject matter, that marked a man who could "really preach."

Not all of the stylists were ministers. There was Deacon Sykes, at West Durham Baptist Church, who sometimes, when the spirit moved him, would run from the amen corner to the back of the church and back again, maintaining a sustained holler all the way. He was the talk of Brookstown (another name for West Durham).

Everything that followed the sermon was done with dispatch: song, call to the altar, benediction. Mount Zion's congregation was saved for another month.

The highlight of the religious year was the revival. Late in the summer, people would knock off from work a little early in the evening, just as the sun turned red and started going down. They'd come in from the fields, draw water from the well, and wash in the ice-cold water. They'd put on clean clothes—not Sunday clothes, but second-best. It was revival time, the great meeting.

About dusk, people would start down the road—some walking, some in cars—on their way to the church. Those who passed our house first were the sisters and brothers on their way to testimony meeting.

It was August and hot in the church. The windows were raised and the overhead lights seemed harsh in the shimmering heat. Despite the heat, however, all the sisters wore hats and some wore gloves. Though the men had just come in from the fields they, too, wore dark suits. Some wore felt hats, even though it was dead summer and sweat ran down from under the inner bands.

Two people took charge of testimony meeting, which was not very spirited, for Mount Zion was a Baptist church and they did not testify, as the Holiness people did. In the Holiness church the testimony meeting was just as important as the sermon, but not so in the Baptist church, where the minister's sermon always had primary importance.

In the Baptist church, someone sang a song—often the singer was one of the night's leaders—and then there was a prayer. This was followed by Scripture reading. Then one of the leaders testified, in a brief set speech telling what God had done for him during the year: he had his health and strength; he still was "clothed in his right mind"; he was not on his "cooling board"; God had brought him through many hard trials—all to the murmured chorus of amens. Then there would be a moment of silence while someone else in the congregation thought of a song he wanted to lead and which he started, somewhat timorously at first until the others joined in.

Gradually, more and more people would participate. One

here and one there would sing a song and testify as other members came in, many coming when it was nearly time for the sermon—they didn't care much for the testimony meeting.

The minister was always a visitor from as far away as possible—distance lent glamour to a speaker. He came recommended as a "fiery speaker" and "a man of God." He wore a dark suit and a white shirt, starched very stiffly. Most of the time he was very black, and he often wore clear, sparkling glasses with gold rims.

He was preceded by a rousing song, different from the somewhat milder singing of the testimony meeting. The best singer in the congregation led the singing, or, as was often the case, the visiting minister himself led it.

Then came the moment that everybody had been waiting for: the call of the sinners to the mourners' bench. "All Christians on my right, raise your hands," the minister would say. The saved would raise their hands, then put them down. "Now all sinners," he would say, his hands still stretched out. Some few would raise their hands, and he would say, "Won't you come?" And some who had made up their minds to get saved at this revival meeting would come. Often sons were there because their mothers had cried and begged them to repent before it was too late and God called their souls into judgment. Then the minister would stretch out his hands to the center aisle and ask the same question. More sinners would come. Then to the left. Always, though, there would be some who wouldn't raise their hands either way, saved or sinner. So, later in the week, he would try a new tactic: he would ask the saved to stand. That strategy exposed the sinners better than the show of hands did.

Once those to be saved were separated from the rest of the congregation, they came to the front and sat in the first two rows, the mourners' bench. They were "in mourning" for their sins. Here they were right under the minister's eye and the sound of his voice, and he would preach to the congregation, but with a text carefully chosen to impress the sinners: the death they would surely die, the hell they would surely go to, and the goodness of God's grace that could save them if only they would accept Him.

After the sermon, the minister and the pastor of the church would come down from the pulpit onto the floor in front of the mourners' bench. There they would be joined by the sisters and brothers from the amen corners and some from the main body of the church. Some would stand and some would kneel—all around, in front, on the sides, and in back of the sinners. Then they would pray for the sinners' souls, often touching the unsaved, asking them, "Won't you trust Him? Accept Him tonight. Tomorrow your soul may be called into judgment. He's standing, waiting, right now. Won't you accept Him? He's knocking. Won't you let Him in? Don't turn Him away." The minister would stand, holding out his hand. If nobody got up from the mourners' bench, they sang another song and prayed another prayer and sang and prayed and sang and prayed. Often a child would get up, and there would be warm hugs. But the real goal was to save hardened sinners, those over eighteen. An older man or woman who got saved would start the whole church shouting. A hardened sinner whose soul was lost had been saved. All heaven would rejoice.

Each night the meetings grew more intense. By Friday night everybody was keyed up. Those who hadn't been coming came to service on Friday night. The testimony meeting was longer and more fervent; the songs were more emotional: "That Awful Day Will Surely Come"; "Come by Here, Lord"; "Remember Me"; "Precious Lord." The minister would preach John on the Island of Patmos and dwell on the part where he looked up and saw the number that no man could number, who had been washed in the blood of the Lamb. All the "saints" gathered round the "mourners." They were determined that no one would leave unsaved that night.

When the last sinner got up, the whole church rejoiced. Grown men put their faces in their hands and women covered their mouths to stifle cries. The revival had been a success.

Although I trace much of my troubling sense of guilt and

an overriding feeling of sin to some of these sermons, I think it is because I took them too literally. My peers took them with many grains of salt and they didn't seem to do them much harm.

The first baptism that I went to was at Eno River. Cars pulled off the highway and parked on the edge, where the dirt was red. Then people climbed down the side of a rocky hill, holding on to trees and bushes to keep from falling. Those who got down first reached a hand up to help the others. It was harder for the women because they had on their Sunday shoes. Some of the boys slid down the slick grass the last few feet.

Once we got down we couldn't see anything but tall trees and the sky and the river. Some of the trees were tall and skinny and had silvery bark; others were tall pines. Some were big and squat, with branches hanging over the water, almost touching it. The river was muddy; there were big rocks sticking up in the middle of the river and near the land. The riverbank was sandy and rocky and not very wide. Far down the river, high up, was a metal bridge that gleamed when the sun struck it.

The whole church came to the river. There were the sisters and the brothers and the choir and other members. Many of the women carried towels and robes to dry the new converts after they were baptized.

The newly saved wore old clothes to be baptized in. They formed a line, held hands, and a deacon led them out in the river to a place where the minister and another deacon were standing in water a little over waist-high. The minister held a tall crooked stick, like a shepherd's crook. The line lengthened out and soon stretched out across the river. The men and women weren't smiling, but they didn't look sad. They held hands.

On the bank the church was singing. There was Scripture reading—about the Dove and This Is My Beloved Son in Whom I Am Well Pleased—and prayer. Then, standing waist-deep in the river, the minister raised his hand over one convert and said, "I baptize you in the name of the Father, of the Son, and of the Holy Ghost." He put his raised hand on top of the convert's head, the other hand across his back, and lowered him into the water. In a little while he raised him up. Then the newly baptized convert was led to the end of the line and another one put in his place. If the convert was a child, the pastor baptized him alone. If it was an adult, one of the deacons helped. People on the banks cried as the baptism continued, and often the convert's family burst into loud crying, and some shouted when he was immersed.

When the last convert had been baptized, the line snaked out of the river and families gathered their own to take them home and put them in dry clothes. At the services afterwards, they would be welcomed into the church—they were now members in good standing.

Dinner on the church grounds was a very special occasion. One such occasion was Baptism Sunday. Every family brought a basket, with enough to share with others. During the latter part of the service, the ladies would quietly "tip" out of the auditorium to go to their cars, where they had left the baskets. The men had constructed makeshift tables under the trees, which were covered with sparkling white tablecloths.

Then the great baskets were opened: huge stacks of fried chicken, dark and crispy brown, nestling next to hills of potato salad, yellow and with green bits of pickles; beef roast already sliced and in its own gravy; giant pink ham slices with a brown-sugar crust; bowls of string beans with a ham slice in them; English peas and freshly sliced country tomatoes; pound cake; sweet-potato pie; blackberry pie; corn bread, biscuits, and light bread.

When the service was over and dinner was served, men and women took plates and moved from dish to dish, taking a piece of chicken from this sister and another specialty from the next. The women encouraged them by saying, "Try a piece of mine." And another would say, "Have a piece of this." By the time they had moved down the length of the table, their plates were piled three or four layers deep—and still there was something left that they had not had a chance to try.

They piled their plates and stood around on the grounds eating and exchanging news of the crops, the weather, the war, President Roosevelt, and what the prospects were for the coming year. I marvel that people who would now be considered below the poverty level on any statistical chart still had enough sense of self, of human worth, to enjoy sharing what they had with others. The meal was the tie that binds.

No one in my family was particularly religious. Rufus Mebane was a worldly man and did not join Mount Olive Baptist Church until less than ten years before his death. My mother, Nonnie, went to church often, but not every Sunday and certainly not to Wednesday-night prayer meeting; and she belonged to no club in the church—not the ladies' auxiliary or choir or anything else. During revival she went, at most, once during the week and then to the final meeting on Friday night.

If my father didn't join the church until late, his sister, Jo, had even less inclination that way. I never heard her say anything against the church; it just didn't interest her. She had her name on the Methodist roll in Brookstown, but as far as I can recall she was an indifferent member. Jesse showed no interest in religion. Ruf Junior avoided the church up to the time of our mother's death. It was left for me, the middle child, to become religious.

I went to the mourners' bench when I was twelve years old. When the minister made the call I stood up. I was scared walking down the aisle but I went and shyly took my seat. Several of us sinners exchanged glances but we didn't smile.

I listened to the minister's sermon, watching the lights gleam on his eyeglasses and his cheeks. I wondered how it would feel at the exact moment that I was saved. I had heard a man testify that when he was saved he saw a light at the back of the church that shone so brightly he had to shield his eyes. Some testified that something or someone touched them and they knew that they had been saved. Sometimes it was a still, small voice calling, and they answered.

I wondered how it would be for me. I sat through the prayers and singing the first night, listening for a voice to tell me to get up and accept Christ as my Savior, but I didn't hear anything. The sisters and brothers were all around me, down on their knees, first singing, then praying, but I didn't hear, see or feel anything. On the second night I concentrated even more intently but I still didn't see or hear what I had heard people testify to. Others around me were getting up, shaking the minister's hand, accepting Christ. They must have heard or felt something that I had missed. I didn't move. I was waiting for a sign.

The next day I decided I would get up and say I felt something whether I did or not—so I did. But I felt that somehow something was wrong. Why should others feel the great magical experience that I couldn't feel?

I was baptized in a farmer's pond. I wanted the sky to open and a voice to speak from heaven or a dove to fly and light on my shoulder. But I heard and saw nothing. I just swallowed a little water as I went under.

The service after the baptism was better, though. I stood in my best dress with the other newly saved ones as the deacons and the missionary sisters shook our hands and welcomed us into the church. For the first time I felt that I truly belonged somewhere.

But my religion was not as good as Inez's, I thought. I started playing with her as soon as they moved from New York. The word soon spread through Wildwood that the Fultons were Holy and Sanctified. The father was a preacher and the mother an evangelist. Their religion was something strange in Wildwood. To me it was wondrous.

When they first moved to Wildwood, the Fultons had service in their living room. As soon as I heard the singing I would beg to go and I would run down the Rock Pile to their house. Though it was a living room in a small cabin, to me it was a magical place, for everyone acted as though it were a large church auditorium. They sang at the tops of their voices. Reverend Fulton played the guitar. Sister Fulton played two gleaming metal instruments called "cymbals," and visiting "saints" brought tambourines, which shimmered in the light as they shook and rattled.

I intensely envied the Holiness children, who sometimes got a chance to play their mothers' tambourines. I wanted so much to shake the tambourine, but I was too shy to ask. I had to content myself with learning the intricate hand-clapping and foot-tapping.

Their order of service was very much like ours, except that it was louder. The Scripture reading got loud amens, as did the prayer. The testimony meeting was longer, with many songs and testimonies. The songs were often interrupted by shouting passages during which the singing stopped while some shouted, the beat being kept up all the while by hand-claps and the rhythmic beat and rattle of the tambourines. This went on until by an unspoken signal the singing started again—right on the beat. Often the same song was interrupted again by someone else who had been touched by the spirit that was "moving from heart to heart and breast to breast" in the room. Often the whole room would stop singing, the only sound being the rhythmic shouting and hand-clapping and the beat of the tambourines. When the song was over, someone led a very quiet, slow song, like "Yeah Lord, yeah Lord, yeah Lord, yeah Lord, yeah Lord . . ." which rose and fell, rose and fell, until everyone was quiet. Then a testimony followed, and another spirited song and more shouting.

Everybody was expected to testify, even small children. Their testimony was, "I thank the Lord for being here /I thank the Lord for my life, health, and strength /I ask you all to pray for me as I journey on in these last and evil days." They got a firm amen, for it was the abiding belief of the Holy and Sanctified that the world was very close to judgment and that only those who had "the full armor" of God were going to be saved. The world was evil; Satan was going to and fro, seeking those whom he could destroy.

I grasped eagerly at this new doctrine. It was a way for me to combat the devil.

11

My mother loved music. Any kind of music. WPTF in Raleigh, North Carolina, had an early-morning country-music show, which she went to work by. For years one of their favorite "wake-'em-up" songs was "They Traced Her Little Footprints in the Snow." A conservative estimate of the number of times I heard that song is five hundred. On Saturday evenings, after television came along, my mother would tune to *Porter Waggoner, The Grand Ole Opry,* and any other country-music show that happened to come on. That taste seemed to be uniquely hers, for no one else in our family ever expressed a liking for "hillbilly music," as we called it before it grew respectable and came to be called "country."

But my mother, Nonnie, liked popular music, too. Perry Como was her absolute favorite, though Andy Williams ran a close second. "Ol' Per is coming on tonight," Nonnie used to say, smiling. I once asked her why she liked him so much. She said that he sang "nice and smooth, as though he didn't want to hurt himself." And we would sit and listen as Perry Como, in his sweater, sat on a stool and sang songs. I liked his show because he had Pearl Bailey on a lot and she was black—at that time my main reason for liking or not liking a show.

Though my mother would probably deny it, thinking it unbecoming a good Christian, gospel music and hymns weren't her thing at all. As a matter of fact, she was not wild about the church in general; though again, she would probably deny that. But she could exist for a long time without going to service. And did. For many years she kept her membership in Brookstown at West Durham Baptist Church, and since she lived in the country and couldn't get there often, she went "when I can." My father didn't go to church at all at that time, either. So sometimes a couple of months would pass before she'd go. Later on, after my father joined Mount Olive Baptist Church in Braggtown, she moved her membership there. But Reverend Graham, the pastor at West Durham Baptist, never stopped making calls, and several times a year he'd come to see us. We knew that he came from town: he always wore a full suit and a hat.

My mother didn't seem to respond to rhythm-and-blues music one way or the other, but she did like older forms of black entertainment. She often quoted a Bert Williams number, something about how poor he was, so that he had on rags "from my coat down to my shoes." Also in our ancient collection of phonograph records there were several Lil Green blues. When Nonnie heard us singing lines from a current rhythm-and-blues song she would scold us about "those ol' reels," but the scolding was mild and I think she felt it her duty as a mother and a religious person to protest, though we knew she didn't really care that much.

Her interest in music extended far back into her past, one of her happiest memories being of the guitar player in Halifax County, Virginia, who would go around from house to house to play for parties on Saturday night. The people of the community followed him week after week, wherever he was playing. Nonnie had been enchanted by his music. Then there was the male relative who long ago had come home from Cincinnati, bringing with him a Victrola for her mother and father as a Christmas present. This, too, would make her smile and she often referred to it. We also had a Victrola, then a radio, and later a television set—all for entertainment after the day was done.

Nonnie led a structured, orderly existence. Before six o'clock in the morning, she was up, starting her day. First she turned on WPTF and listened to the news and the weather and the music. Later, when WDNC in Durham hired Norfleet Whitted, the first black announcer in the area, she listened first to one station, then to the other. Some mornings it would be "They Traced Her Little Footprints in the Snow," and other mornings it would be black gospel-singing and rhythm-and-blues. Then she would make a fire in the wood stove and start her breakfast. She prepared some meat—fried liver pudding or fatback, or a streak-of-fat streak-of-lean—and made a hoecake of bread on top of the stove, which she ate with either Karo syrup or homemade blackberry preserves, occasionally with store-bought strawberry preserves, or sometimes with homemade watermelon-rind preserves that she had canned in the summer. The she would drink her coffee, call me to get up, and leave the house in her blue uniform, blue apron, and blue cap—it would still be dark when she left on winter mornings—and go to catch her ride to the tobacco factory (with Mr. Ralph Baldwin at first, and then, when he retired, with Mr. James Yergan). When Miss Delilah still lived in Wildwood, before she and Mr. Leroy separated, she would come by and call from the road and the two of them would walk together to the end of the road near the highway and wait for Mr. Ralph there.

My job after she left was to see that the fire didn't go out in the wood stove, to see that the pots sitting on the back didn't burn—for in them was our supper, often pinto beans or black-eyed peas or collard greens or turnip salad. Occasionally there was kale or mustard greens or cressy salad. The other pot would have the meat, which most often was neck bones or pig feet or pig ears, and sometimes spareribs. These would cook until it was time for me to go to school; then I would let the fire die down, only to relight it when I came home to let the pots finish cooking.

After Nonnie left, I also had the task of getting Ruf Junior up so that he could get to school on time. This presented no problem to me until Ruf Junior was in high school and started playing basketball. Often he would travel with the team to schools in distant towns, sometimes getting home after midnight, and the next morning he would be tired and sleepy and wouldn't want to get up. I sympathized, but I had my job to do. If I let him oversleep, I knew that Nonnie would fuss when she got home. But on the other hand, no matter how often I called to him, he would murmur sleepily, "All right, all right," then go back to sleep. I solved this problem one bitter-cold winter morning. I jerked all the covers off his bed and ran. I knew that the only place he could get warm again would be in the kitchen. (The only fire was in the wood stove.) The fire was already out, so he'd have to make one. After that, I didn't have such a hard time getting him up.

My mother worked as a cutter, clipping the hard ends of each bundle of tobacco before it was shredded to make cigarettes. At noon she ate the lunch she had brought from home in a brown paper bag: a biscuit with meat in it and a sweet potato or a piece of pie or cake. Some of the women ate in the cafeteria, but in her thirty years at the Liggett and Myers factory, she never once did. She always took her lunch. Then she worked on until closing time, caught her ride back to Wildwood, and started on the evening's activities. First she had supper, which I had finished preparing from the morning. After I got older we sometimes had meat other than what had to be prepared in a "pot." It would be my duty to fry chicken or prepare ham bits and gravy.

After supper, she'd read the Durham *Sun* and see to it that we did the chores if we hadn't done them already: slop the hogs, feed the chickens, get in the wood for the next day. Then we were free. She'd get her blue uniform ready for the next day, then listen to the radio. No later than nine o'clock, she would be in bed. In the morning she would get up, turn on the radio, and start frying some fatback. Another day would have started.

Saturdays were work days, too, the time for washing, ironing, going to the garden, preparing Sunday dinner (no one was supposed to work on the Sabbath, so we ran the chicken down in the yard and Nonnie wrung its neck or chopped its head off with the ax). Sometimes we went to town on Saturday but not often, for Nonnie went to town every day. Sometimes, at lunchtime, she'd go down to Belk's, and always on Friday she went to the A&P on Mangum Street and bought her groceries; then she'd stop at the Big Star in Little Five Points if she had heard that there was a particularly good buy on something. So the Saturday-in-town ritual that is so much a part of the lives of most country children was not mine at all. I myself sometimes went to Brookstown several times a week when my father was alive, because that is where he went to get trash, sell vegetables, and visit his relatives.

Sunday afternoons she would go to see her friends or they would come to see her. She would say, "I believe I'll go up to Miss Angeline's a little while." Or it would be Miss Pauline's or Claudia's. And she would stay until about dusk and come home, listen to the radio, then go to bed, ready to start Monday morning again.

In the spring and summer after work, my mother would plant in her garden: tomatoes, string beans, okra, and she'd sow a turnip patch. Then, every day after work, she'd go over to the garden on the hill to see how it was doing. On Saturdays she'd get her buckets if it was time for us to go berry-picking. And on hot summer evenings, if the peaches man had been around, she'd can them after work because they wouldn't keep until Saturday, the day she did most of her canning.

This was her routine—fixed, without change, unvarying. And she accepted it. She more than accepted it, she embraced it; it gave meaning to her life, it was what she had been put here on this earth to do. It was not to be questioned.

To Nonnie this life was ideal; she saw nothing wrong with it. And she wondered in baffled rage why her daughter didn't value it but rather sought something else, some other rhythm, a more meaningful pattern to human life.

Nonnie Mebane was not political. However, a special awe

would come into her voice when she said, "And Lee *surren-dered.*" She was from Virginia, and I realize now that she probably would have been imbued with Virginia history in her eight years of schooling there. I myself never heard Robert E. Lee's name mentioned in any class at Wildwood School. But my mother loved to say, "And Lee *surrendered.*" She also liked to say sometimes that the Yankee soldiers rode up and said, "Come on out. Ya'll are free this morning."

The way she said it, I could see the men on horseback—the Yankees—coming around to the fields and to the cabins and saying to the blacks who had been slaves for centuries, "Come on out. Ya'll are free this morning." That was a magical moment. I used to get cold chills when she said it, for, I now realize, in her voice I heard the voice of my mother's mother as she told Nonnie and her other children how the Yankees came early one morning and what they had said. My mother's grandmother had heard them.

Nonnie was a good plain cook, but she couldn't sew very well, couldn't fix hair—her own or her daughter's—and, though dutiful, was an indifferent housekeeper. She was thrifty and paid all of her bills on time. Work at the tobacco factory was her life.

Most of Nonnie's brothers and sisters left her alone. There were either thirteen or fifteen of them, depending on who was counting and whether they were counting the ones that died in infancy, and half brothers and half sisters as well. One of my mother's brothers once said to me, "Your mother's 'curious.'" She, for her part, didn't care for most of them, either. Most of them were dedicated drinkers and she didn't want to be around them. As a result, there were aunts and uncles and dozens of first cousins on my mother's side whom I never met. The first time I ever saw a whole convention of them was at my father's funeral, when a goodly number came down from Philadelphia and Virginia. By the time of my mother's death in 1972, there were very few Stephenses left, for oddly enough it was the younger ones, those who went to the city and engaged in the faster pace of life there, who died first.

My Aunt Donna was an exception. I admired her very much. It was her firm belief that families should stay together as a group, so she would write to each member of the family to gather information and then she would disseminate the same to all the other relatives. Nonnie herself wasn't great on writing, and if you made her mad, the way Aunt Cecily did at their mother's funeral, she might wait two years to answer your letter. But Donna persevered. Not only did she write; she also came down from Philadelphia once a year to spend a week "in the country." She divided her time between the relatives in Virginia and my mother. It was always a happy time for me to look up and see that tall pine tree that was Aunt Donna, with two or more skinny little ones running beside her, come down the road to spend two or three days with us.

Cousin Joyce, who was close to my own age, and I would talk. Tall, black, and skinny—she never in her life weighed much more than a hundred pounds—Joyce seemed more like a sister to me than any relative I had in Durham, even though I saw her only once a year. Billie, her little sister, was as mean as she could be, and it was her pleasure to disturb us in any way that she could. One would never have guessed that she would grow up to be the fine person that she is. Then there was Teddy, called Ted-dee. A tall, skinny, sensitive boy, he was friendly but seemed always a little reserved, withdrawn.

Aunt Donna and Uncle Harry had a wonderful relationship, for though she didn't work and there were five children, he always saw to it that Aunt Donna got a chance to take that yearly trip home. He himself would come over every two or three years, sometimes bringing with him the Virginia sisters, Cecily and Shirley, compared to whom Moms Mabley's talk was pious. They would all gather on the front lawn under the trees, and by the time Uncle Harry and Aunt Shirley stopped trading insults and lies, the whole lawn would be in an uproar.

I wanted the warmth, the sense of blood ties, and the good feeling to last always. But when Aunt Donna gathered up her children and they all departed, it would be over until the next year.

One Saturday some people came from town and they brought my cousin Gloria with them. I was glad to see her; she was not stuck-up like my cousin Jerline. Gloria had never been way over in our field, so she and I decided to see the hogs and then go down to the Bottom, where we could slide down the little hills on pine straw.

Since we were going over in the fields, my mother asked me to take the hogs some water; they had been making noise louder than usual. Gloria and I set out with a bucket of water for the hogs. She watched as I poured it in the troughs, wetting their heads. Then we kept on down in the Bottom. On the way, I showed her a pear tree and she picked a green one to take back to town to show what she had got in the country. I showed her the deep gully where we threw our trash. My father was trying to fill it up to make more land. We went to the creek and then we slid down the little hills.

On our way back to the house I saw an enormous spiderweb. I was surprised to see it, for I hadn't noticed it when we'd passed that way before. I stopped and remarked to Gloria that in the morning when spiderwebs caught the dew they glistened like millions of tiny diamonds. Gloria looked at me for a moment and then said, "You sure do talk funny."

"Funny?" I said. I wasn't mad, for Gloria had said it nicely and she wasn't a mean person.

"You don't talk like us," she said.

I was bewildered. "How do you mean?"

"I don't know," Gloria said. "The words you use and the way you say them." That hurt my feelings and Gloria saw it. So she didn't say any more about it and we talked about other things.

I thought how terrible life was, that it could make people so cruel. I wondered about my own suffering, my painful awareness of how different I was from the people around me. Without knowing it, I had absorbed some of the basic structure of the English language and had added enormously to my vocabulary. I had begun to move away from black speech patterns. But I didn't realize it then. I didn't want to be different. Why did doing what I liked to do make me different?

Mr. Harrison, the social studies and arithmetic teacher, was our eighth-grade homeroom teacher. Students laughed and said that you didn't have to do anything in his room because he didn't know anything, and besides, it was rumored that he drank on the sly. True, he didn't show much interest in arithmetic and social studies, but he had one great love: poetry. We read every poem in the literature book. But most of all, he liked for you to say a poem by heart. Any poem would do, but a long one was better. Once he told us that he would give everybody who said "The Midnight Ride of Paul Revere" an A. I learned every stanza: "Listen, my children, and you shall hear / Of the midnight ride of Paul Revere. . . ." Every day for several weeks that was the lesson: "The Midnight Ride of Paul Revere." Some would start and say a page or two, then falter after repeating the same stanza three or four times. Other, hardier souls plodded on to the weary end. As I sat at my seat, I saw the late-night hour and the signal light, "one if by land, two if by sea"; I saw the sparks fly out from under the horse's hooves as Paul Revere rode through every village and hamlet, sounding the alarm.

Mr. Harrison would sit there, his yellow, globular face slightly flushed, nodding his head in time to the rhythm of every hoofbeat. When the reciter stumbled, his head stopped nodding and he looked pained; if the recitation went without a hitch, he was pleased and triumphant at the outcome. "That sure is nice," he'd say. And he never tired of listening to it.

He also let me go around to the high-school part and select a book from the library. Soon I was reading books all day long in school. When I finished one, I would get the one next to it on the shelf. I read everything. I read a book about microbe-hunters and I wanted to be a famous biologist and save the world from cancer. I read a story about Florence Nightingale and I wanted to be a nurse. I read a sea story, a story about the sinking of a ship, and the night was so cold and stormy that I had to hurry up and finish the book because I felt that if I put the book down before I got to the end, the people on the life raft would have to stay out there in the cold until I came back and finished reading. There was an absorbing book about the story of mankind from its beginning to the present. Then there were love stories where the man and woman said tender things to each other and made promises. Each day when I got to school, I quickly did the assignments, then got down to the real business of the day: reading books. The world inside the books was magic and the people in them more real than the world that I lived in.

Sometimes I would take a book home to read, but Nonnie fussed so that often I would simply start reading a book in the library, then replace it on the shelf with a bookmark, then come back the next day.

At home in the late afternoon I listened to the radio: *Stella Dallas, Lorenzo Jones, When a Girl Marries, Our Gal Sunday.* I kept up with each character. At night I liked to listen to *Lux Radio Theatre,* and on Saturday I listened to *Let's Pretend.* I never listened to *Inner Sanctum;* it was too scary. I lived so intensely what I read in books and what I heard on the radio that even though I knew that it wasn't everyday, it was more real than everyday. Sometimes I listened to *The Shadow* because he was a favorite with everybody in school and it gave me something to talk about with them.

All the girls read confession magazines. They would bring them to school and trade with each other. Sometimes at recess two or three girls would go off and sit on the rocks and read a particularly exciting passage in one of the stories. I loved those magazines. I also read detective-story magazines by the dozens. It was mainly boys who read them, but I liked the strange quality of life they portrayed.

The main favorite of all for everybody, though, was comic

books: *Superman, Wonder Woman, Captain Marvel.* The Washington children always had lots of comic books. Their mother liked to read them and they would bring ten and twenty at a time to school. They'd trade with others but sometimes they'd let you read free. I read them by the hundreds.

I dreamed of doing great things in life, of being famous and successful. But I knew that I wasn't being taught in school what I should have been taught. We didn't have the facilities. The high school was four rooms added on to the back of the elementary school, upstairs and downstairs. Upstairs was the ninth-grade classroom, part of which was partitioned off for the principal's office; next door was the eleventh-grade homeroom, where social studies was taught, and around the wall were books and on the sides a newspaper and magazine stand—it also served as the library. Downstairs was the tenth-grade homeroom, with a cabinet of chemicals and a sink to serve as the science laboratory. Beside it was the fourth grade. Several yards away was a barracklike building, in one half of which home economics was taught, with agriculture being taught in the other half. It also served as a rotating homeroom for seniors and other classes. I knew that I was not getting the same education as the students at the white school about two miles away; and it was not even the same education that students at the black school in town received. Yet I wanted to do great things in life. How was I going to do them when I was being crippled at the start?

I had an answer. If only I could go away to boarding school, then I would be safe. I could get a good education and I would be away from my mother, who never stopped criticizing me for reading so much and other "foolishness." But though I pined away and talked about it, I knew that I couldn't go; there was no money.

It was Easter. Several more of us had become women, so we decided to dress like women on Easter Sunday this year and—more important—to wear our Easter clothes to school on Easter Monday. Easter Monday was a bigger holiday than Easter Sunday, for on that day the whole school participated in an Easter-egg hunt.

On Easter Monday each child brought hard-boiled eggs to school. Some of them had been colored and some were plain. The teachers didn't depend on our eggs, however; they brought dozens of eggs themselves, so that there would be enough. They also secretly held back some of the eggs, not hiding them, so that if there were someone who didn't find one, they'd give them one to keep them from crying.

There were so many eggs, however, and everybody traded so freely, often eating two or three before getting to school, that there was never a problem with a child not having enough to eat.

The teachers would assemble all the students in the auditorium and show them a Western movie on a projector that broke down at least five times; they'd leave one teacher with us while the others took baskets and went out in the grove, among the rocks and on the grounds, near big rocks and the bases of trees, and hid the eggs. Some of the boys would pretend that they had to go badly so they could get out of the auditorium to see the good places to look for eggs.

After they had hidden the eggs we ran out, picture forgotten, to search for eggs. When they had all been found, the one who had the largest number got a prize. By then it was lunchtime and we ate eggs. After lunch, the big boys played baseball. Since it was Easter Monday and the men were home on holiday, they came to play baseball, too.

But this Easter we girls weren't going to hunt any eggs. We were going to wear our Easter things and stand around and talk the way grown people did. After all, we were almost grown. We wore our finery proudly. Our notion of fine dressing was low-heeled black patent-leather shoes, most with a flat bow on the toe. Then we wore stockings, and they caused some girls a problem. For the stockings were leg-shaped, curving outward at the calf, while most of the girls had broom-shaped legs, thin and not curving anywhere, so that the stockings stood out from the calf in a little puff. To hold them up we wore garters, which also caused problems, for some legs were so thin that the garters wouldn't hold, not even if they were twisted. That caused the seam to shift, sometimes almost around to the front, causing the wearer to engage in a constant battle with her stockings. We wore stand-out petticoats and constantly adjusted bra straps to let others know we needed one, although most of us had nothing to fill them; Hazel and I were the only ones to have anything that needed support.

We stood around, like our mothers on the church grounds, and talked about intelligent things—like the weather and the teacher and boys. In the afternoon we walked down to the baseball field, where some of the grown men made admiring remarks. Satisfied that we had established our identity, that night we slept peacefully.

12

At first I didn't know any better; I thought that people all over the world washed clothes in the backyard, cooked their supper right out of the garden, churned milk and picked blackberries, got saved and were baptized, and went to church on Sunday. If the work was sheer drudgery, as undoubtedly it was, I didn't feel it as such and perhaps never would have.

But eventually I began to perceive that I was being prepared for my life's work. That's when the trouble really got bad—when I started resisting.

I am going to do great things in life, I secretly vowed.

No, you aren't, said the world around me. You're going to accept your lot just like the rest of us. Black women have always had it hard. Who are you to be so different?

Pick up your cross, said the Sunday school and church. Everyone has a cross to bear.

Black women like me have scrubbed a hundred billion miles of tiled corridors and washed an equal number of dishes. I wasn't going to do that.

I am going to live my own life, I secretly said.

No, you aren't, said an adult. I am going to see to it that you don't. You might as well get those foolish notions out of your head, girl.

That adult was my mother.

Perhaps someday someone will discover the origin of the tension that sometimes develops between black mother and black daughter, especially when the daughter is ambitious. The spark that usually set off the conflict was my interest in things literary and cultural—worthless things for a girl like me, born black in the rural segregated American South. But that was only the tip of the iceberg. Unseen but hulking huge and more deadly was the feeling that there was some basic flaw in a personality that engaged in such pursuits.

Nonnie felt bitterly resentful and rejected when I refused to subscribe to her version of reality. She had managed to project her dislike of my interests so thoroughly into my consciousness that soon I, too, felt that there was something not quite right about valuing ideas. During intermittent periods I would self-consciously cast off the raiment of intellectuality and try on the garment of black folk culture, attempting to convince myself that it was sufficient, that to want more and—even more guilt-producing—to want better was an affectation on my part.

Nevertheless, I began to hope that music would be a way out, and I conceived the idea of becoming a concert pianist. I hadn't taken music lessons for a long time, having stopped when I could play for the Sunday school and the church choir. But I would take piano lessons and practice very hard and then one day I would be a great artist.

I had heard that Mrs. Shearin was the best teacher in town. I called and asked her how much the lessons were. She said one dollar each. I asked if I could work for her to pay for my lessons; she said that she was sure something could be arranged.

Soon I was making a weekly trip to Durham to Mrs. Shearin's studio. I was excited because it was an adventure for me. It was the first time I had been to the heart of the black community in Durham. My father's relatives lived in the northern and western sections of the city, but the center of the black population was in the southern part of the city. Located there were the homes of the "rich" blacks of Durham that I had heard about.

The first time I rode down the main street in the black section I was disappointed. There were a number of big two-story houses, but most of them needed painting, and there were smaller, less-well-kept-up houses nearby and in some cases right next to them. Interspersed among them also were various small businesses, a taxi stand, an ice-cream parlor, a hamburger stand, so that the community did not look like the well-off, prosperous communities in other sections of the city.

Right at the bus stop where I got off was North Carolina College, a state-supported black institution. It was the best-kept piece of property in the neighborhood. It had lustrous green grass kept cut very close, tall trimmed hedges, and red-brick buildings. Saturday mornings I would see students dressed in the latest college fashions waiting for the bus on the other side of the street. I used to look at the buildings and think how nice they were, but I didn't really plan to go to NCC. I wanted desperately to go to one of those great centers of learning I had read about in books and magazines. I wanted to go to Radcliffe or Wellesley.

I liked my music lessons. Mrs. Shearin lived in a Spanish-style house, low and pink. It had nice things but nothing flashy. My tasks were not hard. I vacuumed the living room, made up her son's bed, dusted, and fixed her a large cup of tea for breakfast, which I took to her in the studio, a large room at the back of the house. That over, I waited for my turn.

I was stunned at my total ignorance about music, for I had been playing hymns for a number of years. My teacher in Wildwood had never taught me about the values of notes—that is, that a quarter note gets one beat, a half note gets two beats, and a whole note gets four beats. I had never even heard of an eighth note or a sixteenth note, scales or keys. I was in despair. How was I ever going to be a concert artist when I had never even been taught the basics? I realized then why my teacher in Wildwood practically started her pupils off with hymns, concentrating on the top or melodic line. She knew the familiar hymns by heart and was teaching her students by rote.

Soon I began to understand the new terms, and the joy of learning came back. Mrs. Shearin asked me to subscribe to *Etude* magazine, which started coming to the house every month. I was working for my music, so Nonnie couldn't say much one way or the other. And each student had to buy a little book with the lives of the composers in it. When we played a piece by Mozart or some other composer, before we began we had to tell Mrs. Shearin some facts about his life. We had to be able to spell his name correctly, and she made sure that our pronunciation was correct. I loved it. Scales to me were fun—to be able to go over the whole keyboard, first with one hand, then with two, in key after key, major and minor, was a pleasure. I felt a sense of mastery. It was something new; that meant my world was opening up and I was happy.

Mrs. Shearin herself was very chic. I used to pay her close attention on the sly. She always wore fingernail polish; her hair and face were perfectly groomed and she wore attractive, colorful clothing. But more than what she wore, her manner was gracious and refined, always courteous, though she sometimes yelled at students about their mistakes. She was elegant. That's what I admired about her and my Aunt Jo; they both had style, class, and elegance. Mrs. Shearin had been born to wealth—her father was the best-known black businessman in the United States; Aunt Jo had not been born to wealth, but she had acquired style. They were the only black women that I ever really admired. I've always liked class, style, and elegance.

I was so enthusiastic about my studies in music that soon Esther, a girl in Wildwood, wanted to take piano and I had a partner for my adventures in Durham.

One day I was in my room lying on my bed on my stomach, turning the pages of a magazine on the floor. I liked to read this way. The room was cluttered—the bed was unmade and there were books and records and magazines everywhere.

Nonnie had had a long day at the factory, catching the bundles of tobacco as they came down the belt and cutting off the hard-tied part. (If one of the women on the line failed to turn the bundle of tobacco the right way, the knot end might go into the machine and America would have a bitter cigarette. Nonnie had a responsible job.)

"Mary!" Nonnie yelled.

At first I didn't hear her. I continued to read my book while Beethoven was playing on the record player.

"Mary!"

I put down my book and went to the kitchen.

"What is it, Mama?"

"What is the matter with you, girl?"

"What's wrong, Mama?"

"What's wrong? The okra's burned. That's what's wrong."

"I'm sorry," I said. "It's hard to fry it without burning. I cut it up like you said, but a whole lot of slime ran out; then I rolled it in flour, but I couldn't get it to brown right. I was cooking it longer, trying to make it brown, when it burned."

"You burned up the okra."

Both Nonnie and I knew that I occasionally burned up food. I often put on supper and then got a magazine and thumbed through it while the supper cooked, or started reading a book that I had gotten out of the school library or off the book-mobile that came into the county once a week. But, either way, the results were the same: scorched chicken and leath-erlike fried potatoes—not often, but sometimes.

The quarrel was all the more frustrating because we both knew that it was not really about the scorched food. It was about something else, something I would neither stop doing nor apologize for. Something in me wouldn't let me. But the scene continued.

Nonnie stood there, her glasses glinting with the faint dust that all tobacco workers were covered with. Her blue uniform had dark-brown powder in the folds, and her apron, starched white in the morning, was now slightly beige from the to-bacco. From her clothing came the faint smell of tobacco dust.

"The chicken's all right, isn't it, Mama?" I said.

"I'm not talking about the chicken."

"And I fixed the biscuits all right, too."

I desperately wanted my mother's approval. I wanted to do something that would make her smile at me and say, "That's good. I'm glad that you're my daughter."

"Listen when I'm talking to you, girl."

I knew that I didn't listen. I had learned the practical use of the "tune-out." When the stimuli from the outside world came in too strongly critical of what I was doing, of what I was interested in, I tuned out. The best substitute for lis-tening was a smile. In that way my hearer didn't know that I had long ago ceased to listen. And I had a moment's peace. But Nonnie had me right where she wanted me—in the wrong, with no alibi, and she thoroughly enjoyed her posi-tion.

"And we have some nice Jell-O and I fixed some iced tea," I said. Please, just this one time say something nice, I silently prayed. Iced tea and Jello-O were my mother's favorites.

Nonnie was not to be deterred. "You somewhere with your head in a book and you let my okra burn."

"Mama, it never seems to come out right when I fry it."

"No. You don't watch it. You always got your head in a

103

book or you listening to those old stories or you listening to that music all the time. Burned up my food."

"I'm sorry."

"I go and work hard and when I come home my food's burned."

That hurt, for I knew that my mother worked hard.

"But Mama, I got all A's on my report card this month."

Nonnie wasn't interested in extraneous issues. "And you don't wash the clothes right, either."

I was guilty. Washing and ironing, the measure of achievement for community girls, interested me not at all. For unspoken was the knowledge that these black girls were really being trained to work as domestics, not to keep house for themselves. But they and their mothers played a game that they were learning to be good housekeepers, and their mothers and the neighborhood ladies praised them for all evidence of homemaking skills.

I was later to observe that often cooks who planned, purchased, and prepared attractive menus on their job would at home serve ill-prepared, unbalanced meals. They were too tired to fix better, they said. And women who made their living cleaning and washing and ironing for other people frequently had unironed clothing piled to the ceiling at home and sat down in the midst of untidiness. They, too, were too tired.

But I hadn't trained properly. Instinct had taught me to see through that. It was a trap.

"And my teacher said that I could go far in life, Mama."

"Marguerita makes all of her own clothes." Nonnie neglected to mention that Marguerita's mother was a seamstress herself and that she took time and showed her daughter how to do things. No one took time to show me anything. Most of what I learned, I learned from books.

"And my teacher said that I was smart. You know I can't sew, Mama."

"And Miss Pearl says that Ida Mae does all of her washing and ironing."

"I'm going to play a piece at Mrs. Shearin's piano recital. She asked me to be on the program. She can't have her whole school on the program, just a few that she thinks are playing well. And she asked me to appear."

"You keep your head in a book all the time. What is the matter with you, girl?"

"Mama, I'm sorry that I can't do anything right. I'm sorry."

"No, if I ask you to cook, you hurry up. But if you get a book, you sit back in that room all day Saturday and all day Sunday, reading it. You don't go nowhere. Just sit in that room reading a book. Those old books and those old magazines. You going to end in Goldsboro, right with those other crazy people. You going to be just like Claudia's daughter. She read those books all the time and she went crazy and they sent her to Goldsboro."

"I'm sorry, Mama. I'm sorry, Mama. Sorry that I can't do anything right."

13

Aunt Jo had strange, big-city ways: she smoked cigarettes on the sly, used rouge, introduced strange cuisine in the household, and put unsuitable notions in my head. Getting rid of her was a long-drawn-out campaign, but Nonnie did it—Jo moved to town and shared rooms with two maiden sisters.

When she left, the light went out for me. I never knew again the warmth, feeling, and loving concern that Aunt Jo had shown for me during those years. There was no one to whisper to me about the marvelous things that I was going to accomplish or tell me that I was meant for really great things in life: dancer, pianist, college student. But the damage had been done. In her quiet, determined way, Aunt Jo had planted the seeds so deep that no one could ever uproot them.

Nevertheless, having maneuvered Jo out of the house, Nonnie set herself the task of eradicating those unsuitable notions from her daughter's head. They were nothing but foolishness and would lead Mary to nothing but trouble. She was sorry that Ruf had let Jo stay that long, bringing those Northern ideas and ways that she had learned from rich people into her home. Anything associated with Jo's notions—my being a pianist, an intellectual—she would attack; anything not done properly in the house she would severely condemn.

On my part, I was hardheaded and stubborn. And in spite of all the fussing, I would not change. I brought a book home every day and read it between the time I got home and the time I went to bed. The okra still burned, the chicken burned, and the bread burned. Not really bad, just spots here and there, and I became adept at scraping the burned places off and putting the food back into the frying pan to brown a little more. The flour for the gravy had to be attended to every minute or it would burn so bad I'd have to throw it out and start all over, and Nonnie could not tolerate whitish gravy. So, somewhere down the line I learned about paprika, and for a while produced the reddest, spiciest gravy you ever saw. But Nonnie got wise to that—I probably put in so much that she could taste it—and I learned to cook the flour a little, then use paprika a little, not so you'd notice, but enough to speed the browning time up a bit.

If my cooking was bad, my housekeeping was worse. It would take me half the night to wash the supper dishes, for if the book I was reading was a good one, I'd read a few pages, then go wash a dish or two, then go back and read a few more. The beds got "spreaded up," not made; I took the attitude, What's the difference? You're only going to sleep in them again, anyway. And as Nonnie's fussing became sharper and the negative things she said about me got worse, I hurried even more to finish the chores and get to what I really liked. Maybe I *would* go crazy and wind up in Goldsboro. Maybe I *was* an "odd" child. But I would read that book. I know now that subconsciously I was resisting her in the only way I knew how, not by saying anything but just by not doing what she valued and wanted me to value.

One Sunday morning I had just come in from Sunday school and was sitting in the kitchen, leaning back in a straight chair propped against the wall. It was a warm day; I was slightly sweaty from walking in the heat. I lost my balance and the chair I was sitting in tipped to the left. I fell in the same direction; my head and the knob on the back of the chair hit the window, cracking the pane.

"See what you done!" Nonnie said. "I told you and told you about leaning back in that chair." I was mortified. She had told me before, but what stunned me was the rage and triumph I heard in her voice.

"I'm going to make your daddy whip you. That's what you need. A good whipping! You're getting beside yourself!"

I was too stunned to answer. Aunt Jo was gone, and though my father was sick and irritable most of the time, he let me help him in the little store that he had set up near the house, and asked me to do little things for him—so I knew he liked me. Now she wanted him to turn against me, too.

I thought that there was a magical line that separated children from grown people, that when you reached a certain age you automatically stopped acting "childish"—no longer had such traits as jealousy, spitefulness, meanness—and began acting grown, which was the way the church taught. Those who didn't act that way were sinners. The church taught: "Children, obey your parents, for this is right" and "Honor thy father and mother that thy days may be long upon the land which the Lord thy God giveth thee"; and the minister preached of the Prodigal Son, who took his portion and went and wasted it, but when he came back his father welcomed him with a big feast. In the first grade, their mother loved Dick and Jane, and in the magazines that I read parents loved and cared for their children. So if my mother didn't like and didn't care for me and always spoke to me harshly, she must have a good reason.

I thought and thought as to what the matter was—maybe she knew what had happened to me that night in the rain when I was five years old. I didn't, for I could never clearly remember the part where I fell down. I could remember starting out in the rain and going to the barn and running back to bed, but the part where I was screaming and fell down was cloudy to me and I never could remember. Or maybe my mother knew about my secret longings and my erotic fantasies, though I kept them hidden and never showed any signs of interest in boys.

But today something snapped. Something inside said, No.

"Just wait until he comes to the house. I'm going to make him whip you," she said again.

I wanted to cry, I'm a woman now, I'm not supposed to get any more whippings. But I said nothing.

I wondered about the triumphant tone that I heard in my mother's voice and then realized that it was because at last she could confront my father with something damaging about me. He and Jesse had been bitter enemies for a long time, but my mother liked Jesse, for he had been her firstborn; so it must have been galling to her to have my father talk to him mean and try to whip him—and for Jesse to run away— while he never whipped me and seldom spoke harshly to me, let me go with him everywhere, stand right by him while he poured the steps for the back porch, and ride with him when he peddled vegetables.

I made up my mind then. I would leave and I wasn't ever coming back. Talking to me like that, trying to turn my father against me . . . She wouldn't ever see me anymore.

I went out to the store and asked my father for some money. The store was full of Sunday-school children buying cold drinks and peanuts. I looked at them all dressed up, feeling that if I could get away I'd never see them again. He gave me a quarter and I left the yard, walking with a bunch that was laughing and talking and drinking their cold drinks. One by one they dropped off, but I kept walking. I was on my way to the bus line. I had never ridden the bus, but I knew where it turned around; that was about two miles away. Aunt Jo lived in town now, and so did my father's cousins, and if I could get to them, they would help me; perhaps I could stay with them. I could finish school in town and I wouldn't have to come to Wildwood anymore.

Soon I was near the highway and alone. Everybody else was at home or at a friend's house, where they had asked permission to stop. The highway was different. There were fewer houses, but I had traveled this way hundreds of times on my father's wagon. There was one house close to Wildwood, tall and two-storied, many-windowed, with flapping shutters, that I was afraid of. People said that there was a ghost in it and the ghost made noises late at night. Farther ahead were two homes, one on either side of the highway. Both of the families were rich, but they were not friends, for one family had "old" money and one family had "new" money. Hazel and her family lived with the Richardses, the family with the "old" money, on a "farm" that was really an estate. Hazel was very proud of their house. It had running water and was well kept up, for it was practically in the Richardses' yard. The Ransoms lived in a tree-shaded park, one that occupied the full time of several yard men, practically across the street from the Richardses, but Hazel liked to tell how the people her parents worked for would have nothing to do with them, for they had no "quality."

I walked on past the long hedge that separated the Ransoms' park from the highway, wondering how it must feel to live in a big house in a grove of trees, far away from the highway, never having to do anything, with a swarm of servants doing everything. Then I looked at the four-tiered white fence that surrounded the Richardses' "farm"; it took a long time to drive past it, and I knew that by the time I walked past it, I would be near the bus line.

Once when I was visiting Hazel, she proudly showed me the farm. There was a whole garage of nothing but old cars, all kinds, that used to belong to the family. Then she showed me the swimming pool and the barn where the cows were

109

milked and the tennis courts. She was quite proud of the place; to her it was her "home."

Near the place where the Richardses' fence stopped, but across the highway, were little houses where other white people lived, those who didn't have the money that the Richardses had. Sometimes they sat on the porch and I wondered what they thought when they looked at all the Richardses had and compared it with what they had. From then on to the bus line, there were little houses, boxlike, with little lawns and hedges; the large estate and the farm were past.

When I got to the bus stop, there was no bus. I walked on, not really minding it, for the highway had become a street and now there was a sidewalk and I liked walking; so I continued, mile after mile, passing service stations, little box houses. I met a bus going to the end of the line when I was far down the street, and still I walked—past more service stations and hot-dog stands and small businesses and more houses. I felt so good that I thought that I would walk all the way in to town, thus saving my quarter.

Near the creek at the foot of Mangum Street hill a car passed me. At first I didn't notice it, but when someone yelled I looked up.

There were three or four white boys in the car. I wondered what they had said, but I didn't really pay attention, for I was getting closer and closer to town and I was preoccupied with wondering how I was going to make out. Was someone going to invite me to stay? Would my mother let me stay? Would a new life start for me? I hoped so. I knew that my father would come and get me, and maybe then I could tell him how Nonnie hurt me by talking so mean to me all the time and he would make her stop. But then he was sick all the time and dependent on her, and besides, who would feed me, clothe me, give me money to go to school? There was nobody who could but Aunt Jo, and Nonnie wouldn't, I was sure, let me stay with her. I walked along on a bright Sunday morning—it was near noon by then—hoping that things would work out all right.

Then a black car passed me again and someone threw ice on me. I was scared, for the same car had circled around and come back up on me from behind. White people—they were the evil, the danger, that existed in the world. You avoided them like snakes. I didn't know what to do. Would they harass me from then on, constantly circling and coming up from behind? I looked back and saw the bus coming. It had gone to the end of the line and waited and now was making a return trip; it was Sunday and the buses weren't running frequently. So, never having been on a bus, I stood at the foot of the hill where there was a sign that said BUS, and when it came I got on. A brief conversation with the driver got me three tokens.

I was surprised to see Nancy on the bus; she taught the little children in Sunday school. She was surprised to see me, too. I told her that I was going to town to see my folks. She soon discovered that I knew nothing about changing buses and getting a transfer, and told me how and where to change. I went to the front and got the little pink transfer and got off at Walgreen's at Main Street.

I got to West Durham all right. I was proud of myself for finding the way, the first time on my own. I went to see Aunt Jo, but I felt so sad, for she was living in a small dark room in a house with two unmarried sisters. She didn't like it; I had heard her tell my mother that once. She asked me about everybody and I said they were all right, but I knew that she knew that something was wrong, because I had come alone. I wanted to tell her so much and I started to several times—that I wanted to come to town to live, maybe even stay with her; but I felt so bad that I would be letting her down, for she held me up as a model to her nieces and nephews, and if they knew I was running away from home it would make her look bad for having so much faith in me. I couldn't make the words come out. So we sat and talked, awkwardly, for we hadn't been alone in a long time. She spoke again of education. I must get an education.

I didn't know it then, but she was already dying of cancer. Marva, my older cousin, who lived across the street from Aunt Jo, was surprised to see me, and her daughter Jerline barely spoke—though she had been to visit us in the country—and an older male cousin took the extra token that I had put in a dish on the coffee table. I saw him take it, but he was grown and I was scared to say "Don't."

In the late afternoon I started back home. I rode the bus downtown all right, but at Five Points I didn't know how to change buses and was too scared to ask; so I started walking right on Main Street, in the heart of Durham. I walked the eight miles home.

Near the bus line Jesse met me; he was on his way to town. "Mama's gonna whip you!" He laughed in that special way he had when something bad was going to happen to somebody. I said nothing, but walked on. It was soon deep night. Wildwood was dark and quiet when I got back, with a light here and there. I passed no one.

Nonnie was angry and I was defiant. She got her switches to whip me, but I started yelling that I was going to leave again and I wasn't coming back. She did a lot of fussing, but she hit me only a time or two. I knew that I had won, for I never got another whipping. I had learned the value of protest. And I, too, put my soul on ice. I had to, if I was to survive.

14

My father was a secret dreamer for whom the world had no place, and Aunt Jo was an embittered romantic who gave up the desire for a better life.

Now, from the standpoint of some maturity, I see my father in an entirely different light from the way I saw him as a child, and, indeed, for many years after that. I now realize that my father was the way he was because the social order he was born into could not accommodate him and he either would not or could not fit into the society around him. The irony of the situation is that, though I disapproved of the role my father was playing, I myself, without realizing it, was partly forced into and partly opted for a similar role—that is, a role that was different from, and often hostile to, the expectations of what others thought I should be and become. But, as I say, it wasn't until many years later that I figured all this out, and it took an even longer time for me to accept it on the bedrock emotional level.

Rufus Mebane was born about twenty years after the Civil War, in either Hillsboro or Durham, North Carolina. I've never been sure which. His mother, I know, came from Hillsboro and he was raised in Durham.

I don't know about his father; I didn't hear much talk about him as I was growing up. This is not to say that my father was not the product of a legitimate marriage; it just means that I don't know. I used to hear Aunt Jo say when she was vexed at something my father had done that seemed particularly eccentric to her, "He's just like Ol' Ned Mebane." And my mother would nod. So I think that Ned Mebane was his father, and that he was a noted eccentric.

My grandmother, I believe, was named Sally Mebane before her marriage. (The fact that both of my grandparents, Ned and Sally, had the same last name isn't too surprising because in small communities like theirs it often happens that many people have the same surname, even though they are not necessarily related.) There was a book of my grandmother's that I kept for a long time because it had her handwriting in it. Inscribed on the inside cover of a copy of Shakespeare's *As You Like It* were the words "Sally Mebane her book."

How my grandmother came into possession of a leather-covered volume of Shakespeare that she apparently had read was part of the family shame and secret. It was once whis-

113

pered to me that Sally and her sister were the daughters of a rich man (white, of course) who not only reared them in his house but had them tutored as well. That explained the Shakespeare. The lady of the house knew whose children Sally and her sister were, didn't like it, but couldn't do anything about it, so she said nothing. My father never talked about mother, father, sister, brother. Nobody. It was said that he was "curious" and I suppose that is an instance of it.

I once saw a picture of my father taken in his prime. It startled me, for it in no way resembled the man I knew. He was seated in a chair, looking straight at the camera. He had on a suit with wide pinstripes, and the lapels ended in a sharp upturn. He had on a white shirt and a tie with a stickpin in it and a dark homburg. His face was smooth, with the cheeks a little sunken, and it was obvious that he was very tall. The eyes looked like slate and were opaque. Even though they stared straight at the camera, you had the sense that the eyes consciously did not reveal anything, that they deliberately concealed everything. The eyes frightened me and I put the picture down. The man I knew as a child was stoop-shouldered, long-legged, and mostly bald.

I learned from overhearing adult conversations around me that in his young days he was a rambling, gambling, drinking man—the photograph that I saw was taken in Norfolk, Virginia—and he seems to have had no trade. His childhood must have been an impoverished one, for when his relatives sometimes teased him about the fact that he ran around as a boy in only his shirt, my father would take it up and say, "And there was only one button on it, and that was at the top." But he never talked about his childhood or his schooling. He evidently got to the sixth or seventh grade in the Durham schools, for when he and my mother married and lived in Durham, they both went to night school to get a certificate, and my mother often said that she was ahead of him because she had finished the eighth grade in Halifax County, Virginia.

He didn't marry until his late thirties, and the children came even later, when he was in his middle forties. A gap of four decades can have an adverse effect on parent-child relations. Sometime after his marriage, he decided to leave the Brookstown section in West Durham, even though it was his home. My mother said many, many times, "He didn't like people and he wanted to be away from 'round them." They (I say they, but I have a feeling my mother financed everything) bought a tract of land (thirteen acres) in the wilds of Durham County in a section that later became known as Wildwood. It was truly country, with a house here and there and vast reaches of woods in between. Here he proposed to support himself by farming. When Wildwood got more than a few families, he wanted to move still farther back in the woods, away from people. I often heard him say so. "Nonnie," he would say, "let's us . . ." and he would start to paint an idyllic picture of life still deeper in the woods. I'd get a little chill because I didn't want to go. My mother, who seemed to have been content enough in Brookstown and came to the country just to satisfy him, would always veto that idea. But to the end of his life, at each appearance of a new family in the community he expressed the desire to move.

Ruf Mebane was a man of many hates, some rational, others not. At the top of his hate list were white people. I know from references here and there that it had to do with his mother's light complexion and with the fact that she and her sister were somehow related to someone who was rich. I never did get the straight of it, for it was a taboo subject. Years later, when I first appeared in print, a man who wrote on company stationery from a Texas oil firm sent me a letter inquiring about a sword carried in some war by a Colonel John Mebane, but I never was interested in pursuing the matter. Besides, near Hillsboro, there is a town called Mebane (pronounced "Mebban," like my name), and I am sure there must be hundreds of people in the area with that name. And the name itself has many variations; some of my early school records record the name as "Maban," and I have seen other documents that spell it "Mabane."

But Ruf Mebane never could hold what my mother called

a "public job," for the boss was always white and he couldn't get along with him. In the only job that I ever heard my mother mention that he held, he got into an argument or a fight (I've never been sure which) and was fired. It was at the tobacco factory, and my mother said that after that he couldn't get a job in any factory in town.

I don't doubt the conflict with the boss and the firing, but sometimes I have some doubt about the blacklist in all the other factories. I don't know whether he actually couldn't get another job or whether he found it so repulsive to work under a white boss that he never again tried. I do know that he wouldn't permit a white insurance man to come to the house, and that my mother always paid our insurance at the Metropolitan Life office in Durham. It was not until the 1950s, after his death, when we took out some policies with the North Carolina Mutual Life Insurance Company, a black firm, that an agent started to come to our house to collect, and he, of course, was a black man.

Whenever David Ransom, "the old man," would drive by on the way to his rock quarry at the end of our road, my father would say, "There goes Davy. I played with him when I was a boy, and I knew him when he was grading roads in West Durham with just a mule and wagon." I could hear the bitterness in his voice; as far as he was concerned the only reason Davy had made it and he hadn't was that Davy was white. That is probably the reason Ruf Mebane never went to work for the Ransoms, although a lot of men in his age group in Wildwood certainly did.

Some years later, when my father went to Duke University Hospital for a cancer operation, he had a white nurse who was so impressed by his sweet nature that she wrote my mother a long letter, telling her what a nice man Ruf was, how pleasant it was to take care of him and all (she also gave my mother a pair of draperies to "do up" for her). Those opaque eyes of my father's concealed a great deal indeed.

My father hated any reference to sex, fast women, people who had money, and, in particular, to "that school." Once

Wildwood School got a high school attached to it (four rooms added to the elementary school), Mr. Jackson came to be the principal. And it was a mistake; Mr. Jackson, a plump, short, brown man, was from town, and from his conversation he seemed a rather sophisticated person who was well educated and had traveled. I don't know why he took the job; he probably needed the money, I suppose. But after he came to be principal, the conflict between my father and "that school" grew, for Mr. Jackson, in his daily speeches in chapel, would talk to the student body on various subjects, and sometimes his references were sexual. He once was unhappy because Mary (not me—there must have been fifteen Marys in Wildwood School) didn't bring money for a class project. He asked her about it, telling her what the other girls had done. Mary replied, "I don't have what the other girls have." Mr. Jackson mentioned this in chapel and told us that if it had been a boy who said that, "He and I would be down there in the outdoor toilet with our clothes off right now, looking each other up and down to see what it was that I had that he didn't have."

Mr. Jackson also liked to tell jokes. One morning, he told about separating two boys who were fighting the day before. He inquired as to the cause of the fight, and one told him that the other one had called him the son of a biscuit eater. And Mr. Jackson told us with a straight face, "My mother ate biscuits, so I'm the son of a biscuit eater. I don't see anything to fight about. Don't your mothers eat biscuits? I bet they ate biscuits this morning." And he went on and on, while some took him seriously and others didn't. I, for one, nearly fell out of my seat trying to keep from laughing.

But this and other things didn't sit too well with Ruf Mebane. I don't know who told him about it (I didn't), but he found out about what Mr. Jackson was saying, as did other parents in the school, and there was a lot of mumbling. There was always a lot of mumbling among the blacks, but, as I had observed, nothing was ever done. This time, however, there was a difference. I knew it one day when I came home from school and found my father talking with a white man at the edge of the road, near the fully flowering yellow bush. Just as I walked past (I knew better than to stop or to act in any way as though I were listening), I heard my father tell the white man, who seemed to have a notepad in his hand, "And he also said that no woman up there had a shape like a Coca-Cola bottle," and I knew he was talking about Mr. Jackson, for, though I had never heard him say it, there was common talk on the school grounds that in his classes he commented on the figures of the big girls.

Somehow after that I learned that there had been a meeting at the school; whites had come out from town to hear the complaints, but my father and Mrs. Harris, Hazel's mother, were the only two parents who voiced objections to some of the actions of the principal. I think the meeting did some good, for Mr. Jackson became more circumspect after that. But I was marked, for one day he called me to him on the playground and asked me what my name was. I told him "Mary" and he wanted to know "Mary who?" and when I told him, he said, "So, you're Ruf Mebane's daughter?" I nodded, very scared, for I knew that he knew that my father had gone to the officials and tried to have him fired. Mr. Jackson did eventually leave Wildwood School, but I don't know whether my father's opposition to him had anything to do with it.

My father liked plain, unadorned women. Any decoration at all he regarded as "tempting to men." My mother never wore makeup and had very little jewelry. Her dresses were always subdued-looking. Once she startled me by making some reference to my father as "jealous," and in the 1960s she stunned me by relating that once she and he had been on the verge of separating because, she said, "He claimed that I was going with somebody at the factory." I was astonished at this revelation because I had never heard my father arguing with my mother; in fact, he never raised his voice. But now I can only assume that she knew his nature and had early in their marriage decided to conform to his expectations and never do anything that would arouse his hostility.

"That school" was where they gave his children the "shots" that he was so bitterly opposed to. On one occasion he came to the school and sat in on a teachers' meeting and told them all that he didn't want his children taking shots. Mrs. Thomas, my fourth-grade teacher, came back to the room and asked me in front of the whole class, "What does your father have against shots?" I told her he didn't have anything against shots, though I knew better. "Well," she said, silencing me, "he was just here, upstairs, and he said that he didn't want you to take one." I hadn't known that he was coming that morning at all.

The first time I ever saw my father at the school was during World War II. One summer day he took me and Ruf Junior to Wildwood with him to sign up for ration stamps. I can still see his long legs, crossed at the knees and sticking out into the aisle, as he patiently filled out a form.

If Ruf Mebane didn't like most people and didn't get along with them, he did get along all right with his two youngest children, Ruf Junior and me. He took us with him everywhere. He peddled vegetables on the streets of Durham and we rode along. I can still remember the utter joy I felt when riding along, sitting on the edge of the wagon, drawn by Suki, while inside were cucumbers, onions, squash, tomatoes, okra, unshucked corn, and collard greens. One of his favorite stops was on Mangum Street hill, which is located just after you leave Braggtown but before you get to Durham proper. Someone in one of those big houses used to come out to look at the produce. Later we rode in "the Silver Meteor." My father had taken an old car and cut out the back and fixed it up in such a way that it became a truck. He painted it silver. The bigger children mockingly named it after the crack train that came through Durham and carried people to New York City.

In addition to peddling vegetables from his garden, my father gathered up junk—old clothes and other items. It was these that we used to play house with. Our farm was a long, narrow strip of land and at the back of it, in the Bottom, were many gullies—small canyons, really—and my father wanted to fill these up so that eventually they would be firm land. So he used to put all the unusable junk there. The heavy items that he could sell he took to Sid Rancer's, the junkman in Little Five Points, and we made many, many trips there. He also cleaned out Mr. McDougald's cesspool. But my father never seemed to have any real money. I remember once Aunt Jo came home from town happy because someone had left a pocketbook on the bus and when she got home she found a five-dollar bill inside. My father said, his face all lit up in a big smile, "Hot dog! We've got some real money now!" I remember it well because I had never seen him so emotional. He must have felt his lack of a regular weekly salary very keenly.

Early in the morning when he had been out in the yard, he would sing, but it was really a "holler." It didn't have much tune to it, but it seemed to have a pattern. I was rather ashamed: my father couldn't carry a tune. Not until some years later, when I was reading about the music of black people and I came across a description of the "holler," a form that preceded the blues, did I realize that that was what my father had been doing. It was not his form that was at fault; it was my ignorance.

During the war, when they were building Camp Butner, near Durham, my father got on as a carpenter. He talked with wonder about the money he was making. I had never seen him so proud and happy. When Mr. Reid, a neighbor, came down, he told him how much they were paying an hour, and the other men wondered at that. It had given him a rare status, which he enjoyed. But the job didn't last long, probably because of his poor health.

The thing that I most remember about my father was that he was always sick. He had a stomach ulcer. Most of the time he wouldn't say anything when he felt bad; he would just go lie down. Sometimes I saw him hurt so bad that he would get up from milking the cows or doing some other chores and stretch out on the grass. He took anything that anybody told him was good for it, but he wouldn't go see a doctor. He kept a jar of tar water—water with tar in it—in the icebox all the time because that was supposed to be good for an ulcer. And when he was in the final stages of his cancer, but still didn't want to admit it, he drank a whole lot of beer because someone had told him that beer would cure it. For the first and only time in my life, I saw my father drunk. He was standing at the edge of the road, waving at the neighbors as they passed. He didn't say, "Just read in the Book of Samuel," a remark he was supposed to have made often during his drinking days. He just stood at the edge of the road and waved and generally looked ebullient. The beer didn't work and soon he had to go to a real doctor, but by then the cancer was too far gone.

Never a zealous church member, he decided late in life that he wanted to be a deacon. He got books and studied at night after he came in from the fields or from hauling trash or peddling vegetables. They were books with black-leather covers and small type. He consulted with the deacons after church on Sundays and after a while there came a time when he was to be ordained. I didn't know what it meant, but I knew that it was important. The ordination ceremony was held after the sermon one Sunday. Several deacons from various congregations were ordained at the same time. A lot of ministers came, some from town. Everything was quiet and nobody smiled, but I knew that my father was very pleased, and I was proud.

Near the end of his life he set up "Mr. Ruf's Store" in our yard. Here he had two soft-drink boxes filled with Pepsis, Cokes, Nehis, RCs, Dr Peppers, oranges, and grapes. On the shelves around the walls were crackers and sardines, snuff and tobacco, odds and ends needed by members of the community. In the evening, often the men would come and play checkers under the tree in front of the store, and children always stopped on their way home from school to get a "drank."

My father never mentioned any ambition that he had ever had, but it was obvious that the love of his life was mathematics. Every evening when he came in from the fields or from his day's rounds, he would take down a volume from a set of black cloth-covered books, put on his round yellow-rimmed glasses, and start to read. These were mathematics books. Once I looked inside one of them and could make nothing of the formulas and diagrams that I saw, but my father evidently could, and he would sit sometimes for several hours poring over these books. I sometimes wonder what they meant to him, whether at some time in his life he had wanted to be an architect or builder or engineer or inventor or whatever. Then I wondered where he had bought them. He had a whole set and they obviously were of some value. But he never commented on them, just pored over whatever volume he happened to be concerned with at the time. He may have worked some of the problems in them, but I can't remember.

I do remember that he consulted one volume before he started on a hobby that evidently gave him a lot of pleasure. He liked to make things out of wood. He made a desk that had a small drawer with a glass knob on it; on one side was a deep shelf for magazines.

Later, shortly after he became a deacon, my father decided to build a pulpit for Reverend Whitted. He was a great admirer of his and felt that the stand that Mount Olive Baptist Church had provided for its minister was not fitting. Accordingly, he got down his books and his toolbox. The only instrument in the box that fascinated me was the level. It had a heavy silver substance in it that seemed to wash back and forth, but never fell out. I used to take it up to see if I could shake it out, but my father always made me put it down. He didn't pay anybody much attention one way or the other, for he was totally absorbed in his project. I could tell he was happy and content; it was not the embarrassing sort of happiness I had witnessed when he saw the five-dollar bill that Aunt Jo had found. This was a deeper sort of contentment; he seemed in no hurry to get through.

Day after day, he sawed and measured and sawed. Finally it was done and he stained it. He was quite proud of his handiwork and stood back to admire it. My mother made a heavy cover to go over it until the unveiling at the church.

On the Sunday of the presentation, we went together as a family: my father, my mother, Jesse, Ruf Junior, and I. After the morning service, my father made a formal presentation to the church in a brief, halting speech, and Reverend Whitted and some of the deacons accepted the pulpit. It was quite moving.

On the way home that day, the five of us were very quiet. Something nice had happened and for the first time we seemed all together, "on one accord," no friction or tension dividing us. The prevailing mood that was so striking was one of deep quiet. It was the only time that our family ever showed any unity.

There were constant clashes and arguments between Jesse and my father, ending with my father "whipping" Jesse. My mother once said that they had thought they weren't going to have any children because they had been married nine years and there weren't any. Then, when Jesse was born, my father was so happy to have a son that he spoiled him. But when I came along, Jesse couldn't adjust to sharing his parents' attention and still wanted to act as if he were the baby and the only child. My father tried to break him of this, and that was what caused the tension between them. I remember quite well that one day Jesse and I were having an argument when I was ten or eleven and he was in his early teens. In the midst of the argument, apropos of nothing, he turned to me in startling coldness and said, "What did you have to come here for?" I was surprised by his tone; he had never spoken to me like that. Our arguments were always heated, but these words were deadly. It was pure hate that I had heard, and after that I always tried to keep away from him if I could.

The arguments with my father grew worse, and eventually Jesse started running out into the woods. Sometimes he would slip back into the house at night and my mother would give him some food, and if she indicated that things were a little quieter he would come back and stay, but often he would be gone for two or three days before he could come back, and then my father wouldn't say anything to him. That was the way these quarrels were resolved: with silence, not with words. My father wouldn't get started again, but would be silent when he saw him. The peace never lasted for long, however, and eventually their conflict would take another turn.

One day I came in from school and was speechless with horror to find my father and Jesse standing up on the back porch, fighting with their fists. And Jesse was winning. I wanted to say, "Jesse, please don't hit him. You know he's sick." But I couldn't say anything. Somehow Jesse left, and my father went off to lie down, and I never said a word to anyone about it.

This animosity lasted right up until my father's death in 1947. Jesse never asked him how he was feeling when he had come home from the hospital to die. It worried my father, and I heard him speak about it to my mother several times.

One day when Jesse was in the hall near my father's bedroom, my father called, "Jesse, come here, son."

Jesse came and stood, silent.

"I'm doing very well this morning, son," my father said. "How are you?"

"All right," Jesse said. And walked out of the room.

It was the saddest scene I think I've ever seen in my whole life.

Ruf Mebane was a long time dying and it was very messy. But he never complained and never was demanding.

Near the end, my mother would call the doctor and he would come and lance my father's stomach to relieve the swelling. Then one morning I went to his bed, just before going to school, and my father was making a strange clicking sound in his throat and his eyes were fixed. I called him, but he didn't look at me. I wasn't surprised when later in the morning they came and got me. My father was dead.

After the final rites, we never again went to his grave.

His favorite meal was fresh tomatoes, cut up, with pork grease over them.

Part
TWO

15

The summer after my father's death, my mother took Ruf Junior and me to Philadelphia to visit her sisters and brothers. There had been a whole lot of the Stephenses in southern Virginia, but gradually they left the farm and moved up the eastern seaboard. Most of them settled in Philadelphia. Some were left behind, though. Uncle Josh, my mother's oldest brother, farmed on "halves" in Virginia. Her sister Cecily taught in a country school just outside South Boston, Virginia. Cecily looked out for their brother Sidney, who lived nearby. Another sister, Shirley, divided her time between Virginia and Baltimore. But the main body of the Stephenses had migrated to Philadelphia, one following the other as they were "sent for." Nonnie had four brothers and three sisters in Philadelphia. There were so many that I had a hard time remembering them by name.

The only one of the sisters and brothers that Nonnie liked was Donna. She was the tall, thin lady who came every summer to visit us, bringing her three youngest children, Teddy, Joyce, and Billie. I liked Joyce; she was my age and she and I played so well together that she felt like my own sister.

We would stay with Aunt Donna and Uncle Harry because she was the only one in Philadelphia who, my mother said, "kept a decent house"—that is, she didn't drink and she didn't have people in and out of her house at all hours of the night. The rest of them drank like fish, the men and the women. When we got to Aunt Donna's she made some telephone calls and suddenly the house was filled with big tall men and women, all laughing and hugging and kissing us. They sent out for beer, and soon everyone was telling what used to happen down home. They admired me and slapped Ruf Junior on the back and said he looked just like Sister Nonnie. I didn't hear much because everyone was talking at once, but they told funny jokes and everyone laughed together, for they had heard the same jokes many times.

Cousins whom I had never seen and others whom I had not even heard of came to see us. There must have been twenty of them. Soon we spilled out into the street, going from house to house in the neighborhood, for all of them had settled within five or six blocks of each other. Joyce and Teddy would duck up one street, make a quick turn one way or the other, and soon would be in this or that aunt's kitchen, introducing me as their cousin from down south. Everybody made over me, they were so glad we'd come and they wanted us to have a good time. In a few minutes we were down the stairs again, dodging cars in the street. Several more turns and we were at another cousin's, who was so glad we'd come and hoped we'd enjoy ourselves, and down into the street and running on the sidewalk to somebody else's. Sometimes I didn't know what relation they were to me, but they called each other and me "cousin," even though they were older than Joyce and Teddy and I, so I knew that they were some kin. Teddy told them about the big dinner tonight at Uncle Alexander's house and be sure to come. When I got back to Aunt Donna's I was so tired and sleepy from the long bus trip and all the noise and excitement that I just went to sleep.

Uncle Alexander's house was crowded when we got there. Many people hugged and kissed my mother and us. They were so glad that we had come and hoped we would enjoy ourselves. Best of all I liked the piano player, one of Uncle

Alexander's friends, who'd come around to sing and play for the party. He knew any song you wanted him to sing. All you had to do was tell him and he'd stroke the keys a minute and start singing it. But mostly he sang church songs. One was "The Little Brown Church in the Wildwood." I was amazed. We sang that song in school in Wildwood and I was surprised that someone so far from Durham would know it. I liked his singing so much that I took a chair right beside the piano and sat there while he sang song after song. I didn't want to move to go in to dinner.

The table was the prettiest that I had ever seen. Aunt Donna said that Uncle Alexander had hired a caterer in honor of his sister from down south. The table had all kinds of colors on it and everything was arranged just like a picture. What fascinated me was the Jell-O that looked like it had been beaten into a green cloud, but was still hard. How did they do that? I wondered. All the Jell-O that I'd ever made or seen was firm and clear and smooth. The cloudy kind looked better. Some of the grown folks sat and ate, while the others waited. They were serving two tables, one after the other. They were drinking, but everybody was happy.

On another day we went to Atlantic City, to the beach. I was excited. I had read about the Atlantic Ocean, but I had never seen it. I imagined a long strip of sandy beach with tall, dark-green trees in the background and the blue, clean water that I had seen in magazines. I was worried because I didn't have a swimming suit, but I didn't say anything. Nobody else mentioned it.

Atlantic City looked like Durham to me, only more crowded, the buildings closer together. We went to a cousin's house and it was one of a long row, so that you could sit on your porch and talk to a neighbor just across the railing. It looked something like the "joining rooms" that my father's cousins had in Durham, but longer. The grown people talked, but I was impatient to get to the beach. Aunt Marilyn was drinking and cussing, but not too bad. I was afraid of her. Grown people out of control scared me.

After a while we left our cousin's house to go to the beach. I waited for the trees and sand and blue water to appear. But we got on a long sidewalk made out of boards placed so far apart that if you dropped a penny it would fall through the cracks and you couldn't get it. There were all kinds of shops on either side of the boardwalk and in the distance a long steel bridge that went out in the water and didn't connect with anything.

I asked Uncle Harry where was the beach and he said we were at it. I was stunned. "Where is the water?" I said. He pointed way out from the broadwalk. The water looked like a narrow blue pencil line far in the distance. The people close to the water were so far away that they looked like little insects.

I waited, but Uncle Harry didn't say anything about going to the water. Finally I asked him, "Uncle Harry, when are we going to the water?"

Uncle Harry said, "Our part's down further."

"Our part?" I asked. What did he mean by "our part"?

Finally he said that mostly white used the beach in this section. I listened, amazed. I had been told that things were different up north, yet here on the boardwalk at Atlantic City we couldn't go to the water anywhere we wanted to.

Aunt Marilyn had started up again. The sun and the walking had tired her and made her irritable, and she seemed more drunk than she had been at the house. She staggered along behind and beside us, occasionally lurching sideways, cussing if anyone said anything to her. I was ashamed of her, but she didn't really act bad until we got to the hot-dog stand. It was jammed with people, standing four and five deep, and there was no line. Two teenage white boys were scurrying around, filling the orders that came from every which way. We waited in line and waited and waited, but we never could seem to get their eye. Finally Aunt Marilyn started to cuss out loud.

Uncle Harry remonstrated with her: "People don't like it when you cuss them, Marilyn," he said.

132

"No, they don't like it; they don't like me, my color, not nothing," she said as loud as she could. People turned to look, but our order was quickly filled.

I told everybody in Durham about my trip to Philadelphia. I liked the way the family was close to each other and how all my cousins lived within a few blocks of each other, and I described the party and the man who sang and played "The Little Brown Church in the Wildwood." But I didn't mention our day at the beach, or Aunt Marilyn staggering on the boardwalk. That was the part I wanted to forget.

After my father's death, chaos entered our household. Time and time again, innocent peaceful activity would be punctuated by Ruf Junior's violence, and I would wonder again about my genes, my inheritance. Why did he act like that, and did I have that potential for violence embedded in my personality, waiting to spring out at any time when I least expected it? I sometimes think that perhaps Ruf Junior felt the same lack of love, of warmth, of human feeling that I felt, and it enraged him. His violence was his way of striking out at an environment that met only his physical needs, not his emotional ones.

One day I looked up from my book at the sound of Ruf Junior rushing past me. I didn't know what was the matter, for all afternoon I had heard the shouts of the boys at play in the yard. They laughed sometimes and they argued sometimes—over points, about who was at bat, who was safe, and who was out. But I had grown used to that and, absorbed in my book, heard the sounds as if they were from a far-off world.

Thus I was startled to feel air rushing past as my brother raced into the hall. Before I realized that something was wrong, I looked up to see him with my father's shotgun, which always stood in the hall. My father said it wouldn't work and I had never learned to shoot it, anyway, so since his death it had stood just where he'd left it.

Ruf Junior ran to the doorway and stood in it with the

shotgun in his hand, barrel pointed straight up. I caught up with him just in time to see the boys scatter like a flock of chickens running for their lives. Little Lenny's legs were churning up the road just as fast as they could carry him. I wanted to laugh at Lenny, he looked so funny—his big head, his skinny legs pumping away—and, too, I knew that the gun had no ammunition and that it wouldn't shoot.

I shouldn't have laughed. I didn't know it then, but the terror had started.

Ruf Junior's early adolescence became middle adolescence and the anger continued and increased, but a new and more devastating approach had been added—it was now centered on the family.

On Friday nights, Ruf Junior and Saul and Bad Ear and other boys would disappear across the road into the woods, where some said the bootleggers hid their liquor. Saul and Bad Ear were older than Ruf Junior. They had quit school and were working. Saul had quit because he had difficulty learning to read and write. Neither his mother nor his father was literate. His mother couldn't write her name. She believed in "conjure" and feared that someone was trying to hurt her. His brother had dropped out before the eighth grade, as had his sister. Wildwood disapproved of their values and left them pretty much to themselves; Wildwood felt sorry for the father, felt that he had married badly and that his children had taken after their mother's people—crazy people, Wildwood said. Bad Ear came from a respected family in the community, but his defect, a deformed ear, had made him "different," an outsider in the community, and he soon went bad.

In the woods, they gambled. If the gambling went in his favor in the early part of the evening, and it nearly always did, Ruf Junior wouldn't be back until nearly midnight. But by midnight he'd start to lose, and soon I'd hear the scraping of his metal taps on the front porch, then the front door kicked open.

"I want some money." He would be tall, dark, sweaty, slightly smiling, desperate, mean. He'd lost the money he'd made working after school and was back demanding the five dollars a week he gave his mother.

Nonnie would get up in her nightgown "What's the matter with you, Ruf Junior?" she'd say, dark, fearful, defiant. Sometimes I'd go to see and she'd be standing, slightly trembling, in her nightgown.

"I want some money."

"What do you need money for?" my mother would ask, knowing the answer already.

"The boys got my money and I want to win it back." There would be anger and tears in the voice.

"I done told you about that gambling," Nonnie would say, despair and fear in her voice.

"I want some money." Defiant, Ruf Junior would be trembling with rage.

"I don't have any."

"What about the five dollars I gave you this week to keep for me?"

"You said I could have that."

"I want it." He'd pull out the top bureau drawer and dump its contents on the bed, desperately searching among socks, handkerchiefs, bills, and papers.

"Ruf Junior, stop! I told you I don't have any money." Nonnie would be near tears.

Then he'd dump the middle bureau drawer.

"This ain't nothing but foolishness," she'd say.

He'd pay her no mind, but dump the bottom bureau drawer.

"You ought to be ashamed of yourself," she would say. Then there would be a flight through the house, a searching of crowded shelves, all nooks and crevices, every receptacle holding clothes; clustered items would be rifled and often dumped. If he found as much as a quarter or fifty cents, he'd run out, slamming the door.

I'd lie fearful in my bed, listening, wondering whether there'd be a return.

Then I'd fall into an uneasy sleep, wondering why life had to be like this, hoping that he would stay out till morning.

As things fell apart around me, my fantasizing became an essential aspect of my life. My favorite fantasy was one in which a silver swing held by thick, sparkling silver cords suddenly let down from miles and miles high and I sat in it and was whisked away into the blue, away from the strife and the bleakness and the never having enough and the lack of magic and the desperation in our lives.

16

The summer before ninth grade seemed to be the danger season. One night in the spring we were walking home from a program at the school. When a car would pass, we'd scatter to the sides of the road, and if it was going very fast we might jump the ditch. It was dark and you couldn't really see who was inside, though we could recognize the car. A car passed us and at the same time another one, so that for an instant the second one lighted the first one. In the first car I recognized Maggie. She was laughing, sitting close to Nat. I wondered what she was doing in a car going down the road; she lived near the school. I felt that something was going to happen to Maggie. Then, over the summer, people started talking: Maggie was going to have a baby; Nat was the father and he wasn't going to marry her. I never told anyone that I knew the night that she got pregnant.

Flossie dropped out and sent word that she had changed schools; she was now going to school in town. Some said that she was pregnant.

Minnie, a senior and a "nice" girl, got pregnant. She never would tell who the father was. Folks said that it was a shame, for her father was very civic-minded and a power in the church. Now she had brought shame on her family.

Some dropped out to go north to find work. They weren't interested in school and didn't want to do "days work" or factory work in Durham, so they went north. Others got married; one or two married men in the service and sent letters back home from California or Germany. Still others persevered. They or their parents were determined that they would finish high school.

Dionne, Hazel, and I had been friends since elementary school. Dionne had a heart-shaped face and straw-colored hair. She was very quiet but smiled easily. Hazel had had a hard time when she first entered school, for she had a thyroid condition that distorted her features; her eyes bulged and her mouth hung open most of the time, so much so that in the first and second grades the teachers would say, "Close your mouth, Hazel." Eventually the other children would say, "Close your mouth, Hazel." Hazel would also cry very easily.

To counter this teasing, by the time she was in the fifth grade Hazel had turned into a malicious, lying gossip. She dearly loved hints and innuendo, would spend half of the recess period gathering them up and the other half telling Dionne and me of the terrible things that others had done. The truth was that I really did not like her—I disliked her constant spying and slandering. Yet she was my "friend."

We three were united in believing that celibacy was not only God's way but also the best way to stay in high school and finish. Besides, "nice" girls weren't supposed to know anything about sex, and we were "nice" girls. Formal sex education was unknown; neither our parents nor our teachers ever mentioned the subject, and the nearest any of us ever got to the undressed human body at school was the drawings in the biology book. We had oceans of hearsay information, but no facts from anybody. And when our schoolmates started dropping out because they were pregnant, our mothers' warnings to us were very real.

There was a boy, a classmate, whom I adored from afar. He was a basketball star, and to all intents and purposes that was the only thing he had to recommend him, for even in the eleventh grade he could hardly write his name, depending instead on his prowess on the courts to get him through school, for the principal, a basketball nut, was also the basketball coach. For some reason, I became infatuated with him. It could have been his grace on the court as his lean, very black body went up for a shot. And he was the best scorer on the team, even though he was not the tallest of them. Or it could have been his insouciant manner, never really seeming to care, and being supercool in his conversation. Or it could have been the sense of danger he exuded, for he came to our country school from town, having been expelled from the city schools, and talked of dangerous and sometimes illegal activities on the weekend.

In the spring of our junior year we gave a prom for the seniors. Everybody was going except me, for I didn't know anyone to invite. Hazel, knowing the crush I had on Tom, persuaded me to invite him. I didn't want to, for I felt that he had no particular interest in me, and besides, he was a "bad" boy. But Hazel persisted, and every day during the weeks of planning and preparation she would talk to me of inviting Tom. Finally I gave in and invited him. My mother bought me a beautiful light-green gown at Belk's with a rhinestone-studded waist and long white gloves, and Miss Mattie fixed my hair in an upsweep. I was ready.

On the night of the prom I got dressed and sat and waited and waited, but Tom didn't show. I was so hurt when I realized that he wasn't coming that I went out in the backyard to cry; I didn't want anyone to hear me. To make matters worse, Hazel and some of the other girls in the class came to get me, for Mrs. Lee, the teacher, knowing how hard I had worked on the prom committee and enraged to see Tom there at the dance without me, had sent them. They meant well, I am sure, but to me it was added humiliation, for the whole school knew. Hazel never said anything to me about her part in it, never expressed regret at having insisted that I invite Tom.

It was my association with Hazel that made me wonder about people, why they are the way they are, how they perceive the world and themselves.

I reacted to Hazel in two different ways. I knew how mercilessly the children had teased her when she first came to school, so I knew that her viciousness was an attempt to get back at everyone. But, even more important, I felt guilty because I did not like her. I considered myself a strong church member, and the church taught against having "hatred in your heart" and thinking evil thoughts. So I crushed my feeling of dislike in an effort to conform to the church's teachings. What it was to take me many years to learn was that an absolute conformity to an abstract set of teachings is liable to lead you into great pain in the real world, for in the real world are many people who are not performing according to the principles that you've set down for yourself. Sometimes you have to talk and act toward them in the language and behavior that they understand.

Hazel loved to ridicule people. Often she teased me about Mount Zion, my church. She was a very good mimic, and when she mocked the singing of some of the sisters it did sound very much like them wandering around the key, occasionally hitting it. And the minister, a farmer during the week, loved to tell the latest joke he'd heard while standing around the country store. And our church was "cold," compared to the Holiness churches. That was Hazel's weak point, though, for she belonged to a Holiness church in town that had gotten a little bit sophisticated. They shouted some, but not a whole lot, and they used a book to sing out of. So she didn't want her parents to be compared to the shouting, singing type of Holiness people that we had in Wildwood.

One day Hazel got to talking and laughing about the minister and the singing and the service at Mount Zion and I started laughing and joking about the Holiness people and how they sang and danced all night. She became furious. Her face flushed threateningly and her eyes watered. I kept right on. Then she turned and ran outdoors. Dionne followed her and came back and told me she was crying. I wondered then why it was she felt that she had the right to ridicule my church but that I didn't have the right to ridicule hers. I didn't apologize, and she never brought up Mount Zion again. I had fought back in language that she understood, when Christian patience and suffering hadn't done any good.

Hazel had an interest in other people's sex lives that was incredibly intense. On the pretext of finding out the evil that some of the girls were doing, she'd forsake Dionne and me on Monday and talk to the two Marges. They "did things"—and discussed them quite freely with a chosen few. Hazel made sure that she stayed in good with them, for she wanted to hear the details on Monday. Sometimes it would take only one recess, but most often it would take two. Then on the playground a few minutes after school, she'd start telling Dionne and me, giving us the highlights, saving the best until Tuesday, and for all the rest of the week all we would hear was how terrible Marge S. and Marge W. were; they were so fast; they were just about the worst girls she'd ever seen; she didn't know how a girl could conduct herself like that; she'd be so ashamed if she did things like that.

Dionne and I were supposed to give assent to this general condemnation. If either of us showed the slightest hesitation, Hazel would pounce on us, seeking to find out if maybe we had experienced more than we were admitting to. Dionne would always deny it so vehemently that Hazel would believe her. Sometimes just for meanness I would laugh—a very knowing laugh. Then Hazel would get upset. "Have you? I bet you have and you've been fooling us. Have you? Come on, now, tell me." I'd laugh and laugh. Then after I had worried her to death, I'd say no and she'd accept that, relieved but unsure. Actually, I liked one of the Marges a whole lot. She was fun to be around and would do you a favor. And besides, she was acting while I was still fantasizing. What she did carried more danger than what I did, but I didn't feel that it was any worse.

Hazel took her measure of what was proper from the people

140

her parents worked for: Mrs. Richards said that she hated to see girls with short dresses on, it looked like they'd run out of material; Mrs. Richards had six children, so that was the proper number; Mrs. Richards said ... Hazel had carefully constructed a world and she saw her place in it. The trouble was that she wanted me to have a place there, too; but I was a real challenge to her, for with the ideas that I had, I did not fit into her ideal universe, and if I couldn't be accommodated there, where was I going to exist? Suppose the place I found for myself was in a bigger, better world than the one she had constructed? That would be intolerable.

She would have to search my mind and root out and destroy any thoughts that might lead me to a world outside the "right" one. That would be best. This led to arguments. Most of our arguments ended up with my saying, "I can!" while she maintained over and over, "You can't!" And so it went:

"I can."

"You can't."

"I can."

"You can't."

"I can."

"You can't. The Bible teaches against it. Nobody does that. That's not the way it's supposed to be."

Finally I would tire of the argument and say no more. Hazel would go away, triumphant. She had kept another soul in line for the community that day. Soon I learned a tactic to help me survive. I would venture an opinion. Hazel would say, "You can't do that." And I would say, "Of course, you're right, Hazel. How ridiculous of me." And the argument would end. Hazel would back off, baffled, for she sensed that her victory had been too easy, that even though she should have been triumphant, something let her know that I didn't agree with her at all. It saved me time and energy.

I don't know when I began to fantasize, but it was early. As a young child I used to imagine someone warm and dark enfolding me in a soft embrace. One of the happiest memories

I have of childhood is that of a tall man in a soldier suit picking me up and holding me up to the ceiling. He was a relative who had just come back from overseas during World War II. When he came everyone smiled and gathered around and hugged him and he picked me up, holding me very high.

By the time I was thirteen, the fantasies had become more specific. In one of them, which started very early and continued so long that it seemed to equal the span of my life, I was lying face up and a man was kissing me on my mouth and we'd kiss for hours and hours, sometimes for days. And to me it was the most heavenly fantasy imaginable, to be kissed over and over again. During my high-school years, when I got bored, which was often, I'd summon up the invisible stranger and he would start kissing me. He had no visible features and no distinctive form, but in the fantasy it was always a soft, dark night and he was soft and dark and gentle. I never kissed him back or initiated the encounter, but I looked forward to it.

That fantasy dominated my life until one night I was sleeping with my hands between my legs, and for some reason, I don't know why, I started to rub between by legs, producing a climax so acute that it hurt. After that, I used to imagine that I was lying behind a row of hedges near a highway, and the same dark form that used to come and kiss me would come and lie between my legs, and even though there was no movement (I didn't know what the sex act consisted of at the time), the form's presence on top of me seemed to bring with it a feeling of relief, of protection and support. Whenever I was nervous or harassed or tired I would wander off into this fantasy, sometimes for hours at a time.

Traney's aunt, Miss Lessie, worked for rich white people up north. She came down to Wildwood every summer to see her brother, so I knew her. When she died, the family shipped her things back to Wildwood in boxes.

One day Traney came running through the Rock Pile. She had something to show me. She had found it among her aunt's effects. It was a little book that could almost fit into the palm of one's hand; it had thick, glossy paper, a type of print that seemed to stand out from the page, and pictures that looked like real people or paintings that had been photographed. It was hard to tell because the pictures were rather misty-looking. They showed a naked man and a naked woman in various sexual poses. I was stunned at the existence of such a book, and fascinated. The only other book of that nature that I had seen was a Dagwood and Blondie cartoon book, full of crude drawings, that one of the boys had bought in Durham. He had let one of the "bad" girls have it and she had shown it to the rest of us. The story in Traney's book had to do with a woman whose avocation was taking ocean cruises and engaging in sexual adventures. The language was fluid, "literary," unlike the cartoon language of the Dagwood and Blondie booklet that I had seen. Traney and I had a secret.

Lockhart, my half first cousin, was beautiful. Everything about him was lustrous: eyes so black that they looked liquid, his hair, his skin. "He glittered when he walked." He was nice and would talk to me when I went with my mother to visit Aunt Claudia up on the hill. I knew that he had dropped out of school without finishing, but I didn't know what he did or what he was interested in doing He was more than a "big boy," he was grown, so I was afraid to approach him and start asking questions.

Lockhart didn't enter my consciousness very much until he came back from New York City, for he was at least ten years older than I. I almost didn't recognize him. His beautiful hair was slicked back in an incredibly gooey "process," and he was dressed in the style then known as "sharp." He wore his hair like that for a while, then changed back. But because of other things he had learned in the city, he was never the same again. Word soon circulated through Wildwood that Lockhart was screaming all of the time in his room, trying to climb the wall, and nobody knew what was wrong with him. His relatives took him to Duke Hospital to see what

could be done, but most of what they suggested was inef-
fective. During this period I didn't see Lockhart at all. Then
I heard that he had started to drink heavily.

Although Lockhart was always courteous and soft-spoken,
one Sunday he revealed a side of himself that was unknown
to me. I had just got back from Sunday school when he
stopped by the house. I thought that he had come to say hello
to "Aunt Nonnie" and give her any news that Claudia, his
mother, had sent her. But he had stopped for another reason.
He sat in the covered chair and just started talking in general.
Nonnie came in from the kitchen and said hello to him and
he was his usual polite self, but noticing that he did nothing
to encourage the conversation, she soon went away.

I was very ill at ease. Though I liked him, I had never had
a conversation with him and wondered what it was going to
be about, when he was going to get to the point of asking
what he wanted to ask or telling what he wanted to tell. The
notion of his talking to me, of coming to see me, just because
he liked me was so foreign to me as to be unthinkable. We
sat and talked awhile about this and that; then he asked me
to play for him. I thought he meant a hymn, but no, he wanted me to play something classical. Almost openmouthed with
astonishment, I got out my book of Chopin études and played
him my favorite one. He told me that it was nice, that some
people didn't like that kind of music but he did, and other
nice things.

I wanted to say something warm and friendly back to him.
I only wish I had, for I sensed in him a reaching out to me,
an attempt to let me know that somebody appreciated me
and what I was trying to do. I suspected that he had heard
some people making disparaging remarks about me and my
ambitions and the likelihood of my achieving them. But I,
for my part, had become so numb and brutalized by the coldness and the relentless harsh words that I endured every day
of my life that I couldn't think of an adequate response.

I was suspicious, thinking that he meant to go off and laugh
at me. But I was equally certain that he meant it and that

he wanted to befriend me. I wanted to be friends with him, too, but I didn't know how to. I didn't know what to say or not to say, what to do or not to do, in order to make and keep a friend. So his only attempt to reach out to me was a failure. I very much regret that in my life, for he was truly a gentle, nice person. In Wildwood there was no role for him to play; indeed, at that time in the United States, I doubt if there was any place where a person like him could go to be somebody. Still, my mind wonders, What if?

Lockhart died of alcoholism at an early age. I liked him very much and think of him often.

Lockhart, I learned later, had been a heroin addict.

17

Music was endemic in my culture. Black people all around me could sing so pretty, or play the piano, or play a bright, shiny horn—if they could afford one. Churches had many choirs: the senior choir, the junior choir, the gospel chorus, the male chorus, the women's chorus. Men who every day were tobacco workers, farmers, garbage men, on Sunday joined their voices with those of women who were tobacco workers, maids, and laundry workers, and the resulting music was incredible to hear.

The clear, full soprano tones of one voice I remember, like a crystal glass bell, poured forth, shimmering, touching every soul in the building. Its creator was a dark, stocky woman with an enormous pile of hair on her head. She sounded like a princess high on a mountain telling the people assembled below marvelous news. They could hear and look up, but they could not get to the mountaintop where she was. She was receiving a clear message somewhere far above the place where they were.

The voice invited you to close your eyes and hear the message, feeling that it was coming to you from a great height.

That soprano voice was undergirded by a deep bass voice that went down, down, never straining, always leaving the impression that it could go down even further with no effort at all. Its owner was a mechanic with fingers that had been flattened by falling tires and jacks. He had never heard an opera, and would have been surprised to learn that a voice like his could have made him wealthy. He would have been puzzled, because among his acquaintances were two or three whose voices were as good as his and one whose voice was even better.

The church utilized the community's talent, but still it was not depleted. There was a lot of talent at Wildwood School. The sponsors of the frequent Friday-afternoon talent shows had no trouble finding participants.

The students sang solo and in groups—trios and quartets were the most popular—but they sang. The very latest songs that Norfleet Whitted played on his WDNC radio show were the material. Often the talent at school sounded just as good as the original—they were undiscovered entertainment stars. You could listen to the music and forget the worn clothing and the country haircuts. The four boys standing there in a shallow half-circle were the "Inkspots," singing before a rich audience where all the women had on slinky evening gowns and the men smoked big cigars and waved hundred-dollar bills. "Cab Calloway" appeared, weaving and doubling almost to the floor, singing, "Hi-dee-hi-dee-hi, hi-dee-hi-dee-ho." Displaying tremendous cool, "Billy Eckstine" caressed the mike, looked into the distance, and sang of love. Most of the boys imitating those stars had never been more than a hundred miles from home in their lives. Rural girls combed their hair up in back and made a big roll at the front. They put on an older sister's or an aunt's "cocktail" dress, something black and shiny and ruffled, and dark-red lipstick, and turned into Ruth Brown, Dinah Washington, Ella Fitzgerald.

Those of us who were not so talented sang, anyway. There were nonsense songs, and songs that recounted what happened at a Saturday-night fish fry. We sang of love found, love lost, bad whiskey and its deleterious effects on life and love. And of sex, though many of us didn't know what the lyrics meant. We sang "For You My Love I'd Do Most Anything," "Bless You," "Harbor Lights," "One Scotch, One Bourbon, One Beer," "Bad, Bad Whiskey," "Come On If You're Coming," and "Jelly, Jelly."

I had little talent—the tragedy of my life. With musical talent all around me, most of it being prodigally wasted (what did the possessors care—there was more where that came from, and besides, everybody had some, didn't they?), I, who desperately yearned for it, had so little.

If I had had a great voice, I would have worked hard and studied and become a singer like Marian Anderson. I admired Marian Anderson. She was jet-black—blue-black, people said—and yet she was honored. Her picture was in the paper and she made lots of money and went to the White House.

Or if I couldn't find the money to go overseas and get discovered and be brought back in honor to the United States like Marian Anderson, I would sing with a band like Ella Fitzgerald, and people would try to imitate my singing "A-Tisket, A-Tasket," and they would dance to my music and applaud and the whole world would know how great I was. But I couldn't sing as well as some of the other students in the school. I could have sung better than I did, but my rival Hazel had a better voice and I became self-conscious about mine, though I had a pleasant enough soprano.

I could play the piano, but I played by notes. So many of the black people I knew played by ear. You heard a song on the radio or at church. Then you sat down at the piano and played the chords of the song. You worked at that until you learned how to change them. You had never had a lesson in harmony, but a few days after you first started picking out the tunes by ear you could chord almost any song. Then you added a melody, and you could play the song. And people gathered around and said how good you were. After you had picked out songs by ear for six months or a year, you could instantly play any song you heard. It was a gift. Thousands of blacks have it. Some have developed it; others haven't.

I could not play by ear. I had to have notes. And some snickered behind my back and said, "Inez doesn't have notes. She can hear anything and play it." Or they told me to my face, "Charlie doesn't have to practice. He never had a lesson in his life. All you do is sit and practice." And I cringed inside because I knew they were right. But I persisted, and my knowledge of musical literature increased and I could say names like Bach and Beethoven and Mozart and pronounce them correctly. After a while, though, I didn't mention them because the pronunciation was funny and the children laughed—why play music by those strange foreigners when Inez and Charlie can play the songs on the jukebox? It was a waste of time to them. In their world, nobody black ever got rich or famous playing Bach, Beethoven, or Brahms.

But Mrs. Shearin liked one of the pieces that I had worked up, and she asked me to be in her annual recital at Saint Joseph's Methodist Church. I had never been to a recital or a concert. So, although I was pleased, I was very scared. It was the first time I had played in public from memory. When I noted my place on the program I was satisfied to see that although I wasn't with the real heavyweights in the studio, the marvelously talented, I was listed just before them. My piece was applauded amd members of the audience congratulated me. My hard work at the piano hadn't been for nothing. It had paid off.

The event had such an impact on me that I wrote it up in the form of a story and sent it to *Seventeen* magazine. I wrote about practicing all day Saturday for the Sunday-night recital; about my pink voile dress with the matching petticoat under it; the fear I felt on my way to town; the fact that I listened to most of the other performers with only a part of my mind, for I was really concentrating on trying to make sure that I knew my piece. *Seventeen* magazine said nice things about my story, but they returned it. After that I never tried anymore.

For my peers didn't write stories and send them off to *Seventeen.*

18

Historically, my lifetime is important because I was part of the last generation born into a world of total legal segregation in the Southern United States. When the Supreme Court outlawed segregation in the public schools in 1954, I was twenty-one. When Congress passed the Civil Rights Act of 1964, permitting blacks free access to public places, I was thirty-one. The world I was born into had been segregated for a long time—so long, in fact, that I never met anyone who had lived during the time when restrictive laws were not in existence, although some people spoke of parents and others who had lived during the "free" time. As far as anyone knew, the laws as they then existed would stand forever. They were meant to—and did—create a world that fixed black people at the bottom of society in all aspects of human life. It was a world without options.

Most Americans have never had to live with terror. I had had to live with it all my life—the psychological terror of segregation, in which there was a special set of laws governing your movements. You violated them at your peril, for you knew that if you broke one of them, knowingly or not, physical terror was just around the corner, in the form of policemen and jails, and in some cases and places white vigilante mobs formed for the exclusive purpose of keeping blacks in line.

It was Saturday morning, like any Saturday morning in dozens of Southern towns.

The town had a washed look. The street sweepers had been busy since six o'clock. Now, at eight, they were still slowly moving down the streets, white trucks with clouds of water coming from underneath the swelled tubular sides. Unwary motorists sometimes got a windowful of water as a truck passed by. As it moved on, it left in its wake a clear stream running in the gutters or splashed on the wheels of parked cars.

Homeowners, bent over industriously in the morning sun, were out pushing lawn mowers. The sun was bright, but it wasn't too hot. It was morning and it was May. Most of the mowers were glad that it was finally getting warm enough to go outside.

Traffic was brisk. Country people were coming into town early with their produce; clerks and service workers were getting to the job before the stores opened at ten o'clock. Though the big stores would not be open for another hour or so, the grocery stores, banks, open-air markets, dinettes, were already open and filling with staff and customers.

Everybody was moving toward the heart of Durham's downtown, which waited to receive them rather complacently, little knowing that in a decade the shopping centers far from the center of downtown Durham would create a ghost town in the midst of the busiest blocks on Main Street.

Some moved by car, and some moved by bus. The more affluent used cars, leaving the buses mainly to the poor, black and white, though there were some businesspeople who avoided the trouble of trying to find a parking place downtown by riding the bus.

I didn't mind taking the bus on Saturday. It wasn't so crowded. At night or on Saturday or Sunday was the best time. If there were plenty of seats, the blacks didn't have to worry about being asked to move so that a white person could sit down. And the knot of hatred and fear didn't come into my stomach.

I knew the stop that was the safety point, both going and coming. Leaving town, it was the Little Five Points, about five or six blocks north of the main downtown section. That was the last stop at which four or five people might get on. After that stop, the driver could sometimes pass two or three stops without taking on or letting off a passenger. So the number of seats on the bus usually remained constant on the trip from town to Braggtown. The nearer the bus got to the end of the line, the more I relaxed. For if a white passenger got on near the end of the line, often to catch the return trip back and avoid having to stand in the sun at the bus stop until the bus turned around, he or she would usually stand if there were not seats in the white section, and the driver would say nothing, knowing that the end of the line was near and that the standee would get a seat in a few minutes.

On the trip to town, the Mangum Street A&P was the last point at which the driver picked up more passengers than he let off. These people, though they were just a few blocks from the downtown section, preferred to ride the bus downtown. Those getting on at the A&P were usually on their way to work at the Duke University Hospital—past the downtown section, through a residential neighborhood, and then past the university, before they got to Duke Hospital.

So whether the driver discharged more passengers than he took on near the A&P on Mangum was of great importance. For if he took on more passengers than got off, it meant that some of the newcomers would have to stand. And if they were white, the driver was going to have to ask a black passenger to move so that a white passenger could sit down. Most of the drivers had a rule of thumb, though. By custom the seats behind the exit door had become "colored" seats, and no matter how many whites stood up, anyone sitting behind the exit door knew that he or she wouldn't have to move.

The disputed seat, though, was the one directly opposite the exit door. It was "no-man's-land." White people sat there, and black people sat there. It all depended on whose section was fuller. If the back section was full, the next black passenger who got on sat in the no-man's-land seat; but if the white section filled up, a white person would take the seat. Another thing about the white people: they could sit anywhere they chose, even in the "colored" section. Only the black passengers had to obey segregation laws.

On this Saturday morning Esther and I set out for town for our music lesson. We were going on our weekly big adventure, all the way across town, through the white downtown, then across the railroad tracks, then through the "colored" downtown, a section of run-down dingy shops, through some fading high-class black neighborhoods, past North Carolina College, to Mrs. Shearin's house.

We walked the two miles from Wildwood to the bus line. Though it was a warm day, in the early morning there was dew on the grass and the air still had the night's softness. So we walked along and talked and looked back constantly, hoping someone we knew would stop and pick us up.

I looked back furtively, for in one of the few instances that I remembered my father criticizing me severely, it was for looking back. One day when I was walking from town he had passed in his old truck. I had been looking back and had seen him. "Don't look back," he had said. "People will think that you want them to pick you up." Though he said "people," I knew he meant men—not the men he knew, who lived in the black community, but the black men who were not part of the community, and all of the white men. To be picked up meant that something bad would happen to me. Still, two miles is a long walk and I occasionally joined Esther in looking back to see if anyone we knew was coming.

Esther and I got to the bus and sat on one of the long seats at the back that faced each other. There were three such long seats—one on each side of the bus and a third long seat at the very back that faced the front. I liked to sit on a long seat facing the side because then I didn't have to look at the expressions on the faces of the whites when they put their tokens in and looked at the blacks sitting in the back of the bus. Often I studied my music, looking down and practicing the fingering. I looked up at each stop to see who was getting on and to check on the seating pattern. The seating pattern didn't really bother me that day until the bus started to get unusually full for a Saturday morning. I wondered what was happening, where all these people were coming from. They got on and got on until the white section was almost full and the black section was full.

There was a black man in a blue windbreaker and a gray porkpie hat sitting in no-man's-land, and my stomach tightened. I wondered what would happen. I had never been on a bus on which a black person was asked to give a seat to a white person when there was no other seat empty. Usually, though, I had seen a black person automatically get up and move to an empty seat farther back. But this morning the only empty seat was beside a black person sitting in no-man's-land.

The bus stopped at Little Five Points and one black got off. A young white man was getting on. I tensed. What would happen now? Would the driver ask the black man to get up and move to the empty seat farther back? The white man had a businessman's air about him: suit, shirt, tie, polished brown shoes. He saw the empty seat in the "colored" section and after just a little hesitation went to it, put his briefcase down, and sat with his feet crossed. I relaxed a little when the bus pulled off without the driver saying anything. Evidently he hadn't seen what had happened, or since he was just a few stops from Main Street, he figured the mass exodus there would solve all the problems. Still, I was afraid of a scene.

The next stop was an open-air fruit stand just after Little Five Points, and here another white man got on. Where would he sit? The only available seat was beside the black man. Would he stand the few stops to Main Street or would the driver make the black man move? The whole colored section tensed, but nobody said anything. I looked at Esther, who looked apprehensive. I looked at the other men and women, who studiously avoided my eyes and everybody else's as well, as they maintained a steady gaze at a far-distant land.

Just one woman caught my eye; I had noticed her before, and I had been ashamed of her. She was a stringy little black woman. She could have been forty; she could have been fifty. She looked as if she were a hard drinker. Flat black face with tight features. She was dressed with great insouciance in a tight boy's sweater with horizontal lines running across her flat chest. It pulled down over a nondescript skirt. Laced-up shoes, socks, and a head rag completed her outfit. She looked tense.

The white man who had just gotten on the bus walked to the seat in no-man's-land and stood there. He wouldn't sit down, just stood there. Two adult males, living in the most highly industrialized, most technologically advanced nation in the world, a nation that had devastated two other industrial giants in World War II and had flirted with taking on China in Korea. Both these men, either of whom could have fought for the United States in Germany or Korea, faced each other in mutual rage and hostility. The white one wanted to sit down, but he was going to exert his authority and force the black one to get up first. I watched the driver in the rearview mirror. He was about the same age as the antagonists. The driver wasn't looking for trouble, either.

"Say there, buddy, how about moving back," the driver said, meanwhile driving his bus just as fast as he could. The whole bus froze—whites at the front, blacks at the rear. They didn't want to believe what was happening was really happening.

The seated black man said nothing. The standing white man said nothing.

"Say, buddy, did you hear me? What about moving on back." The driver was scared to death. I could tell that.

"These is the niggers' seats!" the little lady in the strange outfit started screaming. I jumped. I had to shift my attention from the driver to the frieze of the black man seated and white man standing to the articulate little woman who had joined in the fray.

"The government gave us these seats! These is the niggers' seats." I was startled at her statement and her tone. "The president said that these are the niggers' seats!" I expected her to start fighting at any moment.

Evidently the bus driver did, too, because he was driving

faster and faster. I believe that be forgot he was driving a bus and wanted desperately to pull to the side of the street and get out and run.

"I'm going to take you down to the station, buddy," the driver said.

The white man with the briefcase and the polished brown shoes who had taken a seat in the "colored" section looked as though he might die of embarrassment at any moment.

As scared and upset as I was, I didn't miss a thing.

By that time we had come to the stop before Main Street, and the black passenger rose to get off.

"You're not getting off, buddy. I'm going to take you downtown." The driver kept driving as he talked and seemed to be trying to get downtown as fast as he could.

"These are the niggers' seats! The government plainly said these are the niggers' seats!" screamed the little woman in rage.

I was embarrassed at the use of the word "nigger" but I was proud of the lady. I was also proud of the man who wouldn't get up.

The bus driver was afraid, trying to hold on to his job but plainly not willing to get into a row with the blacks.

The bus seemed to be going a hundred miles an hour and everybody was anxious to get off, though only the lady and the driver were saying anything.

The black man stood at the exit door; the driver drove right past the A&P stop. I was terrified. I was sure that the bus was going to the police station to put the black man in jail. The little woman had her hands on her hips and she never stopped yelling. The bus driver kept driving as fast as he could.

Then, somewhere in the back of his mind, he decided to forget the whole thing. The next stop was Main Street, and when he got there, in what seemed to be a flash of lightning, he flung both doors open wide. He and his black antagonist looked at each other in the rearview mirror; in a second the windbreaker and porkpie hat were gone. The little woman was standing, preaching to the whole bus about the government's gift of these seats to the blacks; the man with the brown shoes practically fell out of the door in his hurry; and Esther and I followed the hurrying footsteps.

We walked about three doors down the block, then caught a bus to the black neighborhood. Here we sat on one of the two long seats facing each other, directly behind the driver. It was the custom. Since this bus had a route from a black neighborhood to the downtown section and back, passing through no white residential areas, blacks could sit where they chose. One minute we had been on a bus in which violence was threatened over a seat near the exit door; the next minute we were sitting in the very front behind the driver.

The people who devised this system thought that it was going to last forever

19

It was summer 1949, and I needed a job. Everybody tried to "get on" at the tobacco factory during "green season," when lots of extra workers were hired to "work up" new tobacco—that is, process it for cigarettes. Some people made their chief money of the year during the ten-to-twelve-week green season. The factory paid more money than days work, so lots of women gladly left their housekeeping jobs and went to the factories. In Durham there were two major factories and several smaller ones. The major factories worked up tobacco, but they also made cigarettes and had a shipping department and research laboratories. The smaller factories mainly worked up tobacco for the larger ones, in Durham and in other cities. Of the two major factories in Durham, Liggett and Myers did relatively little hiring in green season; it had a stable year-round force and gave preference to its former workers during the season. My mother worked there. The

American Tobacco Company, the other factory, hired a great many temporary workers.

I was told that my best bet was the American. I wasn't eighteen, but I was tall and stocky and could pass for older, and besides, they never asked to see your birth certificate; so, a few months short of my sixteenth birthday, I went to get work at the American, makers of Lucky Strike cigarettes and other brands. From the start, I knew that I wouldn't get a job on the "cigarette side." That was easy work, and I was told that mostly whites worked over there. I would get a chance on the belt on the "tobacco side." Several women in the neighborhood who had worked at the American during the green season instructed me about how to get on. I was told to get there early and stand on the sidewalk in front of the employment office and just as close as possible to it, so that when they came out to select workers I would be easily seen. Also I was told to say, if they asked me, that I had worked there before. Nobody ever checked the records. So, on the morning that hiring began for green season, I went to Durham.

I accompanied neighbors who had received postcards informing them they could come to work. They left me outside while they went in. I was dismayed, for the whole street in front of the employment office was filled with black women. They crowded around the brick porch leading to the employment office; they were on the sidewalk; they overflowed the street and covered the sidewalk behind. They were directly in front of the office, spreading out fanwise in both directions from it. Nobody was allowed on the porch except those who already had cards.

A pudgy white man with a cigar in his mouth came and stood on the porch and said, "All those who have cards, come forward." Those who had cards held them up over their heads and started pushing through the crowd. Sometimes they had to remonstrate with some stubborn woman who refused to give way: "Let me pass, please! Move out of my way!" Slowly the one blocking her path would grudgingly give ground. Others quickly surged forward, trying to fill the space that was left, taking advantage of the confusion to try to push even nearer the office. When the favored ones got in, there began the long wait for the man to come back and start selecting more "hands" from the crowd of women left standing there. The crowd continued to grow bigger by the minute as new arrivals came.

You could tell the veterans from the rookies by the way they were dressed. The knowledgeable ones had their heads covered by kerchiefs, so that if they were hired, tobacco dust wouldn't get in their hair; they had on clean dresses that by now were faded and shapeless, so that if they were hired they wouldn't get tobacco dust and grime on their best clothes. Those who were trying for the first time had their hair freshly done and wore attractive dresses; they wanted to make a good impression. But the dresses couldn't be seen at the distance that many were standing from the employment office, and they were soon crumpled in the crush.

Some women looked as if they had large families; they looked tired and anxious, but determined. Some looked single; they had on lipstick and eyebrow pencil, and some even wore black patent-leather pumps with stockings.

The morning passed and the sun got hotter; there was no shade on the sidewalks or in the street. The street stayed full, except when trucks edged their way in and the crowd gave way slowly.

After a while, the pudgy white man with the big cigar came to the door and stood and looked. Instantly the whole mass surged forward. The shorter ones tried to stand on tiptoe to be seen over the heads of their taller sisters. Hands shot up in the air, trying to make him notice them. Those at the front who'd gotten shoved against the brick porch shouted, "Stop pushing, stop pushing, ya'll! You're hurting me!"

Finally the pudgy man spoke, standing on the porch with his cigar in his mouth. "Until ya'll stop pushing and shoving I'm not gonna hire none of ya'll." Then he stood for a moment to see what effect his words were having on the crowd. Sensing that they were having no discernible effect, the man went back inside, and the surge forward stopped for the time being.

The women stood and stood; the sun grew hotter. Some grew tired of waiting: "I left my baby with a neighbor. I told her that if I didn't get on I'd be back before twelve. I gotta go." Others left, saying that they were "tired of this mess." One woman said, "All ya'll might as well go home. He's got his number for today. Come back tomorrow when they'll know how many more they'll need." At that, even more women faded away. The mass shrunk, but it was still a mass.

Finally, shortly before noon, the pudgy man came quietly to the porch and pointed quickly to two women standing close by. Before the crowd knew people were getting on, the two women were on the porch and in the hall, following him. The crowd surged forward but the man was gone. "What time is it?" someone said. "Nigh noon" was the answer and everyone seemed to agree that there would be no more hiring until one or two o'clock, after lunch.

Some sat right down on the sidewalk up against the building and took out their sandwiches. Others drifted away from the crowd and down to a nearby luncheonette for cold drinks and sandwiches. I had a tomato sandwich that had become soggy in the press and the heat. I went with some other women far down the street to sit on the grass and eat my sandwich. They talked in front of me as if I were grown, so I knew that I would have no trouble if I got hired. What they said was so interesting that the crowd was re-forming in front of the employment office in the hot, boiling sun before I knew it.

Word came over the grapevine that they needed some more helpers and would hire some more today. This gave everybody courage, so the crowd grew calm. Then the pudgy man came again. He made an announcement: "Any shoving, any pushing, and there'll be no more hiring today." The women grew quiet. Those who had been impatient hadn't come back from lunch, leaving those who were determined to get on.

The man selected two more women; the crowd gave a little surge forward, but nothing like the shoving and pushing of the morning. In another hour he came back for one more, and soon the word came over the grapevine that we might as well go home. The crowd started fading away, but not the diehards. They didn't believe the grapevine and were determined to stay to see what was going to happen. I had no choice; I was staying until the people I rode with got off from work. It was now three o'clock and we all had been standing in the sun since eight o'clock in the morning. When the neighbors I was waiting for came, they said, "Don't worry. You'll get on tomorrow." Besides, they would go in earlier now that they were on.

I lay in bed that night, too tired to do anything else, and thought about the day. Hundreds of women had stood in the hot sun for seven or eight hours under really bad conditions. There was no bathroom, no drinking fountain, no place to sit down. Those who had to leave lost their place in line and, thus, their chance for a job. Why was this? Because they needed work and the factory didn't need them. The factory had more hands available than it could use. That is why they could treat the surplus as they chose, and there was nothing that the women could do about it.

The next day I was there early and standing in place by the steps before the employment office opened. I recognized some of the faces from the day before, and there were some that looked new to me. The crowd stretched out as far as it had the previous day. The sun was already hot when the pudgy man came to the platform with his cigar in his mouth. "Anyone here with a card?" he called. A few women who hadn't come in yesterday came forward. He went back inside.

I was close enough to see into the hall inside and the glass-faced side of the employment office. It was shut off from the hall by glass because it was air-conditioned. There was a man, so slim and shapely that he looked like a girl, who came to the door and watched as the pudgy man came back and stood over the crowd. He watched the crowd surge forward, and he stepped back a little as if all the energy would wash over him. It seemed to give him great satisfaction to see the sea of black women struggling forward, trying to get a job in his factory; he'd stand and watch for a while, then turn and go into the air-conditioned office. At first the women thought that he was going to do some of the hiring and they pressed close to him and looked up. But once they'd determined that he had nothing to do with the hiring, he ceased to exist for them and they paid him no more attention.

More and more women were hired; the pudgy man would point here and there, then take them off. In an hour or so, he'd come back and hire one or two more. Lunch came and the crowd scattered. I'd brought a meat sandwich, hoping that it wouldn't get crumpled and soggy like my tomato sandwich the day before. I knew enough not to leave my good place near the porch, so I ate standing in the hot sun, along with the rest of the women who had good places. I had been listening to the crowd for two days, so now I knew the words and phrases that would make me sound like a veteran, and I employed them. Evidently nothing was wrong with what I said, for no one looked at me "funny."

Around two o'clock the pudgy man came back and his eye fell on me and the woman standing beside me. He motioned us in. I was now a factory hand.

The air-conditioning in the office chilled me after the heat of the street as I gave the necessary information. I made up a birthday and nobody questioned it. Then I was taken to a "line" on the first floor.

It was a cavernous room, long and tall. The man who led me there called to the boss, who came over to tell me what to do, but the machinery was so loud that I couldn't hear him and I was so startled by my new surroundings that I didn't really concentrate on what he said. I was afraid to take a deep breath, for the room was so cloudy with tobacco dust that brown particles hung in the air. I held my breath as long as I could and then took a deep breath. I started to cough and my eyes watered. I saw lots of women and some men, each doing a task seemingly unrelated to the others', but I knew that there must be a plan.

My job had something to do with a conveyor belt. It was shaped like a child's sliding board, only it had a deep trough and it moved. Shredded tobacco was on this belt—I think that it came from upstairs—and my job was to sit by the belt and pick out the pieces whose stems were too large. I tried to determine what kind of stem was too large, for the belt was constantly moving, and obviously I couldn't pick out every single stem on the belt. I looked at the others, but I couldn't see what method they were using. I was in misery, for this was my first "public" job and I didn't want to do badly on it. I did the best that I could, but soon the boss came and told me he was going to put me on the belt upstairs. I was glad, for my back hurt from bending over, trying to pick out stems. Maybe I could do better upstairs.

The air was full of tobacco dust there, too, but not as much as it had been downstairs; also, it was quieter. This belt moved horizontally, from right to left; women stood parallel to it, two women facing each other on the same side of the belt, with a barrel of tied tobacco leaves in front of them. They worked in pairs, taking the tobacco from the barrel, the hogshead, and putting it on the belt. The important thing, as my partner explained to me, was to make sure that the tied ends faced me, for the belt was on its way to the cutter and the machine would cut off the hard tied end—which would not go into the making of cigarettes—while the leaves went another way.

The job seemed easy enough as I picked up bundle after bundle of tobacco and put it on the belt, careful to turn the knot end toward me so that it would be placed right to go under the cutting machine. Gradually, as we worked up our tobacco, I had to bend more, for as we emptied the hogshead we had to stoop over to pick up the tobacco, then straighten up and put it on the belt just right. Then I discovered the hard part of the job: the belt kept moving at the same speed all the time and if the leaves were not placed on the belt at the same tempo there would be a big gap where your bundle should have been. So that meant that when you got down lower, you had to bend down, get the tobacco, straighten up fast, make sure it was placed knot end toward you, place it on the belt, and bend down again. Soon you were bending down, up; down, up; down, up. All along the line, heads were bobbing—down, up; down, up—until you finished the barrel. Then you could rest until the men brought you another one.

To make sure that you kept the belt filled, there was a line boss, a little blond man who looked scared most of the time. He'd walk up and down behind you, saying, "Put the tobacco on the belt, girls. Put the tobacco on the belt. Too many empty spaces, girls. Too many empty spaces." You'd be working away, when suddenly behind you you'd hear this voice: "Put the tobacco on the belt, girls. Put the tobacco on the belt. No empty spaces, girls. No empty spaces." I noticed that no one paid him any mind. He could be standing right by the belt talking, and it was as if he were invisible. The line kept moving, and the women kept bending and putting tobacco on the belt.

Over him was the floor boss. He had charge of all the operations on the floor. He was the line boss's boss, and the line boss was clearly afraid of him. Over the floor boss was the big boss, who seldom came on the floor unless there was real trouble. Most of the women had never seen him, but some had and said that he was mean as the devil.

I bent and straightened and bent and straightened and thought that my back would break. Once in the afternoon I got a ten-minute break in the "house" (toilet). I went there and collapsed into a chair.

That evening on the way home I tried to talk cheerfully to my neighbors about the new job. They were quite pleased that I had gotten on. That was the one thing that kept me from quitting. I didn't want to let them down by telling them that I found the work killing. So I made up my mind to stay, no matter what, for I knew it was a short season.

The most interesting thing about my job was the people

on it. They were grown people that I was seeing for the first time as an equal, not as a child. Some of them commented that I sure looked young, but I smiled and didn't say much and they soon turned the talk to something else. I listened, fascinated.

One woman who worked on a different belt was a schoolteacher during the regular year, and now she had quietly slipped in to take a green-season job. Most of the women commented on her sardonically, not because she was a schoolteacher working in a tobacco factory but because she made sure that they knew that she was a teacher and was to be treated as such. She wore high-heeled shoes to work and smart cotton dresses and kept her hair in an upsweep, not tied in a kerchief like most of the women. At lunchtime she went out to eat. She earned the wrath of the whole floor when she attempted to discipline one of the "girls" for not doing her work properly, threatening to tell the boss and get her fired. At noon the girl involved told everybody what had happened and by the end of the day it had somehow been agreed that from now on we would just leave Schoolteacher alone. I used to look at her. She had been to college. I wanted to go to college, but I didn't want to be like her.

Sometimes in the late afternoon near quitting time, the black men would come by the belt and tease some of the women. They'd say things about sex, and soon the talk would get explicit. I was shocked the first day, but after that I listened. Here were men and women talking like the worst sinners in the world, and God didn't come down out of the sky and cut them down; in fact, He didn't seem to be punishing them at all. I wondered about God and this question quite a bit, particularly when it came to Viola.

Viola was a "bad" woman. I had known some bad girls in school, but none of their activities even began to compare with Viola's. And for the first time I'd met a woman whose sense of her own worth was directly related to how many men wanted her in bed. There had been quite a number. She regarded herself as a queen, and these men were courtiers;

she had the power to reward whichever one was in favor, which she did quite often.

I listened, fascinated, as she regaled us every morning with the considerable doings of the night before. The other women laughed. Occasionally an older woman would remonstrate with her: "You ought not to talk that way in front of that child" (meaning me); but she would be contradicted: "She's old enough to know what life is all about." I expected God to walk on the floor in person and strike Viola dead, but He didn't; I expected the other women to treat Viola with scorn and derision, but although some of the older church-going ladies disapproved, they didn't. Most of them had the attitude that it was her life and her business, and besides, they had problems of their own.

Across the aisle from me was Flora, a very black woman who looked like a "hard knot." She was short and skinny, and she looked as though she drank a lot. She did her work, but not with any enthusiasm. She didn't look up, not even when the floor boss came. The attitude she projected was, "Another day, another dollar, and I've got to work at something."

One day, in the morning, word came over the grapevine that the big boss was coming. We knew that it was true, for the floor boss, a big man whose stomach hung over his belt, started running all over the floor, giving orders right and left. The line boss had lost all semblance of control and was running around like a chicken with its head cut off. Everybody was urging us "girls" to do more and more, to get the tobacco on the belt and not leave any empty spaces. Leaves to the "house" were canceled. It was going to be a trying time for everybody, the workers as well as the bosses.

Every head on my line bobbed up and down, practically in unison. The men who supplied the barrels of tobacco had them lined up two deep behind us, so that when we were out of a barrel they could quickly shove another one in place. There would be no standing and talking while the men brought one down to us.

Soon, word drifted around the room. The big boss was on the floor. I wanted to see him, but I was afraid to stop my work and try to spot him, so I kept working, meanwhile watching the women opposite me so that I could tell by the expressions on their faces if they saw him. That was when I noticed Flora. She was calmly putting tobacco on the belt, no slower and no faster than she had put it on all day. She didn't hurry one bit. I wondered what would happen if the boss came and she acted like that. She saw me looking at her, and she smiled a sort of hard, thin smile. I smiled back, for I saw in Flora's face that if the boss tried messing with her today, he was going to get it. And I wanted to be able to see it.

The whole factory hummed, and we bent and straightened, bent and straightened. Suddenly I looked up to see the big boss, and I nearly laughed out loud. He was about five feet six, with a ruddy complexion that looked as if he were a hard drinker. He had on a straw hat that came down too low on his forehead. But most startling to me was that he had on pants that were obviously too big for him, for they were held almost halfway up his chest by a pair of suspenders. With the hat down too low and the pants up too high, there was very little of the big boss to be seen.

He appeared on the other line, facing me but coming up behind Flora. He stood looking balefully around at the black women, all of whom were working their heads off. All except Flora. Though she must have sensed that he was right behind her, she didn't speed up one bit. She took the bunch of tobacco leaves from the pack and deliberately slapped them down on the belt; then took another bunch and slapped it down. Slap! Slap!

The big boss waited for his presence to be felt, but when it soon became clear to him and to the whole line and the line boss and the floor boss that Flora was going to ignore him the way she ignored the others, the big boss spoke. He had to say something to keep from losing face, so he stood near her side and said, "It looks like you're half-dead this morning."

Flora paused a minute with a bunch of tobacco in her hands and looked dead at him. They looked at each other for a minute; then Flora turned her head and slapped the bunch down on the belt.

I nearly died. I was sure he was going to fire her on the spot, but he didn't. He moved on to another belt. I think that he had recognized a kindred spirit, another mean one like himself, and if he had gotten started he was going to get a good cussing out. That was what her look had told him and he got the message and didn't want to risk a scene right there in front of his subordinates.

Flora had won and I was proud of her. In her way she had protested and was prepared to back it up.

I didn't read at night anymore; I was too tired. I went home, got my supper, and went to bed. Though people told me I would get used to it, I never did. I stayed until there was a "laying off." I was glad when they got to me. Work at the American was hard and mind-numbing, and the factory wasn't doing anything to make it more human.

Aunt Jo was dying. She lay huddled in a small, darkened room with sunlight filtering around the edges of the shade. I sat in a chair in the corner.

For a while we said nothing. Finally she said, "Aren't you going to say anything about the money?" (Sometime before, she had sent for my mother and given her six hundred dollars to be used for my education.)

"Yes'm, Aunt Jo," I said. "Mama told me about it, but she said that you said not to mention it. Thank you, Aunt Jo."

"It's all right," she said. "I gave it to you for your education."

I sat there, wanting to go to the bed and gather her in my arms and tell her, "I'm so sorry that you're sick, you mean so much to me, and thank you so much for caring about me and what is going to happen to me." But I couldn't move from the chair. I was so numbed and frightened by the things that had been said to me and about me that I sat there silent, knowing that after she was gone I'd be alone. I've always regretted that scene and wished I could have been warmer and could have expressed my true feelings.

20

The constrictions, the restraints, the hidden threats that we lived under, that were the conditions of our lives, inevitably produced mutations in the natural human flowering. To me we were like plants that were meant to grow upright but became bent and twisted, stunted, sometimes stretching out and running along the ground, because the conditions of our environment forbade our developing upward naturally. I have observed many such people. Some were grown when I was a child in Wildwood; some I grew up with and observed as they changed and adapted; others I met as an adult in Durham and other Southern settings. But one thing they and I had in common: we were shaped by the same forces.

Here are some of the people of that world without options, people that I knew as a child, in my teens, and later as an adult.

Once, for some reason that I can't remember, I was visiting in the house that Mr. Wells used to live in on the New Road before he and his wife separated. There on the wall was a beautiful pencil or charcoal drawing. It was a bird so full of life and energy that it seemed to burst right off the wall. I just stared at it. And I wanted it. I started to ask to buy it, but didn't, for fear that it would be considered bad manners.

Even more amazing was the name of the artist. I couldn't believe it. It was Charles Black, Wildwood's leading drunk.

Everybody said that he came from educated people and it was true that his two sisters taught school, one in Durham, the other in Durham County. But whenever we in Wildwood saw him, he was falling-down drunk. Yet he had this marvelous talent, which I never ever would have connected with him. It taught me something about our lives and the potential that is there, unrecognized and unrealized.

I used sometimes to look up and see Sugar cruising by in his shiny big car. He drove so slowly that I wondered why the engine didn't stop. Perhaps that was what he was trying to prove—that he could drive at almost "nothing" miles per hour and his car was so fine and his engine so well tuned that it wouldn't stop. There was also another reason—to show the girls what a fine car they could ride in if they went out with him. Cruising by ever so casually, elbow out the window, hat tilted down stylishly over one eye, gap-toothed smile fixed, he surveyed the scene, King of the Hill.

We girls had a game of naming the make and year of every car that passed along the road. I never thought the day would come when there would be so many styles and years I couldn't name them. We would also claim for ourselves the best-looking cars and assign the junkheaps to the others. It didn't really matter. All of the cars would be about the same—dilapidated. Sugar's car, however, was always a standout. All of us would eagerly claim it whenever we saw it.

I first remember seeing Sugar in connection with a car. There had been an accident on Easter Sunday. It was a windy spring day and we girls, coming down the road from the store, stopped to look. It wasn't much—a dented fender or something—but Sugar and the other driver were waiting for someone to investigate. Since we lived way out in the country, they would have a long wait. Accidents seldom happened in Wildwood—there weren't that many cars, just trucks boiling up dust to and from the rock quarry. Naturally, an accident was welcomed; it would provide excitement and give the com-

169

munity something to talk about for a week. So we girls, in our new bras, patent-leather slippers, stockings, and new Easter dresses, came to look.

There stood Sugar with a dent in his car, which was sleek all over, like a shiny, smooth cucumber. The wind was whipping Sugar's pants against his body and I noticed how thin his legs were, but the creamy brown pants kept their knife-edge crease and his shined shoes stayed polished. Occasionally, though, he touched his yellow straw hat, tilted to the side, to make sure it stayed in place; and his face never lost the gap-toothed smile.

We girls looked at him and we looked at the shiny car and we knew he was rich. It was said that he gave his girlfriends nylon stockings and candy.

Sugar was married, but that didn't stop him. He always let Wildwood know that he was still the sharpest man around, and Wildwood always knew the other woman's name. That's why I disliked Sugar: he always named the woman. He used to come down to my father's store at night, when the men sat under the light and played checkers, drank Orange Crush or Nehis, and told the news of the day. His wife, desperately trying to keep up with him, started coming, too. On hot summer nights I would see her alone in the hot car while he stood up under a bare lightbulb that hung from a tree limb and talked to the checker players and the men drinking Orange Crush.

For a long time Sugar kept going strong. He evidently had no problem—with a big, shiny car and money to buy nylon stockings, he had a seemingly inexhaustible supply of women.

But somewhere along the way, women in Wildwood started driving, too, and soon the road was filled with women passing in their own secondhand cars. A few years went by, and girls still in high school were successfully pestering their mothers for a car. Then the women laughed at Sugar's old-fashioned faith in his car; they had cars of their own, and nylon stockings. Time wiped out Sugar's life-style.

One day I was walking up the road when Sugar called me. I stopped and he came to the edge of the road.

"I want to talk to you about something," he said.

"What about?" I said.

"Well, it's not something I want to discuss right out here. Sometime when you have time, I want to talk to you."

"Oh, I see," I said. I wondered what he wanted and I ventured a guess. "Is it about Ruf Junior?"

"Something like that," he said. I wasn't surprised, for my brother hung around Sugar's place. I was still puzzled, however, for Sugar had never interested himself in anything exterior to himself for as long as I had known him.

I thought about it for several days; then I called Sugar and told him I was ready to talk about what it was. Why didn't he come to the house? Ruf Junior was away and wouldn't be back for a while. "No," he said. He didn't want to upset Nonnie, for she would want to know what he had come to talk about. That was reasonable, I thought. He told me he would pick me up around eight o'clock and we would go somewhere and talk. I said all right, but I was uneasy about it.

When he came to get me he had just finished work and hadn't bothered to bathe. I thought that we were going to an eating place in Durham, where we could have a cold drink and talk, but no, he knew a better place. We rode toward Chapel Hill, but just as we got there Sugar turned back, and all of a sudden I was riding on country roads with clouds of dust billowing up outside the windows. What in the world? I thought. But he kept up a steady flow of conversation and never mentioned Ruf Junior.

I expected him to turn around eventually and head back to Durham, for we were in a place that looked like a forest. But we were going deeper and deeper into the woods; I hadn't seen a house for some time, and the roads were narrow and unpaved, with sharp, reddish clay banks on either side. When I stopped concentrating on where we were and started paying attention to what Sugar was saying, I noted that the content and tone of the conversation had shifted. He was now talking about me, how I spoke to everybody and seemed so nice and all, but he'd noticed that he hadn't seen any men around me and he knew that I had been in school all my life and probably hadn't had time to get out much. But, he said, there were things that every girl should know and it was a man's duty to teach it to them, and he was a man and he'd do his duty, just like any man.

I couldn't believe my ears. But I showed no sign of my real feelings. I made a quick assessment of my position. Here I was, miles from home, in a place I knew nothing about, at night. If I flared up at him and he put me out, how would I get back home? I had to play it very cool until I got back on familiar ground. I decided that if he stopped the car I would get out and run, but as long as the car kept moving I was relatively safe.

I responded slowly and carefully, alert to whatever danger there was in the situation. Then it came to me to ask him why he had picked me. He said that some of his friends had bet him money that I'd never been with a man. Something— my cool response, perhaps, or confusion on Sugar's part— made him slow the car down and turn around. In silence he drove me back home.

I was heartsick. Some men in Wildwood had been in a liquor house somewhere, talking about me. I wondered which one of them had brought me into the conversation. These men liked to stand around and speculate about women—who their boyfriends were, what they would do, what they wouldn't do. I am sure that my name had come up many times, but no man in the bunch could comment on me one way or the other, for none of them had anything to tell. No doubt this had piqued Sugar's interest—a young woman walking around untried—so he had probably sounded some of them out, just to make sure, and when they told him that I didn't have a boyfriend and had never had one, Sugar saw his chance.

I said nothing, but my body protested. It broke out in millions of tiny bumps, each of which burned like fire. I lay in bed in agony for several days, all the while reliving that scene again and again. Most women find themselves in situations like that because they have in some way indicated their willingness to be involved. Sugar had come after me because he *couldn't* get any information about my private life.

Miss Angeline had worked for years for all of the Ransoms. She started working for Ransom Senior before his wife died; then, as the children married and established homes of their own, she went to work for them, too. During confinements, periods of illness, or other emergencies, one might call another and borrow Angeline for a day or two, a week, or a month. They swore by her: she was reliable, good, trustworthy. There was no one like Angeline.

She often came to see Nonnie on Sunday after church. She attended a church in another neighborhood, where she had originally belonged before she married and moved to Wildwood. One major topic of her conversation was the rhetorical ability of various ministers. "Didn't he preach!" she'd say. "My my my my *my!* That sure was a preaching man." And her yellowish-brown face would light up like the sun as she took her text right along with the minister and went over it verbatim, pausing to comment on the appropriateness of the illustrations he had used. "He's a preaching man," she would end, "as sure as you're born."

Then she would shift to her other main subject: the Ransoms. They were the devil, she declared, and God was going to punish every one of them. "Yes, He is. Just you wait and see. Take Mrs. Farrow." And Miss Angeline would tell about her latest escapades. Mrs. Farrow was the oldest Ransom daughter, and she had a severe drinking problem. According to Miss Angeline, she went for days on end without ever getting out of bed and coming downstairs. Her husband was a physician and had his practice to think about, and, with her inattention to details, a number of black maids came and went, trying to keep house and take care of the children. Miss

Angeline went in several times a week to clean up, but the day-to-day running of the household eventually fell to Ethelene, the full-time maid, who was evidently something of an organizer and soon had everybody in line. Ethelene ordered the groceries, paid the bills, took the children to their private school in the family station wagon, picked them up after school, made dental appointments and took the children to keep them, and eventually started signing their report cards, for there was no one else to do it.

Mrs. Farrow, resentful that her household was running so smoothly without her, and resentful that Ethelene had assumed so much control, pulled herself together one day and came downstairs to set everything straight. Miss Angeline was there that day. Ethelene, unfazed by this intruder on the order she had established, firmly sent Mrs. Farrow back upstairs, whereupon Mrs. Farrow summoned her father, who came and fired Ethelene. When the children got home and found her gone, they raised such a ruckus that their grandfather had to go get her. She came back—for a handsome raise in salary.

After telling about the sermon and the Ransoms, Miss Angeline frequently ended her visit with a story that she had evidently heard as a small child listening to older poeple talk about slavery. It had so impressed itself on her mind that she told it as if she had been there herself. I heard it so much, and her telling of it was so vivid, that I could see the story being enacted myself:

A woman, the mistress of the house, was very heavy, very cruel, and she sat and rocked in a rocking chair all day. When one of the black children displeased her about something, she would call the child to her and force him to put his hands under her rocking chair. Then she would rock on it, as punishment. Later in life she contracted cancer and died a terrible death. Before her death the palms of her hands rotted and fell away. Over the years I must have heard that story a hundred times, and in my mind's eye I can still see Miss Angeline, her Sunday-afternoon hat on her head, extending her hands with the thumbs turned inward, illustrating how the rotten flesh fell out.

One Friday night at choir practice the president of the choir said that there was going to be a funeral at Mount Zion the next afternoon, and he was wondering if some members of the choir could come to sing. This news startled me; I wondered why the family didn't wait until Sunday, the traditional day for having funerals, for then everybody would be done for the week and would come after their own service. There would be a large crowd. On Saturday afternoon there would be few. But most of the older choir members seemed to know what it was about, and a few raised their hands to indicate that they would come. I said that I would play for them.

On Saturday afternoon there weren't ten people in the church other than the choir and the minister. There were few flowers and the eulogy for the deceased was brief. I wondered about all this but said nothing. When it came time to view the body, I broke my usual rule of never going down to look at the deceased. He was a young man, very black, not yet twenty years old. He had on a dark pinstriped suit and a white shirt. He looked all right except for the fact that the undertaker had obviously been careless, for he had a thick, chalky-white substance between his lips. The minister's words were brief. The family, dark and huddled, did not weep openly. It was the strangest event I had ever seen.

The next day, I tried to find out more about it. Who was he? Who were his people? That I didn't know them meant little, for Mount Zion had moved into Wildwood from Butner when the army built a camp there during World War II, and thus many of its members were from distant communities. No one who knew anything about it would talk. Finally someone said, "He tried to run. They shot him." And I knew the young man had been a prisoner.

175

When I first saw Irene she had on a felt hat and a wool skirt. It was dead summer. Irene was big and strong, "raw-boned." Her voice was harsh and she talked unusually loud. That was hard to do because nearly everyone I knew shouted, and if someone spoke low, people wondered if she was sick or something. But Irene talked louder and stronger than that. When she quit school in the eighth grade to help her mother, she came down to our community and took a job with the Bests as a maid, cook, housekeeper, and taker-care-of-children. Her mother needed help because she had no education and was startlingly unable to cope. Irene loved her mother and looked out for her, but was determined not to be like her. Irene loved education. People talked about her mother and said she sometimes went to men and asked them for flour when her children didn't have anything to eat, and they gave it to her for a price; Irene had had a boyfriend but was now fanatically celibate.

She was determined to prove to herself that she did not have "bad blood," as people sometimes said. So she became a zealous member of a Holiness sect. It was church on Sunday, all day—morning service, afternoon service, and evening service. Often, evening service lasted until one or two in the morning. Then it was Wednesday-night service, Friday-night service, and Saturday-night service, and service in other communities. It was nothing for Irene to work from seven a.m. to six p.m., drive a hundred miles to church, leave church after midnight, arrive home after two a.m., and get up in time to be at her job by seven a.m. the next morning. This was not done occasionally. This was done all the time. So the rounds of her days continued: church, job; church, job; church, job.

She wanted, however, to better herself; so she started going to night school to be able to take her high-school-equivalency test. Sometimes she would talk about it and then her face would gleam with a joy it didn't have when she talked about service, service.

So Irene sat, black, buxom, with her short hair supercurly

around the edges, and mentioned who was doing well in math and who was doing the best in something else. She still worked eleven hours a day, and she still loved the Bests as if they were blood kin, and she still ran all over the countryside going to service, but her world had broadened some.

Weeks faded into months and Irene got her high-school-equivalency certificate and started taking a business course at a black business college in town. I didn't want to tell her that this college had a poor reputation for teaching, because she was so enthusiastic about her typing and shorthand. Irene went and went and went, but she never "finished." Finally the money ran out and she stopped.

Sometime during her business-college days her interest in men broke through again. In her "sinning" days before she became Holy and Sanctified there had been somebody, and moments of groping and panting, but she had given all that up for God and the respectable name that her mother never had. But the interest returned, with one obsession—she was determined that the man she married would be one of the ministers in her sect. In a church where there were few male members and half of the preachers were women, the chances of her marrying a minister were infinitely small, but Irene was undeterred. She had met a man who, though not a minister, was almost as good—he was a gospel singer. He was ideal: he was Holy and Sanctified; he was a gentleman—he never said anything out of the way (made a pass); she was sure he wasn't seeing anybody else; and she talked constantly of marriage.

They didn't see much of each other. He drove a taxi in his spare time and they talked on the phone some and she saw him at church about every two weeks. That sounded a bit infrequent, seeing as how they were in the same town. "But," she told me, "he works at night and I go off a lot, but we see each other in church."

At first I said nothing, although I had heard things about him. Finally I asked her if he ever kissed her.

"Well, once when he brought me back from church, he

177

made as if he was going to kiss me. I moved back, and since then he hasn't tried."

"Is that all?" I said.

"Then once I hadn't seen him in a long time and I went to the Grill in Chapel Hill where he works and asked him what was the matter and we hugged and kissed a lot."

"Is that all?"

"Yes," she said. "You see, in our faith we don't believe in cohabiting before marriage."

In the spring she was sure they were to be married the second Sunday in August. (Good church people often measure time by days of the week: "first Saturday," "second Sunday.")

Through the spring and early summer she gave me progress reports. But I noticed that the intervals between the times they saw each other continued to be two weeks or even more. And when the wedding day grew near, Irene started keeping close to herself.

August passed and there was no announcement. Then September and October. Deep in November, Irene talked about it. During the summer he had grown colder and colder toward her, but when she pressed him he said that everything was all right. "Yes," he said, "we are going to marry." But his strange behavior continued.

Then one night his female cousin paid her a visit and told her, "The mumps went down on him when he was a child, and he is not a man."

By then Irene was so in love with him and with the idea of marrying that she still wanted to marry him. They could be friends. But as far as he was concerned it was no. "Then I hurt so bad I could have died. If I'd had some heroin—anything to numb me—I would have taken that."

Later, she made other attempts at relationships, but these turned out to be disappointments. Education had failed her, men had failed her, and then one day, out of the blue, her main job failed her. Mrs. Best let her go. Irene looked as though she'd been struck by lightning.

She loved the Bests as if they were her own family. She

had gone there in her late teens, fresh out of the country, and was proud of the fact that she had learned city folks' ways so well that she was given the grocery money and bought the food, planned the menu, and cooked the meals. She did not think it odd that after all this handling of the food she should have to come home and cook her own supper. She seemed satisfied with the noon meal they gave her, and if she had a thought to the contrary she never gave it voice. She even accepted it when Mrs. Best forbade her to wash her clothes in *their* washing machine. She helped tend a garden at the back of the Bests' suburban home and picked and canned the vegetables. She told with pride about how much she'd canned.

Folks talked: "Irene's making herself a slave. She's working from sun to sun for practically nothing, and people like her will make it hard for anybody to work 'in service' anymore. The white people will expect a lot for nothing." But Irene was undeterred. The children grew and she had a car. So if they had to go to the dentist, she carried them; if it was the movies, she delivered them and picked them up. And somewhere along the way the Bests' possessions became hers. She spoke of doing "my" floors and doing "our" spring cleaning. She never took off a day; if she needed the time, she asked permission and then waited anxiously for the answer.

So the children grew and the household functioned smoothly and Mrs. Best didn't care because she taught school and it pleased her not to have to be bothered.

There were little warning signs that things were not so rosy, but Irene ignored them. She was satisfied with one thing: she had proved that she was a hard worker, not lazy, and that she was not too "country" to manage a household.

But then Mrs. Best got menopausal and decided to come home for a while and rest her nerves. And this woman, just like Mrs. Farrow, was shocked to find that her household functioned without her. The food was bought, menus planned, and meals prepared without any need of her. Cleaning schedules were arranged and laundry done without any need of her. And the children were starting to go their own separate ways. Who was the culprit who had made her unnecessary at the time of life when she most needed to be needed? Irene.

And the showdown came over half-and-half cream. Mrs. Best told the milkman not to leave it, and Irene said to him, "Leave it today. Mr. Best likes it in his coffee."

And Mrs. Best said, "I am the woman of this house and I told him not to leave it."

The word battle raged, and when it was over, Mrs. Best asked for Irene's key.

Irene gave up on life for herself; overnight she changed into a black matriarch living for others. Her dreams of self-fulfillment unfulfilled and now denied, she became determined that someone in the family would get a good education, and the logical choice was her younger sister, Azell. But Irene ignored such an important thing as Azell's lack of interest and set out to make her sister what she herself wished she could have been, a trained professional woman.

Out of her salary from a professional cleaning service, after buying her mother's groceries, Irene gave Azell money to have her hair done and bought her what the other girls were wearing: "I want her to look like the other kids." She gave Azell lunch money: "Plenty days I went to school with no breakfast and sat there all day hungry." She bought, pushed, and counseled; and Azell smiled her Cheshire-cat smile and accepted everything. Then Irene projected into the future. Azell would become a nurse. She would first become a licensed practical nurse and work awhile. Then she would become a registered nurse. Azell, her eyes flecked with gold, smiled and shyly looked down.

Finally Azell was a senior in high school and Irene spent a great deal of time seeing about where to take nursing courses, when they started, what Azell would need. Azell said nothing. The summer that Azell finished high school, I heard nothing but nurse, fees, hospital, training, nurse, fees, hospital, training. But one day I noticed a fullness in Azell's stomach, and this puzzled me. I thought what I didn't want to think, and I wondered why Irene didn't notice and say something. Her talk of nurse, nurse, became louder and more frantic as Azell's stomach grew larger, and finally everybody knew, and Azell went back up in the country for a year. Irene never mentioned her name. All the going without proper anything so that Azell could have lunch money and new clothes and look like the other girls had been in vain.

But Irene soon found another cause. Her brother's wife, a drinking diabetic, died, and she rented a house and took in her brother and his three children. Her talk shifted to report cards, and get your lessons done, and be back in here before dark. It was as if the black country girl who wanted to be a typist and wear smart dresses and who wanted a husband and children had never existed.

One day a little bug of a car came down the unpaved road, swirling clouds of dust behind it. We dropped everything and ran to look. We always ran to look at anything strange. And we had never seen a little car like that. We had new neighbors, the Fultons. They were from "up north," that mystical place where everyone had money and blacks could do as they pleased. They moved into a little run-down house that had been vacant a long time. It was made of logs and there were wet weeds and rusty tin cans all around it. They never did finish cleaning it up. But then they never finished anything. They had three children, and we were glad because we loved to play and talk and laugh and now we had three more friends to do it with.

I liked Inez right off. She had healthy teeth—black folk back then called anything big "healthy." So Inez had a healthy mouth, a wide grin, smooth brown skin, and thick black hair that glistened when it was straightened. I was jealous of Inez's hair. Mine wasn't long or thick and it was too soft to hold straightening, so it always looked a mess. But Inez was so nice that I didn't let her pretty hair keep me from being friends. Inez had a big mole under her left eye and when she grew older it somehow made her look better. Inez had short, healthy feet, and she knew lots of dirty songs, which she willingly taught me and which I joyfully learned. To this day when I hear "Stars and Stripes Forever," dirty lyrics come into my mind and I smile.

Inez was always unfazed and she was always smiling.

One day, when we were assembled in the auditorium, Inez pulled a chair out from under Cortez, a fellow student, just as he was about to sit down. Cortez protested about this treatment rather loudly from his place on the floor. The teacher remonstrated with Inez about being unladylike; he tried to make her feel guilty by telling her that Cortez was very bitter about it. Inez said that Cortez *looked* bitter and grinned. I nearly died laughing.

Later, when the science teacher objected to her and her gang because they said unkind things about his light-skinned "pets" and remarked pointedly that some people act like fools, Inez was undaunted and took up the cudgels: "I don't know who *acts* like a fool, but you *look* more like a fool than I do." She departed with a suspension from school, trailing the cheers of her classmates behind her.

Inez could take a joke, too. One day when she was going across the rutted, rocky schoolyard, mouth wide open as usual, the principal observed in good humor, "Fulton, you'd better close your mouth before you swallow a fly." Inez grinned even wider, and the principal did, too, and I laughed.

Even her family did not escape her jokes. Her mother had the odd habit of disciplining her children by taking off her "slides" (old shoes whose backs were bent under the feet, like slippers) and throwing them. One day Inez and I were sitting on the sofa and Inez said something—probably something fresh—that her mother didn't like, and she reached down and pulled off her slide and zinged it right at Inez's head. Inez ducked, picked up the slide, drew back her arm, and pretended to make a terrific throw. The shoe never left her hand, but her mother ducked, and I wanted to laugh so bad I went home.

182

Inez and I grew up playing house with the clothes, shoes, hats, and handbags discarded by the white people her mother worked for, the "work ladies." The dresses were long for us, down to the ankle and too big, but we clumped around in high-heeled shoes and thought the old dresses were evening gowns.

We could have all the clothes we wanted after Ann got through with them. Ann was Inez's sister and two years older, and she always got first choice and the best of everything. All Wildwood talked of how unfairly Mrs. Fulton treated her two daughters, buying Ann new outfits, which she demanded every holiday, but giving Inez only things that Ann had tired of or things that the work ladies gave her. Mrs. Fulton's talk was only of Ann, Ann, Ann. She never mentioned Inez. Yet there was only the two-year difference between the sisters' ages. If, after Ann had picked over everything, we put on something that she thought looked good, she'd demand it of me or Inez, and Mrs. Fulton would make Inez give it up. She had no trouble with me; I always gave in. So we wore the work ladies' clothes and tried to find matching handbags, usually with a broken clasp or strap or cracked patent leather, and big flowered hats or drooping-all-around hats, and we thought we were fine ladies.

Inez was always good-humored, never mad, though she'd tell you off in a minute. Anybody. I guess that's why she didn't hold grudges. She always told you just what she thought.

Inez knew how much I liked to read, so she slipped me old newspapers and magazines that her mother brought off the work ladies' jobs. Once she brought me a big newspaper; I had never seen such a big one. It had all sorts of sections— a whole lot of them—and I was marveling at it when Inez appeared a few minutes later and looked ashamed and asked me for it, and I said, "Ann?" She nodded her head and I gave it to her. Ann could not bear for me to read the paper before she did; *she* had to be first.

Inez grew up taking what Ann didn't want, giving up on

demand anything Ann wanted, and grinning, with a joke for everybody.

Inez was musically talented, as were all of the Fultons. She could sing beautifully and played the piano by ear. In the tenth grade, Inez and three girlfriends formed a gospel group and started giving concerts at various local churches.

Though Inez made B's in most of her subjects, she never mentioned going beyond high school. She had sensed that if either sister got further training, it would be Ann. And she never talked of going north, as nearly everybody in the school did. Having come from there, she seemingly had no wish to go back.

When we were teenagers, Inez started joking with the boys. The boys became one boy, and his name was Will. He came from the deep country "up in the woods," and they "courted," though her father fussed and tried to prevent her from seeing him because he was ignorant and didn't have anything. Will couldn't read or write. I saw it on the marriage license that she showed to me. There was a name on it that only by the wildest stretch of the imagination could have been Will's. But Inez asked me to play for her wedding, and Miss Pauline made me a pink voile dress with no sleeves and a low neck, and I played the "Wedding March," and Miss Emma decorated the little Holy church with wild flowers—and one warm Sunday afternoon Inez was married.

Miss Lucy, a mean, gossipy lady, sat next to my mother, and as Inez walked down the aisle she whispered, "That girl is pregnant. I see it."

And my mother said, "Oh hush, Miss Lucy."

But Inez disappeared for two months up at Will's home in the woods, and when she came out she was big, and people wondered how she could have got a baby since her mother was so strict on her and all. Inez looked a little ashamed, but she smiled her healthy smile and joked with everybody.

Later, I unraveled the mystery. Barbara, who was from the country and stayed with Inez's family, told me. Some days when everybody had gone to school Inez doubled back down the power line that ran back of our community and met Will and they both slipped in the back door and stayed there all day while nobody else was home.

Her fanatically religious mother always put her religion before her children and tried to deny Inez everything. But Inez found sex and she found love. I don't know which came first, but she followed them.

When I next saw Inez it was six months after her wedding and I went to see the new baby. She mumbled something about it being "early," but Ann set her straight: "Inez, this baby isn't early. Look at its fingers and toes. They're all right." Inez looked away and didn't say anything.

Then we looked away and looked back and Inez was big again, and everybody marveled that there was so little time between babies. And Inez laughed and joked. If she was treated like dirt, like nothing, she could still be first in something, and she gave the oldest to her husband's mother to raise. Then she had two more, and Will started to "run." "Running" in the black community means "women." And Inez had three more children, and as the babies poured out, Will poured in the liquor and ran some more.

One child, people said, didn't look like Will, and they talked. Then Will fathered a baby by one of his women and brought it home for Inez to keep. His mother backed him and said that if Will could support another man's child, Inez could take care of another woman's child. People stopped laughing so much about Inez's fertility; all those children, improperly fed, improperly clothed, and the rough tobacco barn they lived in was a shame. But Inez grinned and went on.

Finally I decided something should be done about it; I bought a diaphragm and took it to her and tried to tell her how to use it.

"Will doesn't like protection. He says it makes him sore," she said.

"Inez," I said, "put it in before he comes home and take it out after he's gone. He'll never know the difference." I was looking around at the tobacco barn that had been converted into a house, the small, dark, cramped rooms, the crying babies running across the hard-packed earth of the yard. There was no toilet, not even an outdoor one, and one or two of the boys had on shirts but no bottoms. The children were crying all at once, and I marveled that without looking up she could tell by the cry which one was which. They all had nicknames—Footie, Rine, Hah-Hah.

She took the diaphragm, wondering out loud where she would keep it. I suggested that she keep it under her mattress. No one would ever think to look there. She said that she would, and then I didn't see Inez for a long time, and when I did she was big again. I said nothing. Finally she said that Will had caught her rambling under the mattress one night, and when he found out what for, he made her throw the diaphragm away. I said no more. That was child number nine or ten, and if she had a hundred I wasn't going to sympathize, marvel, or comment about it in any way.

I don't know when the pregnancies ceased to be a joke to Inez, but somewhere along the way they did. People in Wildwood tired of the subject; they watched TV, went to ball games, car races, went to the Stallion (a nightclub). Inez was no longer the talk.

Worse yet, her sister-in-law, Will's sister, had begun to accumulate; she built a house and furnished it nicely while Inez lived in a tobacco barn and her children asked her why they could never have seconds at the table. Their diet consisted mostly of beans, peas, and potatoes, and Inez was glad when she could get government-surplus food. She once remarked to me that she was glad that she could read and sign for her commodities because the white landowners in the county were taking government surplus and charging it against their tenants' accounts as though they had bought it in a store.

Inez's children were slow learners. Several of them couldn't read or write their names. And I thought of the crowded little rooms with children sleeping on pallets on the floor, and no privacy, and the things they must have heard and seen, and starch and fat meat day in and day out, week after week, and how they never had a chance.

But I understood, too. She had to have something; her blind love for Will was the only thing in her life that she had ever had—that and the children.

Then Will got a job on a garbage truck in Durham, one of whose stops was at a brothel in a white neighborhood in North Durham, and Inez got word that he was frequenting this house. She and the children were struggling to survive and he was giving a white prostitute fifteen dollars for half an hour.

So one day Inez drove to the house. It was in a peaceful-looking section of town, full of two-story boxlike houses. Most of them were painted white and were well screened, but the grass was stubby. The white mill workers who lived there sometimes sat on their porches in the evening. She went to the front door, rang the bell, and asked for Will.

"Will isn't here," they said.

"Yes, he is here, and I'm going to drive slowly around the block and when I get back I want to see him on the street. If I don't . . ."

She slowly circled the block.

When she returned he was on the street, and she took him home.

She got a job in a school cafeteria, which helped her because she could give the children some leftovers. She slipped and broke her leg, but worked in a heavy cast.

Rine, her daughter, married at fifteen, unlearned in any of the ways of the twentieth century. Inez smiled. One of the boys, who was mentally defective, was accused of a sexual offense. Inez pleaded with the judge, who let him off with a light sentence. Another defective child was put on probation for a misdemeanor. Inez helped him get a "little job." ("Little jobs" are poor-paying jobs for minors.)

Inez early perceived the horrible limitations of her life, and instead of crying out in rage, she turned to embrace them.

Now there are few signs left of the intelligent, talented girl who once walked through Wildwood calling out to people seated on the porch in the summer's heat, "Hi, y'all!"

The last time I saw Daisy she had on sunglasses with white rims; her crinkly hair was fixed in a pompadour with a crinkly pageboy in back; her lips were dark red. She was dressed in high-fashion World War II style, dating from the time when she and Junior had been young and in love. She'd always had a very full bottom, but she'd once had a small waist and a small top. Now bottom and top had simply overflowed, so that there was little distinction between them; the bottom did not identify her as it once had. But the legs were still big and shapely, and she held her head up jauntily. Also, she had her mouth closed, so one couldn't see her snuff-stained, crooked teeth.

Still, Daisy was considered a beauty.

Once, when Junior was in uniform, he had brought Daisy down to the house to see Ruf and Nonnie. She had on a cute dress. Her bottom was big and her teeth were crooked, but she was sort of sassy. She smiled real friendly at me and talked nice.

She was a good wife and stayed home and cared for child after child as it came. She didn't get out much, just visited the neighbors or went where Junior took her. She and Junior still acted like newlyweds.

So the babies came, and whenever I saw her she was smiling.

Junior liked to tell jokes. He told the wonders of his war experiences over and over. He told of playing ball in Europe one night after nine o'clock and "it was as light as day."

One of his stories concerned his attempt to avoid overseas combat. Someone told him while he was stationed in Louisiana that there was a seventh sister of a seventh sister in a nearby town. She was reputed to have great magical powers. So he searched and searched and had to go through all sorts of trouble to find the seventh sister of a seventh sister to ask for help. He found her. He never revealed what mysteries she worked, but he came back from World War II without a scratch.

Then one day Wildwood heard that Daisy had started drinking heavily. Daisy? And, equally incredible, she was going out at night. Daisy? Finally she decided to run. She took her teenage daughter to New York. Close friends wanted to know why, and she wrote that she "wanted to live," that she had been married too long. She had married at sixteen, and she was still in her thirties. People talked: "Married all these years. A nice, quiet person and she wants to live! What in the world is going to happen next?" Junior nearly lost his mind. He couldn't understand it.

Word drifted down to Wildwood from New York. Daisy had a sleep-in job. She worked during the day, but she lived a high life at night. Her daughter did, too.

Her daughter came home first. Pregnant, no husband. People didn't say much. They blamed her mother.

Daisy was made of tougher stuff, but a body and spirit that had known only the somnolence of Wildwood could not stand the work, parties, and pace of New York, and word came down to Wildwood that Daisy had TB.

She soon was back in Durham, but she didn't come out to Wildwood. Those who saw her said she was unrepentant. Nobody could understand why she acted as she did, and she wouldn't enlighten them. They stopped talking after a while, and Daisy came back to Wildwood.

She still wouldn't go back to Junior. Though hurt and humiliated when she walked out on him and the children, he wanted her back. But she stayed with her mother, a ten-minute walk from the house where she and her husband had lived together. It is all boarded up now, that house, and I think it provides a key to the mystery.

Junior's brother Lannie was much younger, so much so that he was of a different generation. When Junior built for Daisy,

189

he put up a little three-room hut of the kind that used to suffice for living many years ago. The children kept coming; the house got fuller, but no larger.

Then Lannie and his wife built next door. Lannie worked for a concrete maker and he built a large house out of cinder blocks. Blacks were building houses larger then, and wives were looking at *House Beautiful* and talking about interiors. Though Daisy had been married for twenty years she was still young, and she saw people all around her getting what she knew she would never have. She looked at her life: many children; an unskilled husband; her youth slipping away. She decided to grab a whole handful of life while she could. She did. Whether it was worth the pain she won't say. She merely walks along with her 1940s sunglasses on and lets Wildwood take it any way it wants to.

Sappho made her appearance in Wildwood and I became aware of it quite by accident. One day I picked up our party line—it always had eight or nine families on it—and found myself listening to the most extraordinary conversation. I didn't put the phone down, but continued to listen.

The first voice belonged to Maria, the daughter of Hettie, the conjure woman. Hettie believed in roots, sticking pins in dolls, and other practices that were foreign to the thinking of most of the people in Wildwood. Maria had dropped out of school early, as had her two brothers. All of them were near-illiterates. Maria once told a woman in Wildwood in confidence that one night her older brother had come home drunk, got in bed with her, and "forced" her.

Maria was harsh and abrupt; she kept to herself most of the time and the other people in Wildwood left her alone. Shocked surprise was the general reaction when Maria grew big. She never named the father of her son, and though there was much speculation, no one ever really knew.

The owner of the other voice on the phone was a shocker. Though I knew that this woman and her husband had had their ups and downs, along with the rest of Wildwood I had assumed that they had a nice marriage. Such evidently was not the case.

"I'm serious about this thing. I'm not fooling," Maria said. The other voice agreed, but it was not so convinced. The conversation continued, and its passionate nature was unmistakable to me. I listened silently, hoping that somehow they wouldn't sense that someone else was on the line—Maria hard, sure, the other voice agreeing but hesitant, doubtful.

I never said anything to anyone about it. To this day I have never heard a breath of it mentioned in Wildwood, and I believe that no one, except the lovers and me, ever knew the relationship existed.

Rita was tired and bedraggled when she moved to Wildwood from a neighboring community. It was still possible, however, to see the once-attractive slimness in the scrawny figure, and what must have been striking good looks in the yellowish, hollow-cheeked face and the cloud of gray-streaked hair. Rita came from good people. They had sent her to college in Durham, during the time when college for black people was a rarity indeed. While in college she had formed a relationship with a prominent middle-aged black businessman—some say he was an undertaker—though he was married. It was easy to see how. She was a young, strikingly attractive girl, who liked to dress well; and he fed her vanity.

But the wife was unforgiving. After her graduation from college, Rita got a job teaching in a small North Carolina community, but she lasted there for only a year. The wife wrote letters to administrative officials in the district and they let Rita go. Then she got another job, and at the end of the year she was again let go; the wife had written letters. Then job after job, each one ending the same way.

And Rita gave up. She started to live off the largesse of men, and soon her drinking became legendary. By the time she moved to Wildwood with her mother, she no longer made any pretense of respectability. Her doings became one of the staples of conversation among the community gossips.

Then one weekend Rita announced to her drinking companions, "I won't be with ya'll next week this time." No one paid her any attention. The next week they were preparing for her funeral. Whether she had premonitions of death or whether she took her own life, no one ever said.

I myself was fascinated by the character of the wife. What was the nature of the woman who would hound someone for years for what obviously was the action of an immature country girl? The wife no doubt considered herself a good Christian who had taught that hussy a lesson. What she did, in fact, was destroy a human life.

21

Most of the black folk in my world were hostile to the notion of celibacy. To them, man was meant for woman and woman was meant for man: that is nature's way, they said, the natural flow of life, rhythmic, like the seasons that flow into each other, each giving way to the next in turn. It is a pro-life stance. Though the church teaches Biblical chastity and preaches that it is better to marry than to burn, still underlying it all is a strong current that says: Better some physical intimacy than none. Marry, yes; but if you don't marry, at least have a boyfriend, by which is meant a lover.

Such a course does follow the flow of life if each member plans to become a part of the community by marrying a member of it and continuing its basic pattern: marriage, job, family. But what if one member wants to break out? Then marriage for him or her is a trap; and at that time intercourse often led to pregnancy, an even worse trap. An illegitimate child would effectively prevent its mother from doing much of anything except providing support for it.

The community expected the sexes to start taking an active interest in each other by the mid-teens. They would hold off inquiries until the member was about twenty; after that the community interested itself in one's private life: Do you have a boyfriend? When are you going to get married? If the answers were negative, the community wondered.

I was outside the pattern. One or two of the boys in school said nice things to me, but I didn't listen. They were country folk like myself, and nice enough, but they were destined for field or factory, and as a part of their lives I would be destined for the same thing. And it was my secret guilt that I had longings to do better than that. I wanted to do great things in life, and go to faraway places.

People said that I got those odd notions out of books; Nonnie said, "Girl, you're going to go crazy"; and now my brothers were hinting that there was something else wrong with me because I didn't seem to like boys. Once, when I crossed Ruf Junior, he said it outright: he called me a "Lesbidan." I wanted to tell him he was pronouncing the word incorrectly and to spell it for him, but I knew better.

Their remarks would have been amusing if they had not been so sinister. Besides, my rich fantasy life showed no signs of abating. In my daydreams I was a very famous person, living in Wildwood incognito. I was frequently the savior of mankind from cancer; I wrote great books; and I startled the world with my artistry at the piano.

My daytime fantasies gave way to vivid nighttime dreams. The dreams were often narratives—events that sometimes were continuations of stories that I was reading; sometimes I used the same characters but rewrote the story. And I could often will myself to continue a story that I had started the night before in a dream.

I often fantasized someone who was on my side, someone whom I could talk to all the time, whom I could tell what I felt inside, who would bolster me and tell me, "Yes, you can do it." But most of all, this someone cared for me, looked out for me, and gratified my longings, gave my heart ease.

I never went to sleep before he came into my thoughts.

It was summer again. I had just finished my junior year in high school, and I needed a job. Betty had told me in Sunday school that the Ransoms were going on a vacation and needed somebody to help with the children. She asked me if I was interested. She usually went, but this year she couldn't.

I had heard a lot about the Ransoms. Hazel lived across the highway from them. Hazel said that Mr. Ransom used to beat his wife with a wet towel.

"A wet towel?" I asked.

"Yes," she said, "so it won't leave marks."

"Why does he do that?"

"She gets to drinking and cutting up when he's not there, so when he comes home he beats her."

Such were the tales that emanated from the big house where these rich white folks lived.

"He would get a divorce, but she says she'll break him if he does." Everybody who'd ever worked for them said that.

Hazel was full of Ransom talk: their comings and goings gave all of Wildwood something to talk about, but to Hazel it was life itself. She herself had been raised in a house on a rich family's estate, the Richardses'. And she regarded their existence with the same wonder as a child regards a fairy tale. The Richardses, "old rich," looked down on the Ransoms, "new rich," and Hazel, ever faithful in identifying with her parents' employers, herself echoed the Richardses' disdain of the Ransoms. I halfway disbelieved much of Hazel's incessant gossip, but I listened.

Thus I heard secondhand about drinking and fighting and divorce in paradise. Certainly the Ransoms lived in paradise. They had a large house, situated on spacious grounds in the midst of a beautiful grove of trees. The whole yard was thickly clustered with trees. In the spring some of them flowered and the others got so thick with leaves that you barely could see the house gleaming in the distance from the highway. In the winter you could see all the way up to the house, which looked high and white and rich, like something in a picture magazine.

There was a waist-high hedge running all around the grounds, and on spring and summer days, if you passed there, you saw many black men patiently grooming the shrubbery. They were all drawn from Wildwood. Some of them had never been on another job. Ambitious men in the community shunned that job; they sought factory work instead. But these men were used to a way of life around white people and were not much lured by the factories, where you had to meet a clock and could not rest when the boss was away. Indeed, the boss was working on his job, like you, and if he didn't meet the clock like you, he could be fired, too. So the Ransoms drew most of their servants from our community. That is why we knew so much about them. I used to wonder why they needed so many servants and how they could afford them. I had not yet read *The Theory of the Leisure Class,* but I did know that the Ransoms paid very low wages—"nothing," people said.

When Mrs. Ransom learned that Betty couldn't go, she called me and asked me to go with her, saying Betty had recommended me. She told me about Roaring Gap, North Carolina, how beautiful it was, and even read parts of a brochure about it to me over the telephone. We agreed on a salary. It was not as good as what I had made the year before during green season at the American Tobacco factory, but it was more than what I could make doing days work, and Mrs. Ransom painted a picture of such easy duties that I accepted.

Early one Sunday morning in June, Mrs. Ransom came to pick me up in her dark-green Cadillac. I knew that the Cadillac would cause some comment in Wildwood, for a car like that was a rare sight. There were two black brothers in our neighborhood who drove big Buicks, but they were very unusual for our community. The brothers had money; one was a brick mason and the other a carpenter-contractor. They had moved into our community from another town; they were outsiders, and thus their standards didn't apply to us. The only Cadillacs we ever saw in Wildwood belonged to folks up north who came down south visiting, driving the very latest cars—long, low, and gleaming, with lots of chrome and white-walled tires. We didn't know how they could afford it, but we were told and believed that in New York City everybody made big money and drove fine cars.

Dorothy Ransom smiled pleasantly enough and I put my suitcase tied with a string into the trunk and we drove along early-Sunday-morning highways, full of traffic. At first I was apprehensive, but presently I started to relax.

Mr. Ransom—"Laddie"—had gone on ahead in the station wagon. He was an older man, but we always called him "Laddie." As he cruised through Wildwood on his way to and from his construction site at the end of the road that ran through the community, we always paused and said, "There goes Laddie." He drove a car with a long, thick aerial that was fastened down at both ends, and he changed cars every year. Libby and Junior and Warren, the baby, were with him. I had heard that Libby and her mother didn't get on well and frequently quarreled, so I wasn't surprised that Libby was not in the Cadillac. The other daughter, Cherry, rode with her mother.

Betty had talked quite a bit about the Ransom children; she and Libby were the same age and often exchanged secrets. Libby liked men an awful lot, and one of the Ransom hands had been fired because she had written in her diary: "Glenn F.K.'d me." Her mother got hold of the diary and thought that it meant "that" word, but Libby told Betty that it meant "French-kissed." But Glenn had to go. I sensed that that was why the wealthy whites didn't hire white servants; they wanted to keep the social classes apart, particularly if they had come from lower classes themselves, as had the grandfather, David, the patriarch of the Ransom clan and the founder of its fortune.

(Hazel once told me of an incident involving "her" family,

the Richardses, and another white family, the McDougalds, who lived nearby. Diana Richards, the youngest, not knowing about social classes, invited the McDougald children over to her house to swim in the pool. Mrs. Richards rushed into the house with a headache, and as soon as Diana's guests were gone she ordered the servants to drain the pool and scrub it, remarking that the McDougalds might have "crabs." I was glad when I heard that, for it had been Mr. McDougald who had stood up in our house talking to my mother with his hat on.)

The patriarch had worked hard to get where he was and didn't see why everybody else shouldn't also. Consequently, he worked people hard and paid them little and got well off indeed. Once the federal government penetrated the South, the old man frequently found himself in trouble with various labor relations boards over the matter of unpaid overtime and other benefits that the employees in his firm were owed but that he evidently felt were modern fringes and frills and totally unnecessary.

Betty had said that Junior was a sex fiend and that Cherry got her name because all she wanted to eat was cherry tarts.

North Carolina prides itself on its scenery. That Sunday, we drove past cows grazing, with their heads low; brown fields, stands of tobacco, ground-hugging vegetable crops. Here and there a patch of brown would meet a patch of green, showing exactly where a farmer had finished his plowing on Saturday and where he would take it up again on Monday. Tobacco barns were weathered gray, with rusty tin roofs; they had stovepipes sticking out of the sides.

There were farmhouses with no underpinnings. You could see underneath, where the rakes and shovels were kept. There were cinder-block churches, some painted white, some left gray. There were graveyards right on the edge of the highway, where any passing motorist could throw things out on them. Brick churches in bare yards, gnarled trees with exposed roots, wooden churches with fresh coats of paint making them starkly outlined against the clear blue sky, rolled by outside the car window.

Cherry launched into "Old Black Joe" and was soon joined by her mother. I wondered if that song was really necessary; but even though I hated Cherry for singing it—for I sensed that it was meant to hurt me—I had to admit that we sang it in school, where everybody was black. But I was really surprised at her mother; Hazel had told me that before she came south, Dorothy Ransom had been a debutante in New York and had had a coming-out party.

I just looked out the window.

The song finished to her satisfaction, Cherry started commenting on the horses, which she pronounced "hosses." She mimicked the men who worked for them and how they talked about "hosses." There was no mistaking Cherry; she was being mean. Betty had told me some of the stories she'd heard about the children and the maids. One time at the beach Junior had enticed a maid out in a motorboat and then had driven very fast and erratically. The maid couldn't swim, became terrified, and started screaming, while he continued to weave all over the water. The whole family considered it funny and laughed about the incident for days.

In Winston-Salem, at the foot of the mountains, we stopped at a little store for the Sunday paper. The clerk had a sturdy figure and sunburned skin. She obviously was the owner. She looked like pictures of mountain women, but softer, as if she had been away from the hills for a long time. Mrs. Ransom bought the paper and then asked her if she had any milk; the clerk got the milk for her. Then, with no warning, Mrs. Ransom's voice changed. "Is this milk fresh?" she said harshly.

I was so stunned that I looked at the milk carton. There were little rivulets of water running down the sides. It looked cold to the touch. The clerk didn't say anything. She seemed to be unable to think up a response.

Mrs. Ransom said again, "Is this milk fresh? I won't buy it if it isn't."

The clerk looked as if she were weighing two things in her mind—whether to try to make a sale or to reply to someone who was insulting her without reason. "Lady, I wouldn't be selling it if it wasn't fresh!" she said, and looked ready to respond further. I was embarrassed to death. Mrs. Ransom paid her silently and without expression.

As we went back to the car, I wondered about that incident. Just as Cherry had wanted to embarrass me by singing "Old Black Joe" and mimicking the men who worked on their place, Dorothy Ransom had wanted to establish her status as a rich woman going on a vacation by trying to humiliate the clerk. I couldn't understand that; if she had money and a big Cadillac car, why did she also need to embarrass people who didn't have those things?

We drove up into the mountains.

I had never seen scenery so beautiful. I couldn't believe we were still in North Carolina. A clear blue haze was on everything, though it was early afternoon; and if you reached your hand out it felt as if you could touch the mountains, even though they were miles away. The blue haze didn't obscure the clearness. It was as though you could see air.

Tennis racquets, noise, enough food and gear to sustain an army—all exploded on a house that was deceptively small from the front. But the back opened out onto a big porch, high, high up from the ground, that looked out on the mountains.

A white panama hat was on the mantelpiece, and I tried covertly to look at its owner. I had never seen him up close. Driving by our house on his way to his business, Laddie was dark and good-looking, like a rich foreigner. Not like Southern whites, who never looked handsome. He seemed nice enough, but he seemed alone, out of place and time, apart from the family. He grabbed *Life* magazine and vanished to the porch.

I was surprised by the magazine. I thought that the rich had their own special world that they inhabited with their own special foods, clothing, and magazines. I read *Life* myself. Later, when I went to thrift shops, I was surprised to see that designer-label clothes looked like other clothes. They had deeper seams and hems and nice materials, but nothing Miss Pauline couldn't make, except maybe the trimmings and buttons.

Soon Laddie went to the airport, where his pilot would get him, and the house settled down to the routine of the week. Every day I fixed breakfast for one adult, three teenagers, and a child; washed the dishes; cleaned the downstairs; fixed lunch; washed the dishes; cleaned the upstairs; fixed dinner; washed the dishes; went downstairs to rest; then baby-sat with Warren at night.

Most of the time I was too tired to read, but I liked to stand on the large porch that extended out from the mountain and look at the scenery as it shifted colors, from blue to dark-green to gray. I wondered what caused the colors to shift that way. Was it my perception or was there some other reason? Sometimes the clouds would form below and shut out everything except what was nearby. Then at night the fog would slowly crawl up the mountain toward the house—first a little puff, then more and more until there were great billows of it, coming up to envelop the house. Then I sometimes imagined that great cats were softly padding outside my basement window, which rested nearly on the ground.

On Friday night, Laddie came back. His straw hat was on the mantelpiece and he was on the porch reading a magazine. I felt uneasy. Were they going to fight or was everything going to be everyday?

I didn't have long to wait. The bickering started almost immediately and went on seemingly forever. Friday night faded into Saturday morning.

Libby and Junior looked weary. Warren had a faraway look. Cherry rifled the cupboards. Peace seemed to fall when the older ones went away, which they did regularly, to the lake or the country club on top of the mountain. They'd be gone about an hour; then come back and stay for an hour or so; then go back; then come home.

Things got quiet near night, when I heard talk of supper at the inn. He didn't want to go, but she insisted: "Get up off your ass, Laddie, and let's go." Finally she told me that they were going out for supper and Junior and Libby were going to visit friends—Cherry was already with friends at the lake—and they were leaving Warren with me.

I was looking through a magazine and had lost track of the time, when Laddie suddenly appeared in the doorway. It was deep night by then and very quiet, and he looked like a figure out of a mystery story. I was too stunned to say anything, but I wondered where Mrs. Ransom was. The thought came to me that he had killed her and thrown her off the mountain. But he merely said, "I'm going down to Winston-Salem for a while." And then he vanished just as quickly as he had come. Warren looked up briefly from his electric train and looked down again.

I wondered what I should do. Should I call the police? Where was Mrs. Ransom? What had happened? Finally I decided that there was nothing I could do except wait until Libby and Junior came back.

Still later, in the deep night, I heard feet crunching on the rocks outside and Mrs. Ransom appeared in her light-blue cocktail dress with matching high-heeled, open-back sling pumps.

I didn't know what to say. She didn't seem too upset, just said that she'd had to walk home from the inn. I breathed easier. Well, maybe everything was okay after all. But it wasn't.

Early the next morning, Sunday, I awoke to screams so loud that they seemed to fall right down the stairs and into my room. I didn't know whether to go up and fix breakfast or not. Finally there was a lull and I ventured up. I shouldn't have, because something was said that set off another round. Libby was trying to calm her mother, who didn't want to get

201

calm: "I had to walk myself home from that damn inn." Something fell with a crash. Laddie, who had returned during the night, whispered and there was talk of a divorce and "I'll break you." He announced that he was going to the lake and asked who wanted to go. All the children made a beeline for the station wagon while things fell crashing in room after room, denoting their mother's furious passage. I breathed for the first time when I heard the wagon pull out of the driveway.

Mrs. Ransom went into her room and got quiet. In a little while she came out with her suitcase. She reached into her pocketbook and pulled out some crumpled bills. "That's all I've got," she said. "I'm going back to Durham. You can go back with Mr. Ransom and the children." She left me in the house alone.

In the afternoon the small station wagon started back to Durham with one adult, three teenagers, one lost-looking little boy, and me, plus every conceivable kind of equipment that one could use to enjoy oneself and enough leftover food to have a giant church picnic.

Dorothy Ransom never called, never said anything about the rest of the money she owed me.

Part

THREE

22

My experiences at the American Tobacco factory and with the Ransoms further convinced me that I had to do something different in life; the factory was so monotonous that it was mind-numbing, and domestic work as I experienced it with the Ransoms had no semblance of human dignity. The only other alternative for a black girl in Durham at that time was work at Duke University Hospital—or "Duke's," as the black folk called it. For some reason, I don't know why, I never tried to get on at Duke's.

The world outside was threatening to me and I was very scared, without self-confidence. What could I do? Who would help me? If people in the outside world were anything like my blood family or the other people around me, they would be harsh, disapproving, and would exert every effort to try to discourage me.

More than anything in the world, I wanted the college or university experience, but I wanted it in the outside world. I had seen enough of segregated black education to develop a lifelong distaste for it, but again I had no choice. I had only the money that Aunt Jo had left me. So I had to stay at home with Nonnie and go to the black college in Durham. The year was 1951.

North Carolina College at Durham (it used to carry the words "for Negroes" in its official title—it said so on the sign right on the lawn) is located in the southern part of the town. Its immaculately groomed lawns and neat, squarish, redbrick classroom buildings and dormitories mark it as an oasis of privilege and ease. Looking at the postcard scenes through the low-hanging branches of the surrounding trees, one would not have believed that this was six minutes away from some of the worst slums in the South. The college hadn't forgotten their existence; it simply never acknowledged that they were there. The black dispossessed murmured against the "big dogs," and bided their time. I often thought that if and when "the revolution" came and the black masses in America awakened from their long sleep, their first target was going to be the black professional class and it would be a horrendous bloodbath.

For most students, the year at North Carolina College starts out like any other year at any black college in the South.

Mama and Papa arrive on campus early with the prized possession—a son or daughter—in tow. (Hereinafter, this possession will be referred to as a "freshman.") Mama is dressed in her summer best—often dark crepe, even though it is too hot for that kind of material. But she is going to the college and she wants to look her best. Her judgment rules over Daddy, too, for she has seen to it that he is dressed in his Sunday suit also—always dark, either brown, blue, or gray, sometimes black. At last they have a son or daughter in college. She will become a teacher and wear Sunday clothes to school every day. He will be a man of importance and will be respected by all.

For Mother and Father this day is the culmination of a long dream. They have struggled so hard and sat around the fire at night and planned for so long. They want their child to go to college and be somebody. Father has worked in the fields, either his own or somebody else's, for years, plowing the earth early, when the sky is still gray with night, and staying in the fields until the sun has turned reddish-gold and set. Mother has worked alongside him or for somebody else, cooking and taking care of children, and then come back home to cook and sew and take care of her own children. But they both have had one thing in mind. One goal. One drive. They have wanted a child to go to college. Somehow, it will all have been worthwhile if someone in the family makes that precious move upward.

For the black working poor do not scorn the trappings of the middle class. They have been deprived of material possessions for four hundred years and know that it is not romantic and blissful to be without them. To *have* to eat neck bones and pig tails and rice and peas and beans is not a glorious thing. To *have* to walk five miles for any reason is not invigorating; it is a chore and an inconvenience. Black folk don't want the simple life. They've had that; they know all about it; they want to try some other life for a change. Social reformers who forget this fact about black life are in for a shock. If you want the simple life, and want to go off somewhere and live in a commune, all well and good, but spare the black folk. They'll ride by in a car and watch you walking, breathing in that bracing air.

Today it is axiomatic in the South that every black family is going to have two things: a car and a TV. The family too poor to have them is poor indeed. As soon as they can afford a car, they buy one. They eat the cheapest cuts of the cheapest meats because they cannot afford steak and veal and lamb. As soon as they can afford them, they buy them. Until the advent of television, they listened to the radio. When television came, bringing with it the wondrous message of the shiny, glamorous, fast-moving world outside, they bought a TV. Some managed to get a color TV.

But the big move upward is the one to college. So, on the Sunday that college opens, the mothers and fathers arrive with their offspring. She is voluble; he is silent. They both are a little scared, but they both are very, very proud.

Bag after suitcase after trunk flows into the dormitories,

for the girls and boys must have the proper clothing. As hard pressed as the parents are, they want their child to look nice. They want him "to look like the other children." Therefore, the students at the average black college always are better dressed than their peers at the white colleges across town or nearby.

The parents depart, and later in the week those privileged characters, upperclassmen, arrive. Then there is the crush in the gym known as registration day, when faculty and students go through a ritual known as registering, which does not mean very much, for much of the work of that day will soon be undone by a process known as "drop/add." Within a few days, students will drop a lot of courses they have registered for and add some they didn't register for.

Then the happy day arrives. The freshmen wander into their first classes, looking expectant and scared. The upperclassmen affect a "suave" air. The school year has started. It will be punctuated by the thump-thump sound of marching feet as the college band turns out early in the morning and at night for practice drills around the campus. The ROTC will march, and one can imagine the young men far away in some foreign country years from now. Long lines form at the cafeteria and the semester is under way.

During my first week of classes as a freshman, I was stopped one day in the hall by the chairman's wife, who was indistinguishable in color from a white woman. She wanted to see me, she said.

This woman had no official position on the faculty, except that she was an instructor in English; nevertheless, her summons had to be obeyed. In the segregated world there were (and remain) gross abuses of authority because those at the pinnacle, and even their spouses, felt that the people "under" them had no recourse except to submit—and they were right, except that sometimes a black who got sick and tired of it would go to the whites and complain. This course of action was severely condemned by the blacks, but an interesting thing happened—such action always got positive results. Power was thought of in negative terms: I can deny someone something, I can strike at someone who can't strike back, I can ride someone down; that proves I am powerful. The concept of power as a force for good, for affirmative response to people or situations, was not in evidence.

When I went to her office, she greeted me with a big smile. "You know," she said, "you made the highest mark on the verbal part of the examination." She was referring to the examination that the entire freshman class took upon entering the college. I looked at her but I didn't feel warmth, for in spite of her smile her eyes and tone of voice were saying, "How could this black-skinned girl score higher on the verbal than some of the students who've had more advantages than she? It must be some sort of fluke. Let me talk to her." I felt it, but I managed to smile my thanks and back off. For here at North Carolina College at Durham, as it had been since the beginning, social class and color were the primary criteria used in determining status on the campus.

First came the children of doctors, lawyers, and college teachers. Next came the children of public-school teachers, businessmen, and anybody else who had access to more money than the poor black working class. After that came the bulk of the student population, the children of the working class, most of whom were the first in their families to go beyond high school. The attitude toward them was: You're here because we need the numbers, but in all other things defer to your betters.

The faculty assumed that light-skinned students were more intelligent, and they were always a bit nonplussed when a dark-skinned student did well, especially if she was a girl. They had reason to be appalled when they discovered that I planned to do not only well but better than my light-skinned peers.

I don't know whether African men recently transported to the New World considered themselves handsome or, more important, whether they considered African women beautiful in comparison with Native American Indian women or immigrant European women. It is a question that I have never heard raised or seen research on. If African men considered African women beautiful, just when their shift in interest away from black black women occurred might prove to be an interesting topic for researchers. But one thing I know for sure: by the twentieth century, really black skin on a woman was considered ugly in this country. This was particularly true among those who were exposed to college.

Hazel, who was light brown, used to say to me, "You are *dark,* but not *too* dark." The saved commiserating with the damned. I had the feeling that if nature had painted one more brushstroke on me, I'd have had to kill myself.

Black skin was to be disguised at all costs. Since a black face is rather hard to disguise, many women took refuge in ludicrous makeup. Mrs. Burry, one of my teachers in elementary school, used white face powder. But she neglected to powder her neck and arms, and even the black on her face gleamed through the white, giving her an eerie appearance. But she did the best she could.

I observed all through elementary and high school that for various entertainments the girls were placed on the stage in order of color. And very black ones didn't get into the front row. If they were past caramel-brown, to the back row they would go. And nobody questioned the justice of these decisions—neither the students nor the teachers.

One of the teachers at Wildwood School, who was from the Deep South and was just as black as she could be, had been a strict enforcer of these standards. That was another irony—that someone who had been judged outside the realm of beauty herself because of her skin tones should have adopted them so wholeheartedly and applied them herself without question.

One girl stymied that teacher, though. Ruby, a black cherry of a girl, not only got off the back row but off the front row as well, to stand alone at stage center. She could outsing, out-dance, and outdeclaim everyone else, and talent proved triumphant over pigmentation. But the May Queen and her Court (and in high school, Miss Wildwood) were always chosen from among the lighter ones.

When I was a freshman in high school, it became clear that a light-skinned sophomore girl named Rose was going to get the "best girl scholar" prize for the next three years, and there was nothing I could do about it, even though I knew I was the better. Rose was caramel-colored and had shoulder-length hair. She was highly favored by the science and math teacher, who figured the averages. I wasn't. There was only one prize. Therefore, Rose would get it until she graduated. I was one year behind her, and I would not get it until after she graduated.

To be held in such low esteem was painful. It was difficult not to feel that I had been cheated out of the medal, which I felt that, in a fair competition, I perhaps would have won. Being unable to protest or do anything about it was a traumatic experience for me. From then on I instinctively tended to avoid the college-exposed dark-skinned male, knowing that when he looked at me he saw himself and, most of the time, his mother and sister as well, and since he had rejected his blackness, he had rejected theirs and mine.

Oddly enough, the lighter-skinned black male did not seem to feel so much prejudice toward the black black woman. It was no accident, I felt, that Mr. Harrison, the eighth-grade teacher, who was reddish-yellow himself, once protested to the science and math teacher about the fact that he always assigned sweeping duties to Doris and Ruby Lee, two black black girls. Mr. Harrison said to them one day, right in the other teacher's presence, "You must be some bad girls. Every day I come down here ya'll are sweeping." The science and math teacher got the point and didn't ask them to sweep anymore.

Uneducated black males, too, sometimes related very well

to the black black woman. They had been less firmly indoctrinated by the white society around them and were more securely rooted in their own culture.

Because of the stigma attached to having dark skin, a black black woman had to do many things to find a place for herself. One possibility was to attach herself to a light-skinned woman, hoping that some of the magic would rub off on her. A second was to make herself sexually available, hoping to attract a mate. Third, she could resign herself to a more chaste life-style—either (for the professional woman) teaching and work in established churches or (for the uneducated woman) domestic work and zealous service in the Holy and Sanctified churches.

Even as a young girl, Lucy had chosen the first route. Lucy was short, skinny, short-haired, and black black, and thus unacceptable. So she made her choice. She selected Patricia, the lightest-skinned girl in the school, as her friend, and followed her around. Patricia and her friends barely tolerated Lucy, but Lucy smiled and doggedly hung on, hoping that some who noticed Patricia might notice her, too. Though I felt shame for her behavior, even then I understood.

As is often the case of the victim agreeing with and adopting the attitudes of the oppressor, so I have seen it with black black women. I have seen them adopt the oppressor's attitude that they are nothing but "sex machines," and their supposedly superior sexual performance becomes their sole reason for being and for esteeming themselves. Such women learn early that in order to make themselves attractive to men they have somehow to shift the emphasis from physical beauty to some other area—usually sexual performance. Their constant talk is of their desirability and their ability to gratify a man sexually.

I knew two such women well—both of them black black. To hear their endless talk of sexual conquests was very sad. I have never seen the category that these women fall into described anywhere. It is not that of promiscuity or nymphomania. It is the category of total self-rejection: "Since I am black, I am ugly, I am nobody. I will perform on the level that they have assigned to me." Such women are the pitiful results of what not only white America but also, and more important, black America has done to them.

Some, not taking the sexuality route but still accepting black society's view of their worthlessness, swing all the way across to intense religiosity. Some are staunch, fervent workers in the more traditional Southern churches—Baptist and Methodist—and others are leaders and ministers in the lower-status, more evangelical Holiness sects.

Another avenue open to the black black woman is excellence in a career. Since in the South the field most accessible to such women is education, a great many of them prepared to become teachers. But here, too, the black black woman had problems. Grades weren't given to her lightly in school, nor were promotions on the job. Consequently, she had to prepare especially well. She had to pass examinations with flying colors or be left behind; she knew that she would receive no special consideration. She had to be overqualified for a job because otherwise she didn't stand a chance of getting it—and she was competing only with other blacks. She had to have something to back her up: not charm, not personality—but training.

The black black woman's training would pay off in the 1970s. With the arrival of integration the black black woman would find, paradoxically enough, that her skin color in an integrated situation was not the handicap it had been in an all-black situation. But it wasn't until the middle and late 1960s, when the post-1945 generation of black males arrived on college campuses, that I noticed any change in the situation at all. *He* wore an afro and *she* wore an afro, and sometimes the only way you could tell them apart was when his afro was taller than hers. Black had become beautiful, and the really black girl was often selected as queen of various campus activities. It was then that the dread I felt at dealing with the college-educated black male began to ease. Even now, though, when I have occasion to engage in any type of transaction with a college-educated black man, I gauge his age. If I guess he was born after 1945, I feel confident that the transaction will turn out all right. If he probably was born before 1945, my stomach tightens, I find myself taking shallow breaths, and I try to state my business and escape as soon as possible.

When I first knew Carroll Light, his world was tight, secure; he knew where he was going and about how soon he would get there. He taught me English in the first quarter of my freshman year at college. He was a big, tall, yellow man, balding on top, with tufts of hair sticking up on either side of the smooth place. Outside the classroom he always wore a hat. He had a deep, resonant laugh, but the defiant thrust of his jaw gave him a somewhat belligerent look that was little softened by his clear-rimmed glasses. He usually wore a sports jacket and slacks, a bit unconventional for male faculty at the college, but his casual dress was a reflection of his interest in sports.

He often missed class. We would go and sit, and after twenty minutes or so, when we realized that he wasn't coming, some would leave. They would be happy to skip class, but a few would be worried, for we knew that all the freshman English classes would be given the same end-of-the-term examination, and if we hadn't had what the other sections had, we would show up poorly on the test. So a few diehards would sometimes just sit and talk in the classroom the whole period, halfway hoping that Mr. Light would come. If the others were worried, I was terrified, for I feared failure more than anything.

One day Mr. Light told me that he wanted to see me about a paper I had written. In it I described the people who came into an all-night café in the inner city of Durham, where I had once worked for about a week. From the end of the workday until about midnight, there were ordinary working folk in the café. They ordered fried chicken and beer and played the jukebox. But at midnight, the first of the "night people" showed up, usually daring teenagers. Between three and five in the morning, the debris of the human community washed in—men and women sodden with drink, their clothes looking as if they'd slept in them for weeks. They didn't seem human—rather, more like filthy, smelly bundles of clothes. Then, after five in the morning, ordinary people started coming in again to get their breakfasts or a cup of coffee before they went to work.

I had observed this phenomenon the first night I went to work and had been fascinated by it. One further part of my paper described two young women with short, straightened hair, who came in. They obviously were from the area surrounding the café, the worst slums in Durham. They had on white sweat shirts and were not very clean, but each one had her white sweat shirt gathered up at the shoulders by pink ribbons. To me they weren't funny; they were sad. They looked about eighteen—my age at the time—and I could sense that these clothes were all that they had; yet they had made enough acknowledgment of their womanhood to want to look attractive and feminine so that they could attract the attention of the men. So they did the best they could, and the pink ribbons on each shoulder were the result.

Mr. Light told me that this description of the girls was the most interesting part of my paper and that I should write more about that. But I was shy, for in some ways I identified with those girls and I didn't want to feel that I was using them to make people laugh. Also, his manner put me off. The whole interview was marked by intense joviality on his part. Because of his humorous manner, I couldn't tell whether he was genuinely interested in me. But I felt that a class and color difference was at the root of it—a light-skinned black professional was amused by my description of the people in Durham's inner city. I didn't write any more on the subject.

When the grades for that first quarter came out, I had the highest average in the freshman class. The chairman's wife called me into her office again. We did a replay of the same

215

scene we had played during the first week of the term. She complimented me on my grades, but her eyes and voice were telling me something different. She asked me to sit down; then she reached into a drawer and pulled out a copy of the freshman English final examination. She asked me to take the exam over again.

At first I couldn't believe what she was saying. I had taken the course under another teacher, and it was so incredible to her that I should have made the highest score in the class that she was trying to test me again personally. For a few moments I knew rage so intense that I wanted to take my fists and start punching her. I have seldom hated anyone so deeply. I handed the examination back to her and walked out.

She had felt quite safe in doing that to me. After all, she was the chairman's wife, and so didn't that give her the right to treat the black farm girl as she chose? (Life is strange. When in the mid-1960s the department started hiring native-born whites, it was she who most bitterly resented their presence.)

It was that incident which caused me to make a very basic decision. I was in the world alone; no one bolstered my ambitions, fed my dreams. I could not quit now, for if I did I would have no future—there would be more incidents like the Ransoms or the American Tobacco factory. If I was going to get through college, I would have to be bland, noncommittal. I would simply hang on. I needed a degree and I would stay until I got it.

But I had to show the chairman's wife what I could do, so I transferred to her section. Let her see for herself, I thought. Her class turned out to be a glorified kindergarten. Every day I expected to hear her say, "Now, children . . ." I didn't see Mr. Light again until three years later, on my graduation day. I had finished first in my class, and the local television station wanted a picture. Carroll Light assisted them. You? You? his eyes asked as he came up and pointed me out to the camera as the honor graduating senior.

Gregory Newton taught political science. During my sophomore year, I took one of his courses as an elective and liked it so well that for a while I thought of majoring in political science. After that I would see him around the campus, and he would always stop and ask me how I was doing, and, what was most unusual for the college, he would ask my opinion on things, particularly current events. I was so starved for talk that then, as now, often words came out, not one at a time but in great gluts, clusters of words.

I had long been a soul on ice at the college. Finally one day when I very much wanted to talk to somebody, I thought of Mr. Newton. One part of my mind said, Go, and the other said, Don't go. What will people say? You're not in his class now; you're not even in his department. But all the while I was debating, I was on my way to see him.

It was late afternoon; the sun just barely came into his office. He greeted me nicely enough and asked what was on my mind. I told him about an hour's worth. I talked so long because it quickly became apparent that he liked and understood me. That day ended perfectly for me; I had found a friend, someone I could talk to, someone whose opinion I respected, someone who always told me just how things looked to him and who was what I greatly admire in a person—a straight talker. He was the first person I had ever really talked to, revealing my dreams, the pain of my life, exploring possibilities for a larger life, a more meaningful one in a larger setting.

He listened and encouraged me, and invited me to come again. I was embarrassed to go back, for I always talked so long and I didn't want to take up his time, but he didn't seem to mind. We became friends. I didn't realize then just how rare real friendship between a man and woman is. I know now.

From that time until I graduated, I had one friend. Sometimes I wouldn't see him more than twice a semester, but when the need to communicate with someone became overwhelming, I would ease into the chair by his desk in the late afternoon and talk.

I sometimes wondered how such a vitally alive, dashing sort of man could empathize so easily with me. But he did, and I had sense enough not to question it further.

One night during my sophomore year there was to be an evening concert that I very much wanted to attend. (Music was part of my double major, along with English.) Though I could catch the city bus afterward, it would be near eleven o'clock before I got to the end of the line, and easily midnight before I could walk home. So I asked my mother to ask Ruf Junior to pick me up. A mistake.

The abuse started as soon as I got into the car. He hadn't wanted to come. Everything was wrong: my staying out so late at night for some damned concert—and the voice went on and on. Everything in God's name was wrong with me. Somewhere something inside me got very quiet, and the next thing I knew, the car had swerved up onto the sidewalk on Fayetteville Street and I was fighting him as hard as I could. He managed to get the car back in the street, but it started to jump the curb on the other side. I saw it moving and knew that I was the cause, but for what seemed like a long time I could do nothing but strike out at this man who was abusing me for no good reason. I stopped and he righted the car and didn't say any more, for in the mood I was in, if he had said one more word there would have been another fight. I realized later that he was stunned—he'd never expected me to strike out at him—and was reassessing the situation, trying to figure out what to do next.

We drove home in complete silence. As soon as Ruf Junior switched off the ignition, he jumped out and ran in the house. I picked up my books and went in behind him. But by then he'd told Nonnie his version of what had happened. Both of them stood in the kitchen, with identical expressions.

"Ruf Junior told me what you did. Acting like you crazy," she spat out at me.

I knew instant and total rage. Without asking me a single question, without even thinking about it, she had heard what he'd had to say, had convinced herself that I was wrong, and was now condemning me. I was so mad I couldn't speak. I turned and ran down to Mount Zion church and sat on the outside steps leading to the choir stall. I tried to think, but I couldn't. I didn't have anywhere to go, anybody to turn to. I felt as though someone had a string wrapped around my chest and was pulling it tighter and tighter. It hurt and I couldn't breathe.

When it eased a little, I went home. The door was open. Nonnie never said anything more to me about the incident.

Dorothy Carrington was not a memorable person. This worried her. She was of average height, a little plump, and she smiled a lot. Although we spent four years at the same college and I must have passed her on the walk or in the halls several hundred times, I remember seeing her there only once.

The first and only time I *saw* her was one late afternoon in April or May of 1953, shortly before the end of the term. I was walking on the campus in front of the dormitories near the Administration Building and diagonally across from the law school. A senior who had been in trouble with the law was walking in front of me, approaching a group of other seniors, Dorothy among them. As he got nearer, everybody paused, as if waiting for a signal as to what to do. Then Dorothy stepped out from the group and embraced the man—maternally—and the others moved in close, hovering, murmuring around him. I passed on by, stepping off the sidewalk and walking around the group.

I knew about the young man, whose last name was Moultrie, for I had read about his troubles in the newspaper and had heard the case discussed on the campus. He was from what the officials at North Carolina College liked to call a "good" family—that is, one in which the mother and father did not make their living in field or factory or in domestic service. Such students were highly prized at the college, which wanted to project a "genteel" image—a bit difficult to do if your students came to school fresh out of the tobacco fields of eastern North Carolina, or if their parents worked in the tobacco factories in Durham or Winston-Salem, or in the housekeeping departments of Duke University or Duke Hospital and other universities and hospitals around the state, or in cafés or service stations. So, the few students who did come from "good" backgrounds were highly prized; they showed the whites that blacks were advancing, that they, too, had an upper class.

(This is not a joke. Students at North Carolina College whose parents were teachers or other members of the professional class were privileged and they knew it. They used to toss their heads and flaunt themselves around the students whose parents were black working class. Yet at that time nobody—neither the children of the professional class, nor the children of the working class, nor the faculty and staff of the college—nobody could sit down and have a sandwich on Main Street in Durham at Kress's, Walgreen's, Rose's, or any other store. One store solved the problem simply by having a stand-up lunch counter for everybody. Some people ate there just so that they would not have to undergo the humiliation of seeing white people sit down while by law they had to stand up or go outside to eat. For people who wonder why segregation lasted so long without effective protest against it, one answer might lie in the notion of a "privileged" class among oppressed people.)

The college hadn't been able to protect young Moultrie, for he had gotten into trouble in the town, and the police and the authorities were not cognizant of the fact that he was from a "good" family and, thus, was not to be treated as your average black.

The young man's brother was a policeman, during a time when Southern towns had just begun to put blacks on the force. Until that time, if one had to call the police, by definition he was "putting the man" on somebody, and "the man" was always white. So, to be a policeman in the early 1950s was a rare honor for a black man. However, Moultrie's brother was an enterprising person and decided to use his position on the force to increase his personal wealth. In short, he approached a liquor seller, a black woman, one who by definition was without status or class or rights in the black community. He, a black man and a policeman, laid down the law to her: she would give him a large sum of money or he would see to it that she had a whole lot of problems. She was to raise the required sum, and he would be back to collect in a few days. Moultrie, the college senior, accompanied his brother, the policeman, during this encounter. The policeman felt that a scared, uneducated black woman, with no status in the community, would have no choice but to do as he had said. But she had called a lawyer and told him about the extortion scheme. When the policeman appeared for the payoff, he walked into a trap, for the police were waiting for *him.*

Everybody at the college waited and wondered. What would happen? The administration was in a bind. On the one hand, Moultrie was one of their own, a model for the other students to look up to; but on the other hand, what would the white community say if he were permitted to continue in school and finish? Finally, the verdict came. When I saw Dorothy embrace Moultrie I had not yet learned what the verdict was, but evidently she and her friends knew. The college had punished Moultrie by requiring him to return for one semester for the next three years in order to get his degree.

I wondered at the time at this outpouring of sympathy for Moultrie, but I felt instinctively why Dorothy was doing it. She was going out with Reginald, a product of one of Durham's professional families, and already she was identifying their cause as her own. I don't know quite why I felt that Dorothy wasn't one of them, but I did.

Years later, when I finally got to know her, I noticed that if she was ever asked where she was from, she mentioned a small town in eastern North Carolina and quickly changed the subject. Since at that time eastern North Carolina was

221

nothing but fields and more fields, I didn't have much trouble filling in the blank spaces. But Dorothy wanted to be from Durham, for in Durham there was a black professional class and her whole ambition in life was to become a part of it.

During my senior year in college, 1955, the Barter Theatre of Virginia came to do *The Merchant of Venice.* It was the first live professional performance I had ever seen. And it was magnificent. The audience was one hundred percent on Shylock's side. They "oohed" and "ahed" at his telling phrases— "If you prick us do we not bleed . . ."—and showed no interest whatever in the quality of mercy's not being strained. The actors themselves were stunned. Plainly, they had not anticipated this reaction. The actor who played Shylock, once he knew that the audience was on his side, really became expansive, with broader and broader gestures, and addressed more and more of his lines directly to the audience. The heretofore hero and heroine were a bit put out, but they did the best they could.

From the moment Shylock swept onto the stage in a coat shot through with metallic threads and in heavy copper makeup, I was entranced. That one could take a few pieces of wood, some suits and dresses, and, using mainly words, create a whole new world, was amazing to me. It was magic. Then, a few minutes after the show, take down the set, pack the costumes, and go to another town, to make the same world live all over again—tonight, or five years from now, or five hundred years from now. It was more fantastic than anything in science. The whole audience thought so, too. The applause was still going on as I slipped away to catch the last bus to Wildwood.

It was the words and how they fitted together that had created the magic. I wanted to know how it was done.

I still frequented the public library and a rental library for recent novels. Thus, by chance, during my senior year I came across *The Dollmaker* by Harriet Arnow. I experienced the same feeling of being stunned by writing that I had known at *The*

Merchant of Venice. In Arnow's book there was a scene so powerful that to me it was real: a mother cuts her child's throat so that he can get air and thus not die from the diphtheria that is strangling him. Later, the family moves to Detroit, and the quality of life there was described so vividly that I felt that if I passed the house I would recognize the characters in the yard. Magic.

I had also become interested in philosophy and taken a course with Dr. Sing-nan Fen. During my senior year Dr. Fen invited me to participate in a discussion group that he was forming. He stressed that it was not going to be "a polite class" but a genuine, "anything goes" type of discussion group where he would be a participant rather than a teacher expecting students to defer to him. I went and enjoyed it very much. Most of the time there were only two or three of us there, but Dr. Fen never failed to come. I was impressed with his sense of professionalism—that he would give so freely of his time after he had met his contractual obligations.

When Dr. Fen learned that I was going to make a trip to New York during the summer of 1954, he gave me a letter of introduction to Dr. Alain Locke. I had read about Dr. Locke and knew that he was one of the most distinguished scholars that black America had produced. But when I got to New York Dr. Locke was very sick, and not long after that I read his obituary in the newspapers.

Dr. Fen was the only professor ever to invite me to dinner. When he asked me I was stunned. I wanted to go but I was too shy about my clothes, my awkwardness. He looked puzzled and I realized that to him these excuses were no excuses at all. So I went. He had a nice family, a wife and two children. They served spaghetti with meat sauce, a vegetable, and fruit for dessert. We talked and laughed about things in general and then I went home. It was my first contact outside my own ethnic group.

"You wanted to see me, Miss Owens?"

I stood uncertainly in the office door. I was surprised when

Miss Owens, an extremely close friend of the chairman and his wife, had said to me after class, smiling a carefully molded smile, that I should stop by her office.

I knew that Miss Owens didn't like me, and I would have avoided her altogether if possible. Alas, it wasn't possible, for she taught one of the courses that I had to have in order to graduate.

Miss Owens, with the smooth brown face and the level eye, represented what I most hated and feared. I hated her because I was sure she wished me to fail. I had the feeling that when the prim, proper black bourgeoisie of Durham looked at me, they somehow wanted to wave a magic wand and make me disappear. For I was that dreaded thing that most of them tried to avoid if possible—the earthy black African peasant. (I often smiled to myself during the late 1960s when there was so much talk in the black community about getting back to "roots." I was part of those roots, had never left them, and thus felt no guilt about looking around for other ways of doing and being.) Miss Owens disliked me because I represented what she had come from, one generation removed, and what she evidently wanted to forget as completely as possible.

So with that knowledge and mutual hate between us we looked at each other that spring morning just before I was to be graduated. I feared her because I needed the course and the credit to graduate, but if Miss Owens crossed the invisible line that separated us, there would be a scene and I might not graduate. So I stood in the door, and my mouth smiled while my eyes measured my opponent and I wondered, Merciful God, why did you let me be born and have to contend with horrible people like this?

"Yes, Miss Mebane," she answered.

I didn't make a move inside the door. Miss Owens wanted me to sit down voluntarily; then she wouldn't have to do the polite thing and ask me. But I waited. And I said nothing. This was another tactic that I had learned. Say nothing and brace yourself for the worst. It was not long in coming.

"I've noticed your clothing," Miss Owens said, still smiling. I bared my teeth in a set smile but said nothing. "For example, today you are wearing a striped blouse, but your skirt is checked. Stripes and checks don't go together."

I felt pain in my chest, but I grimly hung on to my smile and said nothing. The conversation continued on the subject of my clothing, and why didn't I buy some cute little blouses with Peter Pan collars and some nice solid-color skirts?

Nowhere in the conversation did Miss Owens ask me about my financial situation, because she really didn't care. It was axiomatic in the black community of Durham that the less you had, the more "face" you had to put on. Women's assembly at North Carolina College at Durham every other week was devoted largely to how to dress—dress being defined as how to look as though you were affluent on very little money. After all, one had to make some distinction between the social classes. Why not start with one's clothing?

Miss Owens was anxious that I and other black girls like me not present a picture to the outside world—the white world—that would make her ashamed. She would be ashamed of a look that said, Yes, I've had a hard time in life and my mother works in a factory and sometimes there are things that go on at home that I don't want to talk about.

I fought down the hurt in my chest. When it appeared that that was all there was to be to the conversation and I started to take deep breaths again, Miss Owens continued. "Oh, yes. I read your article in the *Campus Echo* in which you express certain strong opinions." She was referring to a book review I had done; it wasn't the nature of the opinions that bothered her, but the fact that I had them. She said that she thought I should be more moderate in expressing my views, less forceful. I had read the book I reviewed in my article—something she had not done—and I had plainly stated what I thought.

Underlying the whole interview, of course, was the official position of Miss Owens and her kind: Be like us; that is the only way you can succeed in life. So far, I had resisted them; but what was more galling to them was that I had been successful in spite of resisting them. Evidently I had been successful in concealing from Miss Owens the absolute horror I felt at what the Miss Owenses of this world were, and I hoped to God I would never ever become one.

They thought that they had a system that would last forever. But it didn't. As soon as the college students finished fighting the racist whites and their system of segregation, they turned their attention to the black campus and the class and color racists on it. The ensuing struggle of the late 1960s was deep and bitter, for it was a class struggle. The children of the black folk were tired of being spat on. And they rebelled. Though there were many excesses committed by the students during that period, they were in no way equal to the excesses that had gone on on black campuses for a long time. The revolution was overdue.

It was hot on the June morning when I went to receive my degree. My mother didn't want to go; she said that it had been too hot in the gym the day before—on Baccalaureate Sunday. So I caught a ride into Durham and went to my graduation alone. There was no close relative there to see me get my degree. Many cars came from all over the state and out of state. The overflowing crowd of mothers, fathers, aunts, uncles, little brothers, little sisters, distant relatives, babies— some of whom had been up most of the night traveling so that they could start right back home without having to spend the night anywhere else—were there to see a member of their family graduate.

I walked across the stage and got my degree—and caught the bus home. I read the program again. I was summa cum laude. I wondered what that really meant—certainly nothing in my life. When I was about a mile down the road after getting off the bus, a neighbor stopped and picked me up.

I tried to get a John Hay Whitney Fellowship but was unsuccessful. A German couple, the Manasses, when they found out that I wasn't going to graduate school, took an interest and came to my home to talk about helping me to get in somewhere. But it was already June and I didn't get anything. It is ironic that the two "foreign elements" on the campus, Professor Fen and Professor and Mrs. Manasse, were the only ones to express an interest in me and my career. I didn't know it then, but the pattern for my life had been established: when help came, it would always be from the outside.

23

Jesse, responding to some inner signal in his own nature or to some external impulse (the absence of an adult male at home, perhaps), had gone into the Army after graduating from high school. He and Belle, a high-school classmate, married and had a child, Diane. Ruf Junior, by the time he was twenty, was married, had a child, and had established his pattern. During the week, he worked hard and functioned in other areas of life as a normal human being. But the weekends were different.

Ruf Junior and Louise and the baby moved in with us, and it was good for Louise that they did. My mother's presence prevented some of the fighting, but not all. When I couldn't bear to see Ruf Junior beating Louise anymore, I would call the police. As a matter of fact, the police came out from Durham so often to put an end to the terror that eventually the neighbors stopped commenting about it.

But the strange thing was that after these horrendous weekends, both Nonnie and Louise acted mad at me for calling in the authorities. It was as though I had done something wrong. This was so even the time when Louise wound up in Duke Hospital and Ruf Junior in court and the whole episode was written up in an embarrassing story in the Durham *Sun*.

I often have thought that it was the madness of of my family relationships that gave me an insider's view of the world occupied by the insane, and throughout my adult life I have on several occasions found myself in some sort of relationship with a deranged person. This fact puzzled me until I realized that in my own home situation I had learned methods of treating aberrant situations as though they were normal. Consequently, people with serious emotional problems gravitated toward me like filings toward a magnet—mainly, I suppose, because I didn't react to them in the way most people do. By the early 1970s, though, I was no longer responsive to such people. I never lost my ability to see clearly the landscape occupied by the deranged, and I can still readily follow the hop, skip, and jump—sideways, forward, backward—of the emotional and mental patterns of such people, but I grew weary of them, for it took too much of my energy to deal with them. I no longer want to pay attention and understand, so I avoid them.

The drunk scenes at home lasted for more than fifteen years—and they blighted and colored my view of human nature, black males, and the world around me. I call these the Nightmare Years. It was as though I lived in a world inside a world, within an inverted bowl of clear, heavy plastic. Through it I could see people going about their daily routines just as clearly as if I were one of them. Only when I tried to move out of my encapsulated world did I realize that the bowl was there; I pressed my hand against it and moved it around and around, looking for an opening. But I couldn't find one; my world was circular and I covered the same ground over and over.

It was summer, in the mid-1950s, and I was on a bus traveling north, going to New York City. It was not the first time I had made this trip. During the summer after my sophomore year in college, I had gone up and had worked at the H. Wolff Book Manufacturing Company. Though I made barely enough money to pay the nine-dollar-per-week rent for a hall bedroom and to maintain myself in the city, I had enjoyed the summer because the city offered so much that Wildwood did not have. (Durham did not really exist for me, for it was a segregated town, and so I was barred from anything of interest.)

That summer in New York, I attended the concerts at Lewisohn Stadium after work and on the weekends I went to the Museum of Modern Art, but never to the Metropolitan Museum of Art—I don't know why, really.

An interesting incident happened that summer, when the Museum of Modern Art advertised on television a painting class in the evenings for the public, and I decided to take it. I was amused at the startled look I got from the girl taking names when I showed up for the class. The look plainly said: *You?* And I looked back at her, a look that said: *Yes, me.* Stereotyping was not unknown in New York City.

On this trip, I was traveling in a mother's role, for I had Diane, Jesse's mentally retarded child with the crippled hand, on my lap.

The trip started the same as always.

If you were going to New York City from Durham, North Carolina, you took the eleven p.m. bus at the Durham bus station. No one I knew ever started a long-distance trip in the daytime. People had to work in the daytime; they caught buses at night. And even if they traveled on Saturday or Sunday, they still caught buses at night. Perhaps the reason was that if they left during the day, they might arrive at their destination late at night when everybody would be asleep and they would have to get someone up out of bed to come down to the bus station to get them, or, just as bad, they would have to catch a taxi and be driven around a strange city at night when they couldn't recognize the landscape and thus might be overcharged.

I was going north because Jesse had called my mother from Brooklyn and said that he and his wife, Belle, had gone back together again and wanted Diane back. After marrying Belle in Wildwood, Jesse took her to Brooklyn to live, while he was stationed at various Army posts. Diane spent her first two years of life in Brooklyn. But Belle left Jesse a couple

229

of times. She believed in having "good buddies," "friend girls," confidantes; when Jesse got out of the Army and came back to Brooklyn, some of Belle's "friend girls" told him some bad things about her, and after that there was no getting along together. During one of these separations, Bellé brought Diane south for Nonnie to keep until she found work; then, she said, she would return and get Diane and take her back north with her. No one suspected at the time that Belle would never set foot in Wildwood again or that, after a while, she would cease to communicate with Nonnie in any way, that she would never write or telephone, that she would never send Diane even a Christmas card. Never. To this day, I cannot comprehend the callousness of a mother capable of cutting off her own blood like that, with never a look back. But Belle did it; she wiped the slate clean of Diane.

I wondered at Jesse's phone call, because it would have been more natural if Belle had called. But Nonnie tightened her jaw in that peculiar way she had when she was going to do something no matter what, and said, "*He* said they've gone back together."

I really didn't want to go on the trip, but I obeyed my mother's wishes and took the eleven p.m. bus. I was dog tired as I settled into a seat with Diane on my lap and a shopping bag on the floor, full of baby bottles, diapers, a coat for me for the after-midnight chill, a blanket and a pacifier for Diane, and a prayer that she would be good on the ten-hour trip and that I wouldn't have any trouble, because I was so exhausted. I knew in my heart of hearts that Jesse and Belle hadn't gone back together, and I wondered about my mother's passivity, her easy acquiescence to his demands. The way she always gave in to him frustrated me so that I often wanted to cry.

As usual, different sorts of people were on the bus. It was hot, and they had pushed all the windows open. There was no air conditioning; there were no rest-room facilities; and there were no rules against standing. The bus driver packed them in as long as they could get in. There were people who would be standing for a good part of the three or more hours that it took to get to Richmond, Virginia. Because there was no rest room, the bus would make frequent stops in the many towns that it went through—the day of the interstate highway had not yet dawned in the South.

The first stop after Raleigh on the way from Durham to New York City was Scotland Neck, North Carolina. There were unimaginably huge yellow-and-red signs at the bus station in Scotland Neck proclaiming WHITE and COLORED. It was obvious that some poor black soul had once made a horrible mistake and entered the wrong waiting room there. The city fathers didn't want that to happen again and had paid for some monster signs to prevent it. But just in case someone couldn't read or was otherwise crazy, fully armed policemen patrolled the bus station, the way they did at every stop between Durham and Washington, D.C. (Even in the mid-1970s in Orangeburg, South Carolina, police cars still met late-night buses—perhaps an unconscious carry-over from the past.)

I didn't get off between Durham and Washington, D.C. It was too risky.

The next stop was Petersburg, Virginia, home of Fort Lee. There were a lot of soldiers standing around the terminal, and also several of the usual police cars. The next stop—Richmond—was a major rest stop. People who hadn't been provident enough (or considered themselves too sophisticated) to bring along a brown paper bag filled with fried chicken, light bread or biscuits, and a slice of pound cake or sweet-potato pie, rushed in to get a fast hamburger, if they could.

An acquaintance once told me of an incident that happened on a bus trip that she made. At one stop, the black girl fixing the hamburgers was working alone. The kitchen was located between the two segregated waiting rooms. The code was that she served one white customer, then turned to the window behind her and served one black customer, then turned again, and so on. But on this particular night the whites were all clamoring for service, and with no one to help her she was unable to take care of both blacks and whites. She was afraid

231

to leave the whites unserved, for if they complained she would certainly lose her job; so she solved her problem by simply refusing to turn around and wait on the blacks. My friend, seeing her dilemma and also the dilemma of the black passengers, entered the kitchen, put her things down, made herself a hamburger, and then started serving the other blacks. They laughed good-naturedly and called her "crazy," but the counter girl was grateful; and soon the bus reloaded and drove away as if nothing out of the ordinary had happened.

In Richmond, I didn't move. Diane was being good. I held her on my lap and hoped that she wouldn't get too wet and that I wouldn't have to change her—at two, Diane was not toilet-trained.

In Richmond a new driver got on for the trip to Washington. He looked around, checked to make sure that every passenger had the proper ticket and was seated in the right place: whites toward the front, blacks toward the rear. His eyes roamed over the no-man's-land in dead center, from which, depending on the racial composition of the bus, you might be told to move.

The next stop was Washington. Everybody breathed a great sigh as the bus came under the yellow lights of the station. The danger was past. Washington was the Mason and Dixon Line. If you were traveling north, segregation stopped in Washington; if, however, you were traveling south, segregation started there. So, in the nation's capital, fear could end or fear could begin.

The next stop was a restaurant on the Pennsylvania Turnpike. Diane and I slept and slept. Diane roused up occasionally, but as long as she had the pacifier, which had distorted her mouth terribly, she was all right. I hated the pacifier and wished I could throw it away, but Nonnie let her have it. Thinking these thoughts I soon fell asleep again. And the bus rolled northward.

Awakening in the morning light, I noticed that the traffic— indeed, everything moving—semed to be drawn by a huge magnet: the city. Cars moved three and four abreast; planes flew overhead; and there were small boats on the water. Everything was activity. Always to me at such a moment, approaching New York City, I feel that America is a great country.

I love the energy of a great city. Soon, there we were: in the city.

There was a struggle with suitcases and diapers and the shopping bag. I had Diane in one arm; there was a sweater dragging here and a blanket dragging there. I wondered why I was always in such a mess, but then I knew the answer. I always tried to be accommodating to my family, but they always repaid me with a hate-filled, harsh, disapproving attitude and made even more impossible demands on me. Still, I clung to them, hoping that somehow, some way, I could earn their affection and thus find a place in a world that seemingly had none for me. Maybe I could please my mother— and lessen Jesse's hostility—with this good deed.

Inside the bus terminal, I just had to stop. I couldn't go any farther. I was so tired. Jesse was not there to meet me. He had given me a new address, different from the one that he and Belle had had the summer I came up and worked.

Though I had good directions to the subway, I found it difficult to carry all that paraphernalia and hold on to a crippled child at the same time. I needed help, so I decided to approach a stranger. He was rather tall, and sort of brown, and he looked South American. He had on a subdued brown tweed suit and was, in general, nonflamboyant, and I said to him, "I can't get all my things to the subway downstairs and hold on to Diane, too. Will you keep an eye on her while I take some of it down and then come back and get her?"

He looked at me and said, "Of course." He sounded very well educated. Still, I was afraid to leave Diane with him; but then, if I didn't leave her with him, I would never get on the subway, and I didn't have enough money to take a taxi from the bus terminal to Brooklyn. So I took one last look at Diane, hoping that the stranger was not a child molester and that I would not come back and find both him and Diane gone, and grabbed up everything that I could and rushed to the down escalator. At the entrance to the subway I put down the bags and packages and, hoping no one would steal them, rushed back upstairs to find Diane.

They were standing right where I left them and were getting along fine. Diane had made a friend, and she was quite comfortable with him, standing right at his knee. I thanked him profusely and for a moment could not help wondering if I would ever find a man like that. (1) He was kind. (2) He was intelligent. (3) He was of assistance to me when I needed him. I very much wanted someone like that, someone whom I could love.

But I could not tarry. I picked up Diane and hurried back downstairs to our things. The suitcases and the bags were still there. No one had bothered them, not even in the supposedly mean city called New York. A stranger took the trouble to help me get on the train with Diane and the luggage. We settled down for the long ride to Brooklyn.

A stranger told me where to get off the train so that I could find the strange address in the strange neighborhood. When I got there I was afraid to go in; it looked like a house where bad things go on. I am psychic about places. I can *feel* them, and they tell me things—sometimes things I don't really want to know. It's as though the air becomes palpable and my whole being becomes like a blind person's hand, carefully exploring an object, finding out its true nature through touch and that intangible intuition that blind people have.

It was an odd-looking house for the city; the front didn't face the street. When you went in, you were in a courtyard, and the sides of the building faced each other across the courtyard. I inquired for my brother and read off the address. The manager looked at me as if I were a criminal and snatched the paper with the address on it out of my hand. "I have to know who I'm giving information to," he said. My God, I thought, what have I gotten myself into?

After the manager had satisfied himself that I was a legitimate visitor, he led me up some stairs and into a dingy room that was sparsely and shabbily furnished, and Diane and I stretched out on the bed to wait.

There was a little food on the shelves—some potted meat, and pork and beans—but I had no can opener. I didn't know where to go to get something to eat. I had a can of milk for Diane, however; so I fixed that for her and decided to wait. It was morning still, but there wasn't much light coming through the window; so I sat in the dark room and looked out on the courtyard and rocked Diane to sleep and wondered what was going to happen.

Then it got to be afternoon; I could tell by the fading light, though I couldn't see the sky. I was so hungry, but this was such a bad place that I just didn't want to venture downstairs. So I waited.

Though I knew I had come in off a city street, by now I was almost convinced that I was in some other place. I saw none of the signs of a city at night: no streams of traffic, with car hoods reflecting the bright red and yellow neon signs of the stores; no strollers escaping the heat of the tenements; no people walking fast on their way to a place of amusement. Nothing. Soon I knew that it was deep night by the reflection of the artificial light striking the window.

Diane was getting restless; I was so hungry. Neither Belle nor Jesse had come. But maybe Belle will come, I thought, trying to cheer myself up. Maybe they both are at work and will come in together to get Diane.

It was really late now. The world was silent. There was just the yellow light of a bare bulb in the ceiling falling on the floor of the otherwise dark, dingy room. I heard no sounds in the building and I wondered where everybody was, but I was afraid to go out looking.

Then I heard a footstep, and the door pushed in, and there was Jesse. Belle wasn't with him. He looked at me with anger in his eyes—he was on the defensive, and he must have been drinking. I wondered why he had lured me up here with his crippled child when he knew that his wife hadn't come back. He picked up Diane and started out the door; it was after eleven p.m.

"Where are you going?" I said.

"We're going to find Belle."

I wanted to say, "But it's after eleven o'clock, way past her bedtime." But I was afraid of him. I didn't even know where I was, I had little money, and I knew nobody.

I lay on the bed, fully dressed, one foot on the floor, a hand across my eyes to shield them from the harsh bulb. I was afraid to turn off the light. I wondered what was going to happen to Diane. Her father had been drinking, and she was crippled, and the long day had made her irritable. What would he do if she started crying while they were out there, walking in the Brooklyn night? And I wondered what was going to happen to me. I fell into a slumber.

Sometime before dawn, the door pushed in and Jesse walked in with Diane in her blue organdy dress riding high in his arms. He put her on the bed, said little, left a can opener, and went out again. Diane was glad to see me; she curled into a warm little knot at my back. I turned out the light, and both of us fell into a deep sleep.

Soon it was morning—I could tell by the quality of the light in the room. It was different from artificial light. I was glad that the night was over, but it was lonely and fear was palpable. Whenever I moved I could feel it, just like a person standing in the room beside me. Diane couldn't tell me what had happened the night before, but she knew that something was wrong, for she didn't cry; and just as black women have for centuries, we silently moved closer together, even though Diane was only two years old.

The day passed; there was no Belle and there was no Jesse. Diane and I were very quiet together. I wondered what to do. I had little money, just a return bus ticket. Should I go back home? Should I stay? Unable to make up my mind, I lay on the bed while Diane played at the foot, and soon it was afternoon.

Night came again, and Jesse hadn't returned. The potted meat and pork and beans were gone, but I still had canned milk for Diane.

Then the door pushed in and there was Jesse, unshaven, with a shirt open over his undershirt and some nondescript pants that were all the worse for wear.

He opened his mouth in a grin, but his eyes weren't smiling. "What ya'll want?" he said.

"There's no food."

"There's a Chinese restaurant right around the corner. I'll go get ya'll something to eat." And he left.

In a little while he was back, with chop suey, rice, and soy sauce. He acted quite pleasant while I divided the food for the three of us, but he said that he didn't want any. Still, he didn't go, and I knew that there was something else. I waited with a feeling of dread. I was being softened up for something; I didn't know what. However, I didn't have to wait long.

Jesse was seated on the chair and I was on the bed beside Diane, feeding her some rice and chop suey. Jesse then told me that he didn't know where Belle was. From what I could gather, he had gone with Diane the night before from house to house where there were people who knew Belle well enough to be able to get in touch with her and tell her that Diane was in Brooklyn. He had hoped that by using the child as bait he would be able to lure Belle from her hiding place. But wherever Belle was, she was lying low.

But Jesse had a plan. He described a long, tortuous route— I should take this bus, go to that stop, get off, cross the street, go to that corner, take the bus going in that direction—and at the end of the route was an agency whose job it was to take care of abandoned babies. I was to go in and tell the lady that I had brought Diane north to her mother but I couldn't find her, so I had to leave the child there. The agency had ways of finding out where the mothers of abandoned babies were.

While he was still speaking, hysteria ran in the door,

237

grabbed me up off the bed so that I instinctively moved between Jesse and Diane, and clutched my throat so tightly that I was strangling for air. I could not speak. I was shaking my head from side to side: No! No! No! I still couldn't get my breath, though I started crying. Hysteria was holding my throat and I couldn't speak. When it finally let go enough so that I could get a little air, I screamed, "No!"

Jesse spewed out curses and dirty names. It was as if he wanted me wiped from the face of the earth, destroyed. Then he ran out of the room, slamming the door.

For a long time I sat on the bed, unable to think. But something told me to get up and leave before he came back. So I started stuffing things into the suitcases and bags and parcels. Every so often I had to stop and sit; I felt so bad and I couldn't stop crying.

Diane, her crippled hand held out in front of her, patted me with the other one. "Don't cry," she said. "Don't cry."

Finally I had everything and rushed out the door, hurrying with Diane. Just as we passed the landing, a voice called my name softly. I didn't wonder at the time how he knew it. He was one of the other tenants. He told me his name was Red and he knew Jesse. He started to help me with Diane and the bags. He was short: about five feet seven. He wore a big hat with a turned-down brim, probably to make him appear heavier; it was of winter material even though it was summer. He looked like a mild-mannered man and he had a small, heart-shaped face.

I asked Red for his address and told him that when I got home I would write to him, but somewhere along the way I lost the address. I have always been sorry about that, for I wanted to tell him how much I appreciated what he did for me.

I went by taxi to the place I had stayed when I worked at the H. Wolff Book Manufacturing Company. The landlady had a vacant room; I explained my situation and told her that I would send her the money as soon as I got home.

When I got back to Wildwood, I told Nonnie what had

happened; she didn't comment. I never mentioned to anyone else how Jesse had tricked us.

24

Ever since my junior year in college I had been enormously interested in psychology. For a long time I had noticed how people acted, and often tried to figure out the reason for their quirks, their idiosyncrasies. Now I started a more systematic study on my own. What made my mother the way she was? Or my brothers? I learned the importance of early childhood experiences and started piecing together some of Nonnie Stephens Mebane's past.

She had loved school. She had been taught in a one-room schoolhouse in Virginia by a Baptist minister. He taught well, for Nonnie had a clear handwriting and she could figure whole numbers, something we were never taught to do in school. That is, she could add numbers like 48 and 56 in her head without adding first the right column and then the left. I never knew how she did it. She was an avid reader of the newspaper, especially the comics. As a child, I often heard her talk of Roosevelt—so much that I thought he had some special interest in our family.

However, she was unable to go to high school, for the high school was a boarding school in another county. And her parents could send only one, the oldest child, Cecily. Nonnie wanted to stay in school so badly that she went for two years to the eighth grade; then the teacher told her she would have to stop. To the end of her life, she always spoke of Cecily with great bitterness. "She thinks that she's so much, just 'cause she's got that little education."

Soon Nonnie left home and went to work as a cook in a boardinghouse in Petersburg, Virginia. She had left a young man back home and wrote messages to her sister to give to him. When she returned home, she found that her sister had married him. This was evidently a very bitter thing to have happen to her; she felt betrayed by a member of her own family. Perhaps, I thought, that is why she showed so little warmth toward them, writing regularly only to Aunt Donna. The rest of them she could take or leave alone, and they responded in kind. Once, when he was drinking, Uncle Roland told me that the rest of her brothers and sisters considered Nonnie "curious."

Eventually she made her way to Philadelphia; then she visited Durham for a while, living with a cousin while she worked in the tobacco factories. During her stay in Durham, she met Ruf Mebane; they corresponded when she moved to Philadelphia, and soon she returned to Durham to marry him. Ruf himself, as I've said, was considered "curious" by many; he didn't like to be around people, though he had been born in the town. So, as soon as they were able, they bought land far out in the country, away from everybody else.

Their marriage seemed to have been a conventional one, except that apparently they could have no children. But finally Jesse was born, and they were overjoyed and tried to give him everything that he wanted. Then there was the stillborn child; then I was born, then Ruf Junior, and that ended their family. Ruf and Nonnie lived a conventional life, she working in the factory, he working on the farm and at odd jobs.

That pattern seemed solid and good enough, but something happened. What was it? As nearly as I can figure out, the trouble started when two forces left the house: Aunt Jo moved out and my father died. Within eight years both of the sons had become hostile. I wondered about the hostility and its origin. Could it be that the same lack of feeling that had been so traumatic to me had affected them? I didn't understand how my brothers and our mother interacted, but I know that she never spoke harshly to them, as she ordinarily did to me.

But did they, too, suffer from her lack of feeling, and was their hostility a result of their reaction to a sense of deprivation? Or was there something more subtle at work? Were they responding to some silent signal from our mother that made them act out the passive feelings that she had never been able to express?

Then where did I fit into the picture? Could it be that I had miscued, had scrambled the signals and thus was not acting out my mother's hostility and aggression toward society as I should have been?

My mother had done some nice things for me in life. I had got the piano when I was quite young. It is true that some of my peers had pianos, too. Was that the reason? Jealousy? But a piano cost fifty dollars and that was a lot of money. When I was ten, eleven, and twelve I had begged my mother and she had let me have birthday parties. It is true that my peers had birthday parties, too, but my mother had bought the ice cream and cookies and the cake with the pink candles.

But all of that had ceased with Aunt Jo's removal and my father's death. It was true that I could not have finished college without Nonnie's financial help. Did that not prove her regard for me? But on the other hand, there was her unending criticism of everything I did—though I tried to be absolutely perfect to keep the criticism down—and there was the most damaging of all things to me, the abrupt turning away when I brought honor home.

I couldn't figure it out. A necessary part of the equation was missing. I didn't know what it was; the only possibility that I could think of was the old one that I had thought of many times over the years: that I had somehow greatly offended my mother. I have never been able to resolve the question. Perhaps she was jealous of me.

I was never a Lesbian, but Ruf Junior continued to talk and the infection spread.

I sometimes went around to talk to the college psychologist, a black woman who had many problems of her own. She was a nice person and was interesting to talk to. But soon I instinctively realized one thing: I was asking someone who was locked in how to get out. How could she help me when she couldn't help herself? That was when I first realized, subconsciously, that in a way I was going to explore what no one I knew had ever consciously explored: how to break out. And what was more, I'd have to chart my own course, for there were no plans available, no one to tell me which way to go.

I made it the main aim of my life to find someone who was understanding and sensitive, and to find an environment in which I could develop and flourish. Beyond me lay the great world, the white world, the world that I had been taught was my implacable enemy. I didn't know how I was going to get out, but I was going to try. I had to.